We Hope to Get Word Tomorrow

In remembrance of all those who died on the Somme,
and all those who survived.

❖

'They were above all that was ever dreamed of,
uttermost courage, honour, truth to
something above self.'
(J. L. Garvin, The Observer*, 22 July 1917)*

Second-Lieutenant R. G. Garvin ('Ged'), aged nineteen, in the uniform of the 7th South Lancashire Regiment, April–June 1915

We Hope to Get Word Tomorrow

The letters of James Louis ('J. L.') Garvin,
his wife Christina and their son
Roland Gerard ('Ged')
1914–1916

Edited by
Mark Pottle and John G. G. Ledingham

Foreword by Hew Strachan

Frontline Books, London

We Hope to Get Word Tomorrow

This edition published in 2009 by Frontline Books, an imprint of Pen & Sword Books Limited, 47 Church Street, Barnsley, S. Yorkshire, S70 2AS
www.frontline-books.com

ISBN: 978-1-84832-545-6

A CIP data record for this title is available from the British Library.

For more information on our books, please visit
www.frontline-books.com, email info@frontline-books.com
or write to us at the above address.

Typeset by JCS Publishing Services Ltd, www.jcs-publishing.co.uk

Maps drawn by Red Lion Prints

Printed in the UK by MPG Books Ltd.

Contents

Illustrations

Frontispiece

Second-Lieutenant R. G. Garvin ('Ged'), aged nineteen, in the uniform of the 7th South Lancashire Regiment, April–June 1915

Plates

Text illustrations

Maps

Foreword

A war is a rite of passage for all those who are caught up in it, but it is especially so for those who enter it as adolescents and then become adults. 'Ged' Garvin was in his last term at Westminster School and due to go up to Oxford when the Archduke Franz Ferdinand was assassinated at Sarajevo on 28 June 1914. Instead, at the age of eighteen, he took a commission in an infantry battalion. Two years later, now a captain and as such responsible for the lives of many others, 'a sort of little father' in the words of one the last letters he received from his own father, he was killed on the Somme. He was still too young to vote.

His story is sickeningly familiar; it evokes that of 'the three musketeers', the trio of friends who, like Ged, left school (in their case Uppingham) in 1914, postponed university to go off to the war, and did not come back. Those boys were immortalised by Vera Brittain in *Testament of Youth*, a book that has its charge for all sorts of reasons that reach beyond its evocation of time and place; it is after all a lament for lost love. *We Hope to Get Word Tomorrow* is also much more than another story of a literate subaltern, able to articulate what he saw and experienced. At its heart too is the lament for lost love, in this case not that between star-crossed lovers, but that between parents and son. Nor are they simply grieving Ged's death in anticipation of the fact; they are also mourning the loss of the little boy who is growing to maturity thanks to the inevitability of time as much as through the accident of war.

Ged's mother and father wrote to him as often as he wrote to them, and so their correspondence is the story of their relationship and its evolution under the strains of war. Ged's parents tried to live normally, and to tell their son that his home continued its domestic routine, when they were living each day under enormous stress. That emotional intensity, even more than the war itself, is the dominant theme of their letters: their uncertainty as to where their son was, what he was doing and whether he was even alive, and his concern to reassure them. 'Of course', Ged's father wrote to his son ten days before he was killed, 'parents at home go through a thousand deaths.'

The image of the grieving mother is one perpetuated for us in countless war memorials. Christina's letters, and her son's replies, are both open in their love. She worries about his fitness and comforts, sublimating her maternalism by sending out food and equipment. He responds with warm endearments, and is anxious about her fragile health. What is really revealing in these letters is the manifestation of love between father and son. Ged's father, J. L. Garvin, found words in his letters that might – like much affection between father and son – have remained otherwise unspoken face to face. As Ged was about to go overseas, his father could console himself knowing that he had made his feelings for his first-born clear enough. 'Though a certain stoppage in all decent souls makes full speech impossible on things too dear and deep to be expressed between father and son (being menfolk and denied emotional relief),' he wrote on 9 July 1915, 'yet there never was in the world a son dearer to a father nor a better son.'

Within a year, although the mutual love was undimmed, the relationship between father and son had changed. Its epistolary nature meant that it could not be exclusive. Ged urged his father to share the more confidential aspects of his letters only with his mother, but both men knew that they also shared them with the censor. The quality and quantity of the postal services sustained by all the armies on the Western Front in the First World War is one reason why we have so much purchase on the experience of that war. But Ged, not least because, as an officer, he had to censor the letters of those under his command, knew that there were things that he could not tell his father, however insistent the latter's quest for information. Two more obstacles came between them. The first was of course the war itself. Often Ged was simply too exhausted to write at all or to write much.

Even when he had the energy, he confronted the challenge of what he should tell his parents of an experience that would only increase their anxieties.

Then there was the further challenge of finding the right words. Like others of their background and education, Ged and his father fell back on literature and history for their shared vocabulary. Ged read voraciously and his father supplied the books his son sought. More jarring than the contrast between the reality of war and the words of Meredith or Wordsworth, which both of them quoted, was the use of earlier forms of fighting as analogies for those of 1915–16. Garvin senior spoke of 'trailing pikes', a reference that presumably made sense to a son studying the campaigns of Turenne and himself ready to refer not only to the practices of seventeenth-century siege warfare but also to Henry V and Agincourt. Garvin junior kept alive his filial obligations by consulting his father on his drinking habits, wondering whether he was old enough to drink crème de menthe. His father reassured him that his parents had no right to 'order your conduct now that you are passing through that last test of manhood'. Nonetheless he could not resist also telling him that the principles to follow when drinking were 'neither asceticism, nor indulgence, but controlled enjoyment'.

The gap between them was opening up as his son was indeed becoming a man, a process accelerated by the war but not initiated by it: 'then the war came and you grew a man unawares', Garvin senior wrote on 27 April 1916. Unable to serve in the army himself, J. L. Garvin felt 'superannuated' and 'decrepit'. The normal balance between the generations was being inverted, with the younger suffering and dying at the front, and the older unsure how best to provide support. J. L. Garvin's frustration, however deeply felt, had less reason than most. As one of the most influential newspaper editors of his age, who made the *Observer* a voice of formidable comment, he was close to the centre of events and had the power to help shape them. Garvin's commentary on the policies of the day is important in its own right, not only because what he expressed to his son would find its way into print but also because he had the ear of many great men. A Unionist but an Irish Catholic, he was critical of the wartime administrations of H. H. Asquith – both Liberal and, after May 1915, coalition. Shilly-shallying over conscription and uncertainty over strategy were for him the hallmarks of Asquith's premiership. Recent scholars have been kinder, arguing that Asquith kept a consensus going and eventually adopted the measures that Garvin wanted. But for Garvin himself the political heroes of the day were his friend, Winston Churchill, and Asquith's eventual successor as Prime Minister, David Lloyd George.

J. L. Garvin never wavered in his conviction that the war was just, and was accordingly determined that all the nation's resources should be bent to its prosecution. Chief among these was manpower. He favoured national service and he recognised that the fight would be long and the losses consequently high. That was what his head told him was right, but it cannot have spared his heart when the news of one particular death did finally reach London.

Hew Strachan
Chichele Professor of the History of War
All Souls College, Oxford

Editorial Note

In the early morning of Friday 21 July 1916 J. L. Garvin, editor of the *Observer*, awoke suddenly from his sleep and exclaimed to his startled wife Christina: 'Good heavens, I haven't written to Ged.' He had been so busy the day before that he had forgotten to write to his son, who was about to go into battle on the Somme, and in a letter to Ged written later that day he described how the incident had amused Ged's mother: 'She feels under God that you will surely come back to her and will be guarded through the war: that is why she is bright to a degree that will do you good to think of.' It was the penultimate letter that Garvin wrote to his son, who did not live to receive it.

Between September 1914, when he gained his commission, and his death on 23 July 1916, Roland Gerard Garvin ('Ged') wrote to his parents several times a week, and they responded with similar regularity. The majority of their letters has survived: some 340 letters from Ged, 190 from his father and 140 from his mother. Most of Ged's letters from the front were written in pencil on small pieces of paper that came from a writing 'block' that he carried with him, protected from the elements in a leather wallet. He expected his parents to share his letters, and about three in every four were addressed to his mother, who replied less frequently than his father. On Sunday 16 July 1916, while his battalion was resting at an encampment about six miles from the battle front, Ged sent his parents' letters home for safe keeping. He had made a realistic assessment of his chances of survival and wrote simply: 'I'm getting straight again with various papers and arrangements . . . I'm lightening my kit. All the old letters from both of you are coming home – will you put them in my bureau.' In his letter of Friday 21 July his father acknowledged their receipt:

> Your returned letters came in a batch today. What a funny little lump they make: one would have thought there would be a pile of stuff big enough to relieve the paper famine. They shall all be preserved for you like the others and what a sifting you will have and what huge archives you will have accumulated at your age. Of course there's no fresh letter from you and we didn't expect it. *But we hope, all the same, to get word tomorrow . . .*

Ged's letters, together with those of his parents, were kept by two generations of the Garvin family before being placed in the British Library in 2003. None of Ged's parents' letters from September to December 1914 have survived, and this period is covered in the Prologue with selected quotations from Ged's letters alone. Chapter 1 thus begins in January 1915. As might be expected, there was a dramatic increase in the number of letters exchanged after Ged went to France on 17 July 1915. While he was training in England he saw his parents fairly regularly, but once at the front he had only two periods of leave, giving him sixteen days at home in a little over a year. Letters then became more important as the only link between people who had previously been accustomed to seeing each other every day. If one omits the days when he was on leave or in transit, or when he sent only a field card, Ged wrote to his parents and/or they to him on almost nine out of every ten days from 23 July 1915 to 22 July 1916. Even given that letter writing was a skill so much better performed and so much more common then than it is now, it is still remarkable that they wrote as often, and so well, as they did.

The total number of words in the extant letters is just over 280,000, of which it has been possible to reproduce only about one quarter. This was a very difficult task and much remarkable and interesting material has had to be omitted. The largest cuts have been made in the letters of J. L. Garvin, who invariably wrote at great length, and some major themes of his have had to be left out almost completely. He had an encyclopedic knowledge, for instance, of the Eastern Front and would speculate on all manner of subjects related to the war as well as to literature, but this material adds little to our understanding of Ged, his relationship with his parents, or his experience of the war – the essential themes of this book. The complete collection of the letters is of undoubted historical value, but can only be a given a scholarly treatment elsewhere. The editors have sought to present a readable and illuminating narrative, and have tried not to be intrusive in their editing, but they have had to make some alterations to the punctuation, grammar and use of capitals. Cuts have been marked by a three-point ellipsis, and words that have been added to clarify the meaning are enclosed in square brackets. Spelling mistakes and errors in the dating of letters have been corrected. Where the location from which Ged wrote is the subject of a guess – as is often the case when he was moving between billets near the front – it appears in square brackets. For obvious reasons relatively few of his letters were written in a front-line trench, as opposed to a reserve trench or a billet close to the line.

Ged served first on the Lys front, August 1915 to May 1916, and then on the Somme front, May to July 1916, and there are five maps illustrating this. The first three, which follow directly after this Editorial Note, are large-scale overviews covering: (1) the Western Front 1914–16; (2) the Lys front in November 1915; and (3) the Somme front July–November 1916. There are in addition two detailed maps offering background to the night attack on the German line north of Bazentin-le-Petit, 22–23 July 1916, in which Ged died: both appear in the Epilogue, which offers a detailed account of the engagement in which Ged fell.

In an effort not to interrupt the flow of the correspondence the editors have made sparing use of footnotes and linking passages. These are applied only when the reader is likely to need additional information to understand the immediate context. There are, however, several appendices, including a Chronology, Biographical Notes and Glossary, which explain and amplify a number of features, some otherwise obscure, in the letters. The index cross-references between the text and the appendices.

Acknowledgements

We are grateful to a number of people. Professor Jon Stallworthy introduced the two editors to one another and was encouraging in persuading JGGL that the project was worth pursuing. Richard Charkin and Alessandra Bastagli helped steer us to our publisher. William Frame and the team at the Manuscripts Department of the British Library gave unstinting and expert help with the Garvin archive, and we are equally grateful to Peter Robinson of the library's imaging service, and to its picture researcher, Auste Mickunaite. Jonathan Young reworked our rough drawings of the battlefields that Ged experienced into five excellent maps. We also wish to thank Mark Warby, editor of the 'Old Bill Newsletter', for advising us about the late Captain Bruce Bairnsfather. Jane Davies, the curator of the Museum of the Queen's Lancashire Regiment in Preston, and regimental secretaries Lieutenant-Colonel E. J. Downham, MBE, and Major Doug Farrington, have been a mine of information and encouragement – as has Eddie Smith, honorary archivist at Westminster School. Frank Blamey read the text and gave us good advice, and we were assisted also by J. L. Garvin's granddaughter Patricia Wildblood and his godson, Mark Barrington Ward. Without the help and encouragement of John Wilson the letters might never have left JGGL's attic, while Dr Michael Brock has expertly clarified a number of historical points for us. We are indebted to Professor Hew Strachan for a foreword that is full of insight, and we are grateful also to our families, who have given time, patience, advice and support. Finally, we thank our publishing team at Frontline Books, Michael Leventhal, Kate Baker and Deborah Hercun, from whom there has been such an enthusiastic welcome.

JGGL and MP

Overviews of the Battle Fronts

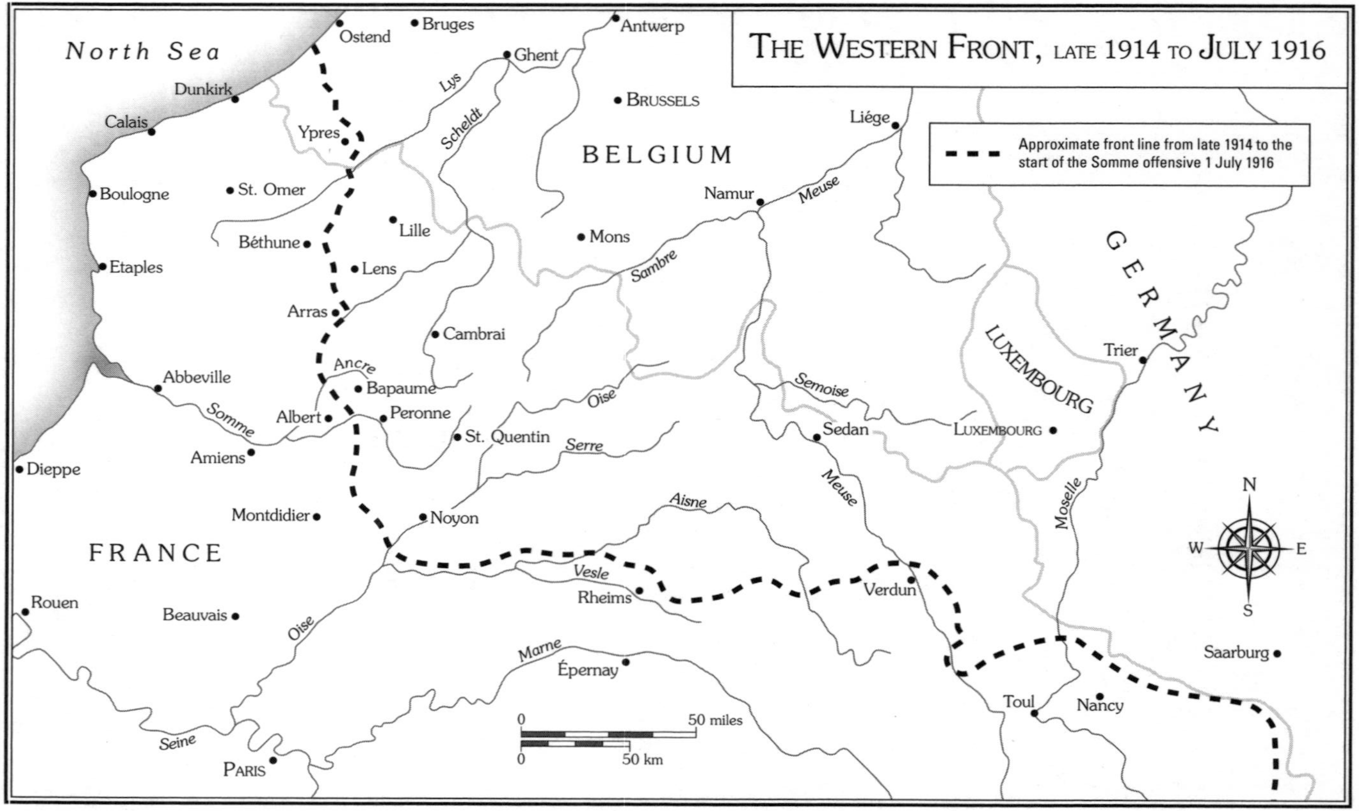
THE WESTERN FRONT, LATE 1914 TO JULY 1916
Approximate front line from late 1914 to the start of the Somme offensive 1 July 1916
North Sea
BELGIUM
FRANCE
GERMANY
LUXEMBOURG
Ostend
Bruges
Antwerp
Ghent
Dunkirk
Calais
Ypres
Boulogne
St. Omer
BRUSSELS
Liége
Namur
Mons
Lille
Béthune
Lens
Etaples
Arras
Cambrai
Abbeville
Bapaume
Albert
Peronne
St. Quentin
Amiens
Dieppe
Montdidier
Noyon
Sedan
LUXEMBOURG
Trier
Rheims
Verdun
Rouen
Beauvais
Épernay
Toul
Nancy
Saarburg
PARIS
Lys
Scheldt
Meuse
Sambre
Semoise
Ancre
Somme
Oise
Serre
Aisne
Vesle
Marne
Seine
Moselle
N
S
E
W
0
50 miles
0
50 km

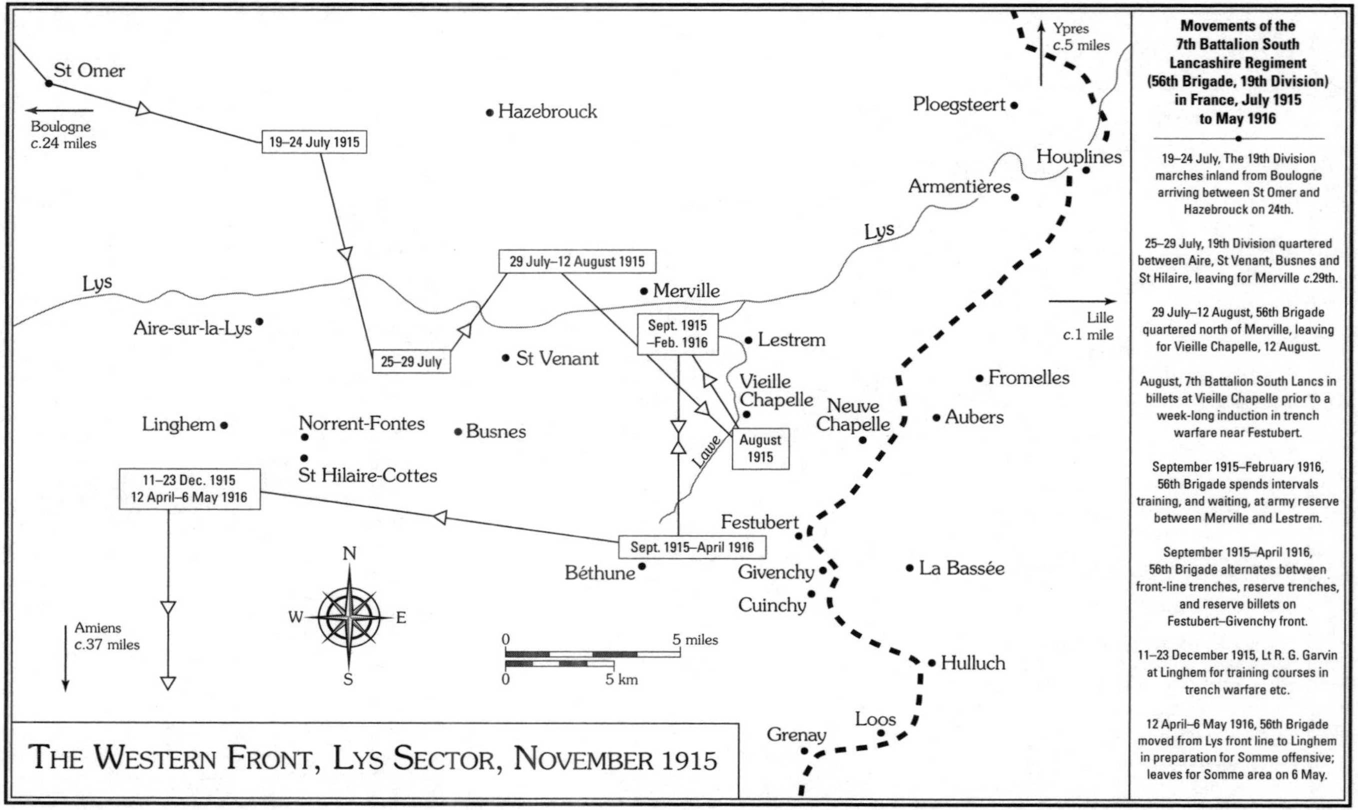
St Omer
Boulogne c.24 miles
19–24 July 1915
Hazebrouck
Ypres c.5 miles
Ploegsteert
Houplines
Armentières
Lys
Lys
29 July–12 August 1915
Merville
Aire-sur-la-Lys
25–29 July
St Venant
Sept. 1915 –Feb. 1916
Lestrem
Lille c.1 mile
Fromelles
Vieille Chapelle
Neuve Chapelle
Aubers
Linghem
Norrent-Fontes
Busnes
St Hilaire-Cottes
August 1915
Lawe
11–23 Dec. 1915 12 April–6 May 1916
Festubert
Sept. 1915–April 1916
Béthune
Givenchy
La Bassée
Cuinchy
N
W
E
S
Amiens c.37 miles
0
5 miles
0
5 km
Hulluch
Loos
Grenay
Movements of the 7th Battalion South Lancashire Regiment (56th Brigade, 19th Division) in France, July 1915 to May 1916
19–24 July, The 19th Division marches inland from Boulogne arriving between St Omer and Hazebrouck on 24th.
25–29 July, 19th Division quartered between Aire, St Venant, Busnes and St Hilaire, leaving for Merville c.29th.
29 July–12 August, 56th Brigade quartered north of Merville, leaving for Vieille Chapelle, 12 August.
August, 7th Battalion South Lancs in billets at Vieille Chapelle prior to a week-long induction in trench warfare near Festubert.
September 1915–February 1916, 56th Brigade spends intervals training, and waiting, at army reserve between Merville and Lestrem.
September 1915–April 1916, 56th Brigade alternates between front-line trenches, reserve trenches, and reserve billets on Festubert–Givenchy front.
11–23 December 1915, Lt R. G. Garvin at Linghem for training courses in trench warfare etc.
12 April–6 May 1916, 56th Brigade moved from Lys front line to Linghem in preparation for Somme offensive; leaves for Somme area on 6 May.

THE WESTERN FRONT, LYS SECTOR, NOVEMBER 1915

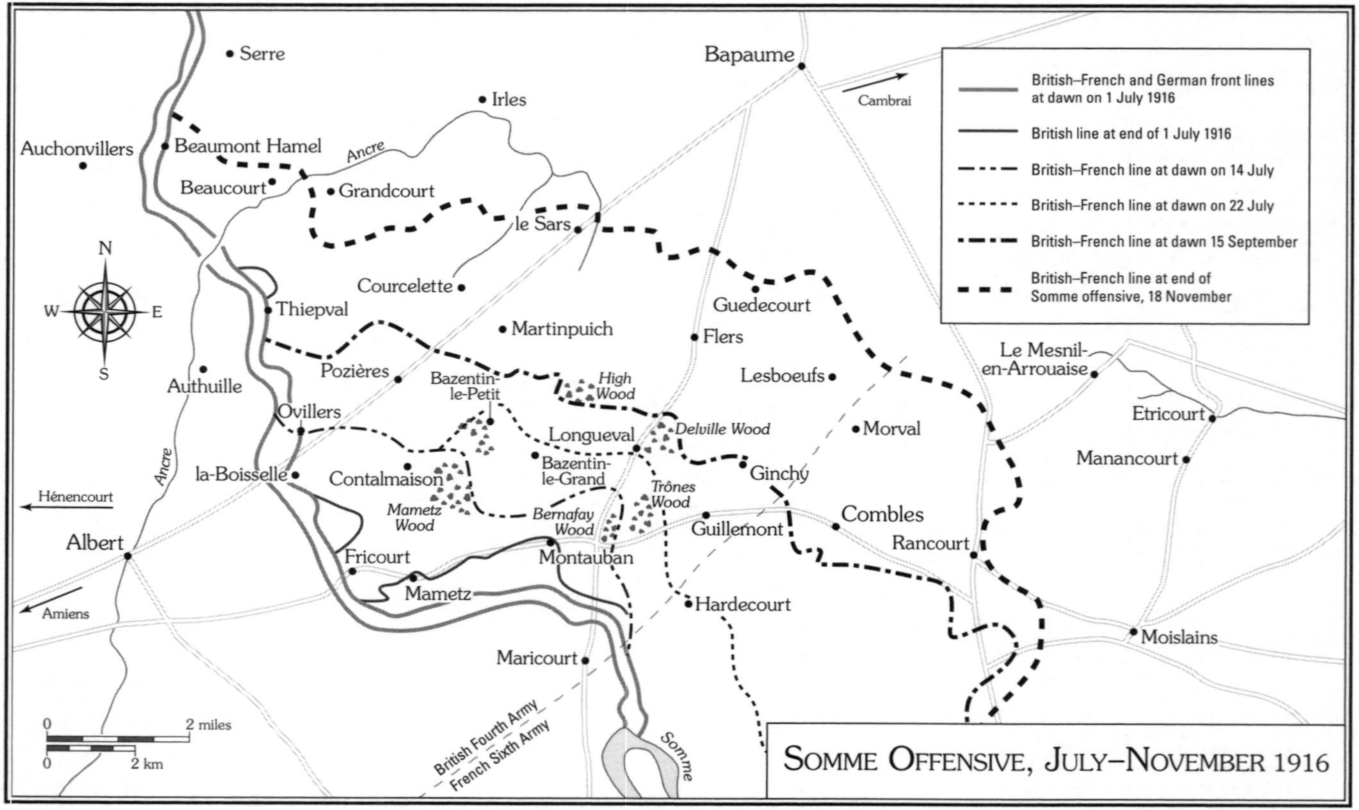
Somme Offensive, July–November 1916
British–French and German front lines at dawn on 1 July 1916
British line at end of 1 July 1916
British–French line at dawn on 14 July
British–French line at dawn on 22 July
British–French line at dawn 15 September
British–French line at end of Somme offensive, 18 November
Serre
Irles
Bapaume
Cambrai
Auchonvillers
Beaumont Hamel
Ancre
Beaucourt
Grandcourt
le Sars
N
W
E
S
Courcelette
Thiepval
Martinpuich
Guedecourt
Flers
Lesboeufs
Le Mesnil-en-Arrouaise
Pozières
Bazentin-le-Petit
High Wood
Authuille
Ovillers
Longueval
Delville Wood
Morval
Etricourt
Manancourt
la-Boisselle
Contalmaison
Bazentin-le-Grand
Ginchy
Hénencourt
Mametz Wood
Bernafay Wood
Trônes Wood
Combles
Guillemont
Rancourt
Albert
Fricourt
Montauban
Mametz
Amiens
Hardecourt
Moislains
Maricourt
0
2 miles
0
2 km
British Fourth Army
French Sixth Army
Somme

Prologue

The Volunteer

In July 1914 Roland Gerard Garvin – 'Ged' to his family – was eighteen years old, and approaching the end of his final term at Westminster School. Contrasting images of him emerge from this period. One is of a boisterous, confident schoolboy, tall and good-looking, who was to be found 'climbing over the Abbey roof, plotting against masters' and joining in 'free fights in the house'.[1] The other is of a thoughtful, diffident young man, whose habitual reserve concealed emotional depth and many talents. Ged was an accomplished flautist and pianist, a fine linguist and a champion fencer. He read avidly, in French and German as well as in English, and was awarded the Goodenough Medal for languages at Westminster. In his final year at school he won a history scholarship to Christ Church, Oxford, and he was due to take his place at the university that October. The summer of 1914 marked a rite of passage from schoolboy to young man.

Ged's father, James Louis Garvin, came from an impoverished background and had left school at thirteen. He was largely self-educated, but rose to be the editor of the *Observer* newspaper and a figure of national importance. His father had left Ireland to escape the potato famine and died at sea in 1870, leaving Garvin, then aged two, and his older brother Michael to the sole care of their widowed mother Catherine. The family drew support from the strong Irish Catholic community in Birkenhead, where Garvin was born, and his mother hoped that her younger son would enter the priesthood. There was a deeply spiritual side to Garvin's character, but he was

1 The words of Ged's school friend, Hume Chidson, in a letter to Ged's mother, Christina, 23 August 1916: Garvin Papers, British Library.

also a free thinker, and his wide reading led him to doubt the faith in which he was raised, although he never entirely rejected it.

Garvin was ambitious and prodigiously hard-working. He studied at the public library, went to night school, taught himself French, German and Spanish, and, while delivering newspapers, dreamed of becoming a newspaper editor. It seemed an unlikely prospect, but in Newcastle, where his brother Michael had secured work as a schoolmaster, he began writing unpaid articles for the local press. On the strength of these he was given a junior post with the *Newcastle Daily Chronicle* in 1891. A few months later a vivid account of the funeral of Charles Stewart Parnell brought Garvin national acclaim. He soon earned enough money from journalism to allow him to contemplate marriage, and one evening in 1893 he beheld Christina Ellen Wilson, the daughter of a police superintendent, singing at a friend's party. 'Tina' was also from an Irish Catholic background, a dark-haired beauty of seventeen, just out of convent school. That night Garvin vowed: 'By the grace of God, that is the woman I shall marry.' He proposed eight days later and she accepted: 'Well, Jim, I don't mind trying,' was her reply. They were married in 1894 and their first child Roland Gerard was born the following year. Four daughters followed – Viola in 1898, Una Christina in 1900, Katharine in 1904 and Ursula in 1907.

By the time that the last was born 'J. L.' Garvin (as he was commonly known) was an established name in London literary and journalistic circles. He had arrived in the capital as leader writer for the *Daily Telegraph* in 1899, and in 1908 his growing reputation and driving ambition secured for him the editorship of Lord Northcliffe's *Observer*. Founded in 1791 the *Observer* was Britain's oldest Sunday newspaper, but it was of limited importance when Garvin took over. He revolutionised its format and content, and dramatically increased the circulation.[2] As well as contributing to the paper's literary pages Garvin wrote a penetrating leading article each week. At a time

---

2 The circulation rose from under 5,000 in 1905 to *c.*80,000 on the eve of war and *c.*180,000 in 1915.

of bitter controversy in domestic politics, and growing tension in foreign affairs, these articles became essential reading and earned him a national and international reputation. Garvin was a passionate supporter of the Unionist Party – some would have argued, its effective leader – and he was also an expert on European affairs, and he used the *Observer* to warn of the dangers posed by the growth of German militarism. Garvin was no jingoist, and had great reverence for German culture, but he regarded Britain's energetic preparation for war as the best guarantee of peace. He had considerably more success in strengthening the navy than the army, and joined Admiral Sir John ('Jacky') Fisher, first sea lord from 1904 to 1910, in the successful campaign to build more Dreadnoughts. He also formed a close political friendship with Winston Churchill, first lord of the admiralty from 1911.

On the eve of war Garvin was at the height of his powers, but success came at a price for family life at home. In a typical week he was occupied day and night in reading and writing, and the floor of his study became almost impassable because of the rising piles of journals, both British and foreign, by which he kept himself so well informed. Tension would rise every Friday and Saturday as the deadline for the next *Observer* approached. Often there would be last-minute changes to the leading article, so that his finished piece only reached the paper's offices late on Saturday night. Sunday was generally a day of recovery, and on Monday the cycle began again. As the war progressed Garvin worked longer and longer hours, and this put a particular strain on Christina, who was often ill, having never fully recovered from recurrent middle-ear disease and chest infections that first afflicted her in 1904. The move to London had brought her into contact with the highest echelons of London political and intellectual society, an abrupt and demanding change from the environment of her youth. Her husband's chaotic hours of work, together with a flow of important and often unexpected visitors to their home at 9 Greville Place, greatly increased the burden of managing a large household with five children at day school. Throughout her married life she had to share her home with her mother-in-law, and when obliged to entertain her brother-in-law as well during the summer of 1914 she came near to a breakdown.

Tina was a devoted mother, and Ged's decision that August to join Kitchener's new armies filled her with pride, but also with fear. She faced the constant anxiety of the next two years with great courage. The hostilities opened on Ged's last day at school, Tuesday 28 July, when the Austro-Hungarian army began the bombardment of the Serbian capital Belgrade. What began as a regional conflict quickly became a European war, and for a week Britain's neutrality hung in the balance. The issue was decided early on Tuesday 4 August when German armies invaded Belgium. Britain declared war at eleven o'clock that evening. One of the first acts of the Prime Minister, H. H. Asquith, was to appoint Lord Kitchener of Khartoum – 'K. of K.' as he was universally known – Secretary of State for War. Kitchener had the prescience to foresee that the conflict would be long, and that this necessitated the raising and training of new armies. Since Britain did not have conscription he called for volunteers, and on 7 August, the day after his appointment, he launched his famous appeal for 'the first hundred thousand': placards simultaneously announced 'Your King and Country Need You. A Call To Arms'. The response was overwhelming. The invasion of Belgium had given the British public a straightforward and enduring moral argument for war, and neither the recruitment offices nor the professional army could cope with the numbers willing to fight. From 4 August to 12 September 478,893 enlisted, more than 300,000 of them in the fortnight after 30 August.[3] By the end of that month the first of the new armies, 'K.1', was formed, and on 11 September the Second New Army, 'K.2', was created.

Ged must have abandoned his plans to go to Oxford within days of the declaration of war, because on 17 August Churchill's private secretary, Eddie Marsh, passed a message to J. L. Garvin from Lord Kitchener to the effect that no decision had been reached on commissions for Ged and his school friend Hume Chidson. Garvin

---

3 Peter Simkins, *Kitchener's Army: The Raising of the New Armies, 1914–16*, Manchester, 1988, p. 75.

had tried to arrange for them to serve together in the Irish Guards, but by this date Chidson had already joined the East Surreys. Ged was not prepared to wait either, and on Friday 28 August he enlisted in the 7th (Service) Battalion of the South Lancashire Regiment – 'The Prince of Wales's Volunteers' – which belonged to the 56th Brigade of the 19th (Western) Division of 'K.2'. Ged had a single weekend in which to reflect on what he had done. The following Monday he found himself marched around Andover in Hampshire with other tired recruits looking for non-existent billets. The town, he noted, was 'horrible rowdy that night'.

The new armies needed leadership, and a large number of the officers came from the public schools and universities. Many had received basic military training in a cadet force, as indeed had Ged at Westminster – in 1913 his platoon had won the interhouse drill competition.[4] But these boy soldiers were not much older at the outbreak of war, and even Ged, who was commissioned on 19 September, thought his brother officers 'very raw'. His battalion was fortunate in having two ex-regulars and a serving lieutenant assigned to it, but its early history was nevertheless chaotic. It was not fully uniformed or equipped until March 1915, and in their first uncomfortable weeks on Salisbury Plain the new recruits had to wear their civilian clothes. Ged wrote home at the end of September: 'The officers are almost all young; the regiment – or my battalion – ragged as to the trousers, coatless mainly, and garbed in black wool waistcoats, with scarfed throats.' He was then inhabiting an empty tent, devoid of even a groundsheet, and had to improvise a bed out of his kitbag: 'As the whole thing is waterproof', he wrote home, 'I was quite comfy even on the grass!'

Throughout his training in England, and later when he was at the front, Ged relied on his parents to supplement his meagre army equipment and rations. They met his needs just as if he were still at school and wanted new sports kit: in October they sent a uniform, a chair and food parcels, and he was aware that he was fortunate in having this kind of support. The 7th South Lancs reflected the much broader

---

4 See plate section, figure 9.

cross-section of society that distinguished the new armies from the British Expeditionary Force (BEF), and Ged had under his command men whose experience of life was very different to his own privileged upbringing. By early November the officers were well quartered, and Ged even had a batman to make his bed, but he recognised that 'for the men, who sleep on straw palliasses on the earth, many in a tent, things are rather worse.'

The battalion's preliminary training was rudimentary at best. There were insufficient rifles to equip the new armies, and when Ged and five other officers were given revolver practice they were limited to three shots each at twenty yards, only three of which hit the target. Shortages of equipment were exacerbated by the cold, and at the end of October a sudden freeze prevented washing and shaving. Ged noted that the men 'seem rather down in the mouth, and get fits of disgusting slackness'. Days later the North Lancashire's store tent blew away in a storm that turned the camp into 'a sliding swamp'. The mud had to be cleared with buckets – it was apt training for what was to come, and, ominously, there were courses on 'trenching' in early November. Life in camp had become so tedious that everyone was in sore need of a break by December, but visions of Christmas at home were overshadowed by a serious (although exaggerated) fear of a German invasion. Ill-prepared as they were, the fledgling new armies had to be ready to repel this, and on 16 December Ged wrote home about his uncertain prospects of leave:

> Just possibly, the Kaiser may have been thoughtless enough to nip our furlough in the bud. We may rush off to greet him with a reasonable warmth on the east or some other coast (of course we hear nothing official, and have confidence in the Navy), but I agree with the man who said today in an aggrieved tone: 'Can't they wait till the New Year?' . . .

1

Training in England

After spending Christmas leave at home in London Ged returned to his battalion in Andover, Hampshire. He and three comrades were billeted in a single room in the town's vicarage, but they were nevertheless comfortable, and well looked after by the vicar and his family. Towards the end of the month they moved to the harsher regime of fixed huts in the regimental training camp at Perham Down.

❖

Thursday 21st January 1915
'The Huts', Perham Down, Andover

Dear Mummy

. . . I pen this in a moderately warm hut, the mess anteroom, beautifully situate on an open hillside with a spacious view in every direction; within two miles of the range.

The camp looks exactly like a gold-rush, and feels like Yukon most of the time. Our rooms haven't got stoves yet, and the nights are freezing. Thank goodness we are off in a fortnight, or ten days if we have luck. I've been on the range all day, from half past nine – we marched off at eight thirty – to half past four. We got home about an hour later, which gave us tea a bit before six. I lunched on a cheese sandwich, a beef sandwich and half a box of Brund's Meat Lozenges (put in my bag by your forethought). Please send me things to eat. That Wither's chocolate would be ideal on the range. I'm half deafened. I'll put cotton-wool in my ears tomorrow if I can get any. These cartridges go off with a noise like a railway accident (continued in Dad's letter).

Friday 22nd January
'The Huts', Perham Down, Andover

Dear Dad

This carries on Mummy's letter. Read hers first – or get her to read it to you.

The shooting wasn't very good. One or two men were alright, but only one or two. I got bored to death, standing there watching them fire; with hardly anything to do myself, as the platoon sergeant, an old and experienced man, was doing the coaching. It rained once or twice, and snowed for a minute or so . . .

Lots of love to you all, you and Mummy, Granny and all the kiddies. Remember me to the maids. Bye-bye. Ged.

Friday 22nd January
'Shootlands', Nr Dorking, Surrey[1]

My dearest Laddie

I have not written sooner, because I had hoped there would be a wire to say if you had been moved or not . . .

We came to Dorking and stayed the night there, but I didn't sleep, not more than two hours – church bells every quarter-hour all night. Then we drove here on Wednesday morning . . . We walked yesterday through wonderful woods about eight miles . . . Today the snow has fallen so thickly that we had only one and a half hours' walk this morning, and now the snow is over a foot deep and I'm wondering how it is with you, and what you are doing, and where you are, and how your men are . . .

This house is quite the most lovely spot you can imagine and Dad is bent on trying to get it, or something like it. That always worries me, because nothing seems to be the thing he wants but what he can't always have – and to hear it constantly does worry. He says he'll never have health till he gets air outside his door, and that London stifles him . . .

---

1 'Shootlands' was a country house taken by the Garvins for weekends: see the Note on Places below.

With dearest dearest love and prayers and blessings to my boy. Mummy . . .

Monday 25th January
'Shootlands', Nr Dorking, Surrey

My dearest boy

I am afraid you are having the beastliest time, and picture rigours in the snow, and horrors when the thaw drips and the huts are surrounded by churned slush . . . I want to know how your cold is, and when you are likely to move from such hungry quarters in the howling waste – as you must last week have been occupying. Mummy is better in several ways than I have seen her in a long time, and we have had walks together like old times. We must get a small burrow of our own in the country. I covet this one, but we shall never possess it. It is high up among the pines and firs over one side of that deep, solitary, so long-beloved valley of ours, running down for some miles from Leith Hill, with miles of woods near in several directions and wide prospects from the higher points of the road, and very little of mankind . . .

The change is so great that one feels as though one had been a month away, and one finds oneself again, and wonders how one's wife and children ever put up with the confined champing creature one always is, openly or secretly, in the town; and wonders, too, how one puts up with the town, where one is not one's very self . . .

I hope you can make out this scrawl. Of war next week. I have kept off it for some days so as to think better about it afterwards.

All the unspoken to you – well known to us. Dad.

Sunday 31st January
'The Huts', Perham Down, Andover

Dear Dad

I'd better tell you while I remember: we go away on Tuesday to Clevedon. I'm awfully glad you and Mummy were happy at Shootlands . . .

Here things have been fairly comfy since we got stoves in the rooms. The weather is shocking again this morning. The men are shooting pretty well. It's doing them a lot of good. I'm not much of a shot myself, though I can manage a respectable score once in a way. Every day we have been on the range here from about eight to three, lunching in the middle off German sausage sandwiches, or ration beef . . . cake and biscuits. Drinks: stout, which I haven't tried, and port, which I have. It's so cold that one can drink port in fair quantities without feeling more than a glow, which passes away in a few minutes. My British Warm and Jaeger scarf are invaluable. Thank Mummy for the chocolate, and Edith for sending the fruit.

Bye-bye, love to you and everybody. Ged.

Sunday 7th February
Norfolk Hotel, Clevedon, Somerset

Dear Mummy

These words is penned in a small drawing-room, filled with temporary officers singing *Old King Cole*, a popular military ballad . . . We're doing field training here in a country cut up like a patchwork quilt by streams and ditches running at the feet of rough and prickly hedges that feel as though they hadn't been combed since Creation. First day I went in above the ankles. Second day I jumped in the middle of a ditch, leading the way for my troops. Friday night did outpost duty from nine to eight in a howling gale (that was the evening I fell in the ditch). You should have seen me, wet to the knees, muffled in British Warm, posting sentries on the brink of the beach and beating up against the wind on a narrow dyke, where the ground felt like bananas and cream; the rain poured and the wind drove straight in one's face. I found six posts, upholding a tiled roof eight feet square (holed in places of course) and put my picket underneath, where we huddled together and reflected (I did, anyway) on the foolishness of generals and the vileness of mud. I was warm all the same, though my British Warm is still soaked nearly through. Thank you very much for the furry poncho.

Curiously enough the country north of us runs in a beautiful valley. It would be like one of the Lake dales, but for the villages, with tiled roofs and coloured walls. On Friday morning, when we fought a rearguard action, the sunshine made it like what one imagines the valleys of the Apennine. Over the hills to the west, not half a mile away, the sea lies between us and the coast of Wales. We got a wonderful view that morning, across the Severn estuary to the Welsh hills, with the wind chasing the cloud shadows, and the sunlight full. A glorious opening for the spring . . .

Love to you and Dad and all at home. Bye-bye Ged.

PS I'm kept up so late because the Officer of the Day has to turn out the guard after 11.00 p.m. (and hated doing it).

Monday 8th February
9 Greville Place, London NW

My Dear Old Son

Clevedon seems so much further than anywhere before, and it's like an age since we foregathered. We must run down to you Sunday after next at latest . . .

As you may have heard from your mother, Jacky was delightful to her and to me and gave us his signature to the portrait for the Red Cross Sale.[2] I suppose some proud possessor a hundred years hence will say 'That was signed by Lord Fisher in the Great War.' There will hardly be a greater to write out the name. He was surprisingly young and his face never looked so irregular, visionary, original and ruthless. Much talk not to be set down . . . 'By hook or by crook' is his favourite motto: 'Hit first, hit hard and keep on hitting' . . .

About the army I know less. People are cheered by seeing so many new guns going about the streets and country roads on their way to

---

2 'Jacky' refers to Admiral Lord Fisher, the first sea lord. Biographical details on Fisher, and the other prominent persons mentioned in the text, are to be found in the Biographical Notes below. Nicknames and Christian names are cross-referenced to surnames in the Index.

destinations unknown, and I fancy the way in which we have turned out guns of all sorts, military and naval, in the last three months or four must have broken every record. They will be a big factor when it comes into visible play in both elements. Amery, who has some sort of official job, is home from the trenches for a week or so. He tells an odd story on how keen on defence are both sides. 'Our fellows were putting up, a bit forward from their diggings, a new barbed-wire entanglement. The weather was so bad, we knocked off before it was finished. When we came back next day the Germans had come out and finished it most carefully!' They were of course not far away. What we all think is that we want younger men in higher positions in the army . . .

I met at lunch the Major Farquarson who was kind to you at the War Office, a nice fellow and able. It is clear that they don't want to make officers of men like [Sergeant] Melican, no matter how highly qualified.[3] I soon realised that, though approaching the matter very very delicately. The change in the weather will be an encouragement to you all. *The Times* swears the little coltsfoot . . . is out near London, and even in London, but I have not seen it. Nothing is, in our garden, but I have never heard its birds better at the same time of year as now – all the usual blackbirds, thrushes, robins, tits in capital form, and through the open window when one wakened on Sunday morning one heard a wren pop off again and again like a jolly little whizzing of sound. But I must leave the chatter to them and shut up . . . Dad.

Friday 12th February
9 Greville Place, London NW

Dearest lad of mine

. . . It was a real joy to get your letter of three days ago and it was also good to hear McClinton's voice on the phone, it was most recognisable. I have heard from Hume, who says he really would

---

3 Sergeant Melican was the physical training instructor at Westminster School, and taught Ged foils: he is pictured in figure 7 of the plate section.

rather not have fruit sent weekly, but just now and again.[4]

Couldn't you say, just now, if there is anything you'd like specially? It would so help the ordering of your extras. Did you get dates, pineapple, chocolates, pears, apples, socks, ginger, biscuits, cheese, books from Solano (any extra hand on to anyone you care for), fur cuirasse, a belt, lucky half-crown? All this I'd like to know . . .

Dad seems seedyish . . . Viola very bad cold, being looked after by the Irish family.[5] I'm awfully well and most cheerful. Grandma wanting to know if I saw the pheasant before it was cooked – very tiresome! Dad longs for a sight of you – and talks of coming next week. But we'll see. Anyhow do send me a word – or phone at some definite time. I'll pay – cos I've still £30 left of my Xmas box.

Love and blessings and prayers. Mummy.

Thursday 18th February
Norfolk Hotel, Clevedon, Somerset

Dear Dad

Thanks awfully for the letters. It livens me up no end when I hear from you and Mummy. We've had our first complete brigade manoeuvres today. We, the East Lancs, and the King's Own marched out about seven miles to attack the North Lancs. They represented a section of the advanced line thrown out by a force holding Clevedon, and were supposed to be holding a long spur – like a finger laid on a map – running down from the tablelands near Bristol to Clevedon. We had to reconnoitre the position of this imaginary force and break or push back the screen of covering troops. The North Lancs held a line very much advanced and very hard to retire from (in my humble opinion, very badly chosen). Then – at least where I was – they engaged much larger numbers of our men and stood their ground

---

4 Ged's school friend Hume Chidson was undergoing training with the East Surreys: see Biographical Notes.

5 The 'Irish family' were the O'Sullivans, close friends of the Garvins, who lived in Lansdowne Road: see Biographical Notes and Note on Places.

till we reached almost bayonet range (two hundred yards or so). I think we'd have wiped them out, as they had a hedge just behind them which held them up under a heavy fire when they did retire . . .

Lots of love as always. Bye bye Ged

Thursday 4th March
9 Greville Place, London NW

Dear Son

The last ten days have passed without a word from me. I scarcely know why except one has been a good deal rushed . . . For me, weeks pass and one never has time enough for thought about the various aspects of the war, and reads no books – not one. I amuse myself with strategical schemes for solving the deadlock in Flanders and north France and, of course, think my own system to be as good as any in the wariness and decision that the job requires.

In Flanders they are simply mud-logged; everything one hears gives one a fresh understanding of that hopeless slough, and I see no reason why we should merely stick, or crudely try to flounder on, just where trenches are most detestable, movement most difficult, and artillery positions most lacking. I wish we could have a talk about it over the map . . .

The Dardanelles business delights me after prophesising these two or three months that Constantinople was the master key for the Allies in the war as a whole. I lunched with Winston yesterday – he asked about you as always – but we talked more about the spirit than the detail of things. I didn't ask him much – it's my rule – and he didn't tell me what he ought not, but there seems no doubt that we are smashing at Kilid Bahr and Chanak at the entrance of the Narrows . . .[6] The Turks have big forts on land and are certain to fight fiercely. There can be no failure on our side now, at any cost.

---

6 The Allied naval bombardment of the outer defences of the Dardanelles straits had begun on 19 February and continued until mid-March, when the loss of three battleships to mines led to its abandonment. Thereafter bold plans were drawn up for an amphibious invasion of the Gallipoli peninsula.

Whatever – we must get through. Winston has fibre . . .

I'm to breakfast with Lloyd George soon, so am moving once more in the atmosphere of affairs. He made a splendid speech last Sunday, which was nothing less than magnificent in its appeal to the people. They don't come near yet to realising what a business we are in.

Things are quiet at home . . . Poor Maima is worried about the Germans and is evidently by no means sure in her heart that they won't gobble us all up. When she saw 'War to the Knife' in the headlines the other night she asked with horror 'Was it true?' and I had to explain that it was a newspaper metaphor . . .

Bless you – Dad.

Friday 5th March
Norfolk Hotel, Clevedon, Somerset

Dear Mummy

Thanks awfully for the letter, or two letters. Also for the consignment. The wire-cutters and medicine box look good; I haven't opened the hamper yet because the previous supplies are still going on.

We had a field-day this morning. I was detached with two men to wreck a railway with two imaginary slabs of guncotton. That meant scouting over a mile or more of country cut up by river and ditch, as though it had been harrowed by Titans; no cover except the only sparse hedges in the country, so far as I can see; and the water – much of it – stagnant and evil-smelling, enough to give typhoid to an army corps. We had wild adventures, bridging a flooded river . . . wading up to the neck (that was me) . . . [*page torn and text missing*] . . . changed and had a hot bath on return. Best love to you and Dad.

Wednesday 10th March
9 Greville Place, London NW

Dear Son

Here it is Wednesday again and I haven't written, but what with the transfer of the *Observer* to Waldorf, to be completed tomorrow, and more going out to lunches and dinners than your mother and I have done this twelve months, it has been a distracted interval.[7] It won't be so bad after this. The said Mummy is much better . . .

I breakfasted with Lloyd George at 11 Downing Street on Tuesday morning – the first breakfast with him for several years – nearly four years, I think. We were alone. He was excellent – full of pluck, vision and common sense. His unkempt hair, now that it has rapidly turned to grey, looks almost bard-like. We have always been sympathetic towards each other (except for the Marconi interval) since 1910, and the talk was worth all the other talks I have had with people of importance since the beginning of the war. Winston has been so much attacked and crabbed, often most unfairly, on the charge of letting out secrets, that he is now too guarded even with his nearest friends, but Lloyd George talked with the frank audacity of Jacky, and just as [Joseph] Chamberlain used to. He is worried about the slowness in turning the whole industrial organisation of the Country on to the manufacture of munitions of war, just as the French have done. We want far more resources for turning out rifles, guns, and above all shells, shells, shells. He told me about the Bill brought in yesterday for enabling the Government to order any manufactory whatever to stop its present business and make war materials: an extraordinary measure for a free Country, a tremendous measure, and it ought to have been brought forward months ago, but better late than never.[8] It

7 In 1915, after failing to find a buyer for the *Observer* and *Pall Mall Gazette*, William Waldorf Astor gave both titles to his son, Waldorf. This ended a period of great uncertainty for Garvin, and when the younger Astor sold the *Pall Mall Gazette* a short time later he was also released from an editorial obligation that had long been onerous. See Glossary, '*Pall Mall Gazette*'.

8 On Tuesday 9 March Lloyd George had surprised the Commons by proposing a new Defence of the Realm Bill – in the opinion of *The Times* 'the most far-reaching of the series'. The Government could already commandeer works where war material was being produced: the new legislation would give it control over works in which war materials were not being made, but could be: *The Times*, 10 March 1915. In a long article on the war in the *Observer* the following Sunday Garvin amplified Lloyd George's call for more guns, more ammunition and more men.

is still infinitely difficult to get into the War Office the sheer driving power and, at need, rushing power, of the Admiralty on the other side of the street . . .

Practise your riding as hard as you can – you never know when it may be useful to you or how much. More of all these things when we meet. Meanwhile my greetings to McClinton . . . Bless you! Dad

Wednesday 24th March
Norfolk Hotel, Clevedon, Somerset

Dear Mummy

Here is the letter you asked for. I can't give you much news because hardly anything of note has happened. We've drafted the recruits into the company, so my platoon shows a total now of fifty-five men on the muster roll. Actually, owing to men being taken away for other duties, we parade a little over thirty. Still, I'm better satisfied than before. One feels a tremendous responsibility in controlling and looking after even a platoon, the smallest unit commanded by a commissioned officer.

Turning away from business, I had a delightful afternoon last Sunday. I went away into the woods to pick white violets. I got a tiny bunch of them and then found a slope where I basked in the sun and read Meredith . . . The primroses cluster thicker and thicker among the woods, and by the edge of the forest paths I found the wild anemone in flower on Sunday, smelling deliciously, with a faint perfume like that of the orange blossom.

For me so much. Please look after yourself. I wish you could come here to rest, but I think we really shall change quarters on Monday to Tidworth . . . I've sent all my washing back in the box. It should arrive before this letter. Please have it washed and forward it to my new address, which I'll give you as soon as I learn it . . .

Bye-bye – fondest love . . . Ged.

Thursday 25th March
9 Greville Place, London NW

Delay, delay, dearest lad, owing to the economic arrangements and endless small struggles at the *Pall Mall Gazette*, where one must write short war notes three days a week to help save the staff there, though I myself will be as glad to get out of it as the ancient mariner to get rid of the albatross . . .

Very glad to meet Austen Chamberlain the other night at Colefaxes, but it was dreadful to hear Gwynne of the *Morning Post* talk of the Balkans and Hungary. I have given my laborious years to know the details of these things, and his moralising mind was like a dust sheet . . . Next night at McKenna's, the Home Secretary . . . and I had a real good talk with him. Unpopular persons attract me. I can see that there is a lot of jealousy and friction between ministers. I told him that nothing could save the Cabinet but 'vigour, vigour, vigour'. I added that decision at the head was required and my impression was that the Prime Minister was not doing his duty. He denied it, but the charge will do good. There is a real movement brewing to get rid of Asquith and make Lloyd George Prime Minister, which would be a good thing in some ways. But Asquith is an extraordinarily difficult person to get rid of, and as soon as his premiership evidently depends on his waking up, he will wake up . . .

I sleep in your little room now . . . Wiffles mumbled your coverlet, bemused to find me there and doggy brains vaguely besieged by such a mixture of associations. When your dirty clothes came home yesterday and he nosed them he had a fit almost, and raced up and down the house seeking his young master. Well well! God bless you. Dad.

❖

Tuesday 6 April to Tuesday 6 May – The Staff College, Camberley, Surrey

Ged spent almost the whole of April, and the first week of May, at the army staff college in Camberley, Surrey. Its proximity to London allowed him to spend most weekends at home, and so he wrote few letters during this period. He was also kept very busy. The syllabus covered everything from tactical instruction and topography to military hygiene and law. The young officers were also given trenchant advice: 'Alcohol in excess fosters disease . . . Forbid smoking when men are doing hard work . . . In defending a house get rid of all glass as far and as quickly as possible . . . Aircraft find things by shadow.' Ged observed divisional manoeuvres involving 19,000 men, and wrote home about experiments 'in blowing up a tree, a wire entanglement, and a bit of railway line'. As he put it in another letter: 'Truly we are scaling the sides of Pelion . . .' In keeping with this classical allusion he wished that he 'were out in Turkey' once the Allied invasion of Gallipoli had begun, on 25 April. He imagined that it would be 'a splendid battle among the hills above the Dardanelles' and his father agreed: 'We have got such a footing they will never shift us now, but there may be a month or more of the stiffest fighting.' Events on the peninsula soon showed how misplaced was the optimism of the father, and the romanticism of the son. Early in May Ged returned to his battalion and he spent the remainder of his training in England at Jellalabad Barracks in Tidworth, Hampshire. Increasingly his thoughts, and those of his parents, turned to the day when the 19th Division would leave for one of the fronts.

❖

Saturday 22nd May
Jellalabad Barracks, Tidworth, Hants.

Dear Mummy

Here's the letter I promised you last night. There are no indications as to when we shall go out. All next week we shall spend on the ranges, firing. The men shoot really quite well, with a pretty good allowance of good shots.

Major-General Fasken sent a letter to the troops today, intimating his satisfaction with their work, and saying that now we are to begin divisional training; that is, our ten thousand infantry and our five batteries will work together, and we shall manoeuvre with cyclists and a squadron (150 men) of cavalry. All very nice: but some of us forebode a further stay here of six weeks *si di mali faveant* – which means 'if the bad gods cherish us'.

The mess has improved notably in the last few days. The country I find adorable. White chestnuts bloom everywhere about the park here, and the buttercups twinkle in the grass like golden carp swimming just below the surface of a pond. I draw an increasing delight and refreshment from 'ye ingenious and delightful poem of Mr John Milton'. And really, when I have penned that, I've very little more to tell you.

Bye-bye – best love . . . Ged.

Tuesday 25th May
9 Greville Place, London NW

Very Private

Our Son

We loved all your letters. I wish this parent also could read John Milton in these times . . . and see a bit of nature at this season. However, there has been glorious blue over this patch of garden . . . so thick is the lilac and laburnum. If I don't write, it is for reasons. My thoughts are always with you. You mingle with all I do – I do it better therefore.

Last week was like nothing ever before – living in taxis or at the end of a telephone or over the writing pad. The Government came down, after nearly ten years of power that so often seemed unshakable, and of good luck that would never end.[9] The coalition was formed that I had worked for more steadily than any man . . . but either what you

9 Between March and May 1915 Asquith's Liberal Government was severely weakened by military reverses – at the Dardanelles and on the Western Front – and a growing crisis over a shortage of shells. Admiral 'Jacky' Fisher's dramatic resignation on 15 May, primarily because of Churchill's ambitious Dardanelles' policy, brought matters to a head, and Asquith was compelled by the Unionist opposition, led by Bonar Law, to form a coalition. The Unionists distrusted Churchill and it was made clear that he could not remain at the Admiralty: he was replaced by A. J. Balfour. By May 1915 the Liberals had been continuously in office for almost a decade, having come to power under Campbell-Bannerman in December 1905.

want hardly ever comes, or hardly ever as you wanted. Winston and Jacky are both out of the Admiralty, Jacky dead wrong this time; he tried to upset Winston by one violent impulse, and did, but upset himself too. He left the Admiralty in the middle of wartime, pending the concession of his demands. A First Sea Lord can no more rightly leave his post in that way than a captain his ship. Winston has been nearly heartbroken after all his splendid work, and the bitter injustice of villainous attacks, which he has borne in silence, but his career is only beginning.

I am determined to have the truth out when it can be said without hurting the Country. Of course one must be very tender towards Jacky – old and overstrained. Mr Balfour becomes First Lord. I dined on his right hand last Friday night and we had a great talk – philosophy and books as well as war. He said Winston was not 'rash' with [a] sense of levity, but had the true 'lionhearted courage', and I feel certain that Balfour means to stick to Winston's Dardanelles policy and put it right through . . .

Solano was up here in khaki yesterday, bringing his little machine-gun manual just out. It seems very clear and useful. I am having it sent to you at once. I also commissioned him to get you the best of all army pistols, the Smith and Wesson .45, just adapted for officers and takes army ammunition – the handle and action far better than revolvers, and tremendous stopping power. Solano says you throw out your arm straight, aim straight, look straight with both eyes at the object, and you must hit . . .

I don't think there's anything more to say . . . Dardanelles, very bloody and 'super-Homeric' indeed, will probably take two months; as for Flanders, not only French himself, but his whole staff are optimistic, and convinced that with plenty of high explosive we shall break the German line and shove them back a long way this summer. Man for man they are not up to our staff.

All the household loves you, our son. Dad

Tuesday 1st June
'D Range', Bulford, Wiltshire

Dear Mummy

I'm snatching a moment to write you this in the butts, in a spasm of rapid firing which I have to mark. Up at ten minutes to six this morning (it's now a quarter to nine). The battalion is firing a course of musketry. I suddenly find the position more comfortable, although I can't say my shooting improves. So far I've felt the usual lying position an awful strain. I got all you sent. Thank you awfully. The pistol looks fine. I've only used it once, and didn't hit the target above once. Perhaps because I was trying to aim with both eyes. Generally one closes one eye.

The fruit supplies us on the range. The chocolate we ate yesterday; and Williams helped me demolish the strawberries and cream, Stuart having gone off to Andover.[10] I'm looking to see you on Sunday . . .

Best love to you both. Get a really good rest. Ged.

Monday 14th June
Jellalabad Barracks, Tidworth, Hants.

Dear Mummy

I've no reason for writing; no atom of news offers. We fired on the range this morning, and heard a lecture in the afternoon. I think I've now been taking a cold bath every morning for a week. McClinton avers that it makes me fitter, but that probably indicates prejudice. He, I, and Maynard – another very nice fellow – went for a ride yesterday. I bear myself shockingly on a horse, but it was good fun.

The spring flowers have all gone, and this bit of country appears to bear few summer ones. The landscape looks mainly dull and grey-green. The days are very hot and the dust on the roads chokes one anywhere but at the head of a column; if a wagon passes the clouds expand like the genie in the bottle . . .

If I get leave I'll wire as soon as possible. Best love to all. Ged.

---

10 Stuart McClinton, whom Ged first met in the 7th South Lancs, and who became a close friend: see Biographical Notes.

Monday 21st June
Jellalabad Barracks, Tidworth, Hants.

Dear Mummy

I'm come back to a very busy existence.[11] Like the swallow I eat on the wing. All today I've been learning 'Physical Training and Bayonet Fighting' (9.30–12.30: 2.30–4.30). It sounds less exhausting than it feels.

In a few minutes I go on duty as member of a Court of Enquiry, to take evidence about the absence of one of the men, before declaring him a deserter. You'll be glad to hear that owing to a Royal review on Wednesday the three days' march has been put off. We got in about two this morning. I slept in the train almost continuously, so I experienced no unusual weariness when I had to get up at six. Most of the battalion has been digging. I've been by myself, except for one corporal, on the drill course, so representative of the battalion.

No further news. Write me when you have time – don't hurry on any account – and let me know how you go on, and Dad. I loved seeing you both, and all these two days. Bye-bye . . . Ged.

Tuesday 22nd June
9 Greville Place, London NW

Dearest Son

How glad you will be to get off the route march for the time, though I suppose the days of heavy labour are only postponed. The weather is clouded, yet very bright, and the wind comes in dry gusts: even our little garden . . . is baked, so I conceive what a Sahara of dust and 'dancing devils' your Tidworth will be presently, unless rain comes . . .

There called upon me in the afternoon a gentleman called Waldo representing *The Philadelphia Public Ledger* and other respectable American journals – an earnest gentleman, and able, but more ponderously fluent and full of clichés, and all the more obvious

11 Ged had spent the weekend 19–20 June at home on leave.

quotations, than any gentleman without exception it has ever been my lot to sit under. He is doing all Europe in wartime in about nine days, and simply packing little notebooks with impressions scribbled down . . . He asked me to excuse him while he scribbled a few impressions in my presence, and I did excuse him, as he was evidently a very true friend of the Allies. I liked him all the same and only feared for his health and brain, dizzying round like that on the wings of the whirlwind; but then his countenance was solid, suggesting Puritan ancestry, and he neither smokes, drinks, nor takes afternoon tea, so probably can stand a lot – like the Russians. Our poor friends, the said Russians are the most astonishing and lovable brave people in the amount of hammering they can stand without breaking up . . .[12]

Wiffles at this moment is following his missus about with his normal absurd devotion. All the dear loves to you from us singly and severally, as well as all the natural and acquired affection that can possibly be contained in the person of the parent who is your Daddy (and hoped you can read this . . . scribble, worthy of Wm Waldo).

Tuesday 22nd June
Jellalabad Barracks, Tidworth, Hants.

Dear Dad

I can't give you any fresh news. Even the barber says 'I never takes rumours for anything now.' Still, he appears to think that the King is coming tomorrow, by way of saying good-bye to his men. Maybe.

I think everyone waits confidently, and meanwhile all are healthy enough and happy.

When we do go, I think the best way of indicating our whereabouts will be by reference to some poet: say – for London 'Longfellow' or

12 At the beginning of May German and Austrian forces in Galicia forced a Russian retreat along a 160-km front, inflicting heavy casualties and taking as many as 140,000 prisoners. The Russians' 'entire position in the Carpathians was unhinged' (Hew Strachan, *The First World War: A New Illustrated History*, London, 2003, p. 139) and on 3 June the city of Przemysl was retaken by the Central Powers. On 22 June Lvov (Lemberg) also fell.

I J. L. Garvin by Alick Ritchie, *Vanity Fair* Supplement
('Fifty to sixty cigars a week': CG to RGG, 14 September 1915)

for Bethune 'Browning', the first letter giving the initial in each case. Your wits will have to complete the name . . . So if I were near Souchez and said casually in the middle of the letter 'I'm just indulging in a little Shakespeare' you would do your best to understand. I'm certain to be in the British sector, which is small enough for this to work, I think. I'll make no other mention of poets' names; and while I think of it – 'Wyatt' stands for 'Wypers'.

Dearest love . . . Ged.

Wednesday 23rd June
9 Greville Place, London NW

My Dear Old Boy

It was good to get another letter this morning. We wait very attentively to hear whether the rumours are right this time. We will interpret the posts geographically as you say. I feel somehow that the move will come soon. We dined with the Chancellor of the Exchequer last night. He thinks it more than possible that your division may go to the Dardanelles, where we need to be heavily strengthened, but considerable reinforcements have gone out there already; and the fighting in the French sector north of Arras has been about as terrific as ever was raged in the world, far more so than the official communiqués suggest . . .

Between Flanders and Dardanelles there's not much to choose is there? Except the smells may be milder in the latter, and the winter less damp and gloomy. I hope that by the time I am writing this His Majesty will have been bucked up by the sight of your division, and partly compensated for the loss of his whisky and soda.[13] But we would like to know whither it is to be and when. God bless you. Young [Harry] Butters came in last night from Mrs O'Sullivan's. He has joined the field artillery and just finished his battery training. He

13 Alcohol consumption was believed to be seriously impeding production in armaments factories, and at the end of March George V offered to set an example by giving up drink for the duration of the war. Lord Kitchener was one of those who immediately followed suit: *The Times*, 1 April 1915.

looks every inch a soldier . . .

Mummy is more composed now we have discovered that what has been the matter with her is hay fever, that most troublesome but not dangerous complaint. I am relieved to know what it is . . . Of course we will talk of nothing but you now – and long to know more. I will write again tomorrow. Meanwhile my dearest we have you wholly in our hearts and our prayers. Dad.

Saturday 26th June
Jellalabad Barracks, Tidworth, Hants.

Dear Mummy

I got your letter today. Thank you ever so much for writing. I can hardly believe we shall go to the Dardanelles. We have no oriental or summer kit, whereas for Flanders we have nearly everything necessary.

Next week, on Tuesday I think, the brigade goes on a route march, bivouacking the night and returning on the morning after. That'll be good fun; I'll thoroughly enjoy it. On Tuesday week next we occupy our trenches from ten o'clock one night until relieved about that time the next night. The scheme sounds good, but I think twenty-four hours for practice will be quite enough. I can pose now, after my class, as an expert bayonet-fighter, able to spear any Prussian . . . By the way, do you mind sending me a box of tooth-soap and a wee box (metal if procurable) of boracic ointment? I often get little cuts that poison slightly, and would rather doctor them myself.

Dearest love to you, Dad, Granny, Vi, Noonie, Kitty and Bunny.[14]
Ged xxxxxxxxx

Monday 28th June
9 Greville Place, London NW

Dearest Lad

We went to Miss Heynemann's yesterday and saw the sketch of

14 The girls were known by family nicknames – Viola was 'Vi' or 'Viva'; Una 'Noonie' or 'John'; Katharine 'Kitty' or 'Gipsy'; and Ursula 'Bunny' or 'Jimmy'. Ged used all of these variants in his letters home.

you which pleased us both very much. It was absurdly like Dad, and also like me. So you are the Harmony. Did Dad tell you that Charlie Sargent had lost an eye somewhere in Flanders. His mother, very well intentioned and equally wooden, wired on Saturday week last for us to get her a passport (she didn't know where he was, how he was injured, or anything). Of course we could only get a form, and, equally of course, as the War Office told me a few nights ago, you can't get out unless the Commandant makes a request for you to go. His father writes broken-heartedly.

Dad is so pleased when you write that I wish you'd forget me and write to him.

I expect he has told you all the political and war news . . .

Dearest love, blessings – oh such blessings my beloved lad, and prayers. Mammy.

Monday 28th June
9 Greville Place, London NW

Dear Old son

. . . It's hard now to know what will happen or when you will go out. Everything is altered. I should think there can be no question of a grand offensive of the Allies in the west until ammunition and machine guns are piled up far more on the British front and certain other improvements made in our own artillery.[15] The neglect or want of pre-vision appears more maddening the more one learns. Do you know that the French and British artilleries never had a meeting to interchange views until Lloyd George brought a little conference of gunners, with most valuable results, when he went over to Boulogne the other day? Again the French have tried their big push – that, as

15 A succession of British failures, beginning with Neuve Chapelle in March, coupled with the frustration of French efforts to achieve a breakthrough, induced a sense of greater realism about the war in Britain, and in June *The Times* warned: 'This country has got to set its teeth . . . [and] face the probability of a prolonged unprogressive campaign in the West': 25 June 1915, p. 9. The importance of industrial-scale quantities of shells, machine guns and heavy artillery was beginning to be properly understood.

I hinted yesterday, was what the battle of Artois was – and have not got through, though they did prodigies of heroism and skill, and lost 300,000 men in seven weeks . . . In a word, for offensive purposes (except at the Dardanelles) this year's campaign is gone. The Allies must reorganise for the spring and the world's fate absolutely depends on our new armies, including McClinton and you, my son.

Well it's all stern and in a way disappointing – bitterly so considering what might have been done – but there's something inspiring in it too. If need be we, at the last, shall fight Germany single-handed, but it won't come to that. Lloyd George, electrifying man, is really doing wonders . . .

I suppose you won't go out till August or later. All the love – Mummy rather better. Dad

Thursday 1st July
Jellalabad Barracks, Tidworth, Hants.

Dear Mummy

I've been too tired to take up the pen this evening in time. We made a sixteen-mile march yesterday, between two and half past nine. Today I can scarcely move for fatigue. Tomorrow evening we go into the trenches for practice in the relief of another battalion. On Sunday we begin our twenty-four hours. We shall have immense excitement – live bombs in places, and miniature rifle cartridges to shoot miniature targets at one stated time. All perfectly safe and great fun . . .

Bye-bye. Dearest love to you and Dad, Granny, Vi, Noonie, Gipsy, Bunny. Remembrances to the maids.

Sunday 4th July
Jellalabad Barracks, Tidworth, Hants.

Dear Dad

I fear rain will descend on our trenches tonight. We shall pace our fosses like the hidalgo, dull and damp, and above all cursing the Germans and the weather. A terrible heat has drugged the air all today, heralding a thunderstorm which will just catch us.

I shall not be able to write before Tuesday, if the programme takes effect as given out. I wish I could send you the staff-map of our trenches, an admirable piece of work, about fifty yards to the inch. Phew! that thunderclap sounded horrid. There's another, banging and rumbling as though nothing else in the world deserved a hearing. The North Lancs face us in the opposite line. *Gott Strafe* the North Lancs, a hateful and treacherous foe, who will not jib even at the killing of our brave soldiers. You may tell Granny that a real Catholic priest, an old army chaplain, has been attached to us for rations; though as yet we see little of him. The gentle rain drops from Heaven at this point. Otherwise I should have to cease from holding forth . . .

Could Mummy get hold of bags for my trenchscope like McClinton's? And are the trenchscopes on the market? One of our officers clamours for one.

Dearest love to you and Mummy, Granny, Vi, Noonie, Kitty and Bunny. Ged.

Monday 5th July
'7.55 a.m. Salisbury Plain'

Dear Mummy

Here's my first really truly letter from the trenches. Quite good trenches too. Nothing much has happened so far. Of course we got next to no sleep. The men behaved very well, holding their tongues in the main and gathering quietly for the attack. We attacked the North Lancs about half past two, but the company we were attached to sprinkled up our men with its own, and muddled the arrangements. We thought the attack very weak and hardly even exciting.

The night rattled with shooting, less in our lines than in those to the left. The sentries lost no opportunity of obeying the order to fire on all scouts of the enemy. I remained awake – on duty – patrolling the trenches all night until we stood to arms. 'Standing to Arms' means waking up everybody and getting ready to smite or be smitten; the function takes place an hour before dawn . . . The sky looked beautiful just before our attack, the night paling to a cloudy blue and the waning moon brightening opposite to a big lonely star.

After the assault a rest was declared from 3.15 until 10.15. Helped by a couple of sips from your brandy to warm me up and fortify me against an uncommonly chill morning and draughty shelter, I filched three hours' sleep. Then to breakfast – tea and bread and butter, which I enjoyed immensely. A wash and then this letter. There you have the full chronicle . . .

Another attack of some kind is expected this afternoon. I shan't be able to give you an account of it today. Bye-bye. With dearest love . . . Ged.

Monday 5th July
9 Greville Place, London NW

Good Correspondent

We Garvins are in our nature northerners and do better – I mean flourish – in the cold weather than in the hot. If it were not for the heat that softens the marrow of the Indian races every season at this time of the year, we could never hold India. I maintain stoutly that Japan must not be thought of as oriental, but as northern, sea nursed and mountain bred. What it must be among the red grit and dirty scrub of the Dardanelles . . . All this means that I think of you going sixteen miles with your pack in the dog days. From the beginning of time it was a hard life being a soldier . . . I think irrelevantly next of cream-sodas at Selfridges, and wish I were beside you in all things, and that father and son were going to the front together. That impossibility is always in my head . . .

If I don't answer everything you tell me about, know that I note all with seeing mind, and long to have a full and particular account of the days in the trenches. As for your trenchscope questions: bags are sent to you direct, but the thing isn't on the market properly yet. Let your officer friends who want one write direct to 'W. J. McAlice Esq., c/o The *Observer*' . . . who will pass the letter on to the agent . . .

I spent hours with Winston until deep in the morning. We talked at his mother's and walked home still talking and let ourselves in at Arlington Street and still talked. Leaving the Admiralty has given him a better chance to look into the whole war, and his grasp of the full problem is now astonishingly good.[16] He and Lloyd George are likely to make it up, God be praised. I loathe my friends not being friends with each other . . . Dardanelles supremely important now, nothing less . . . I should not in the least wonder if you went to Gallipoli after all.

All the deep loves go to you. Dad.

Tuesday 6th July
Jellalabad Barracks, Tidworth, Hants.

Dear Dad

I jumped for joy when I was handed two long letters for breakfast. I'm answering both tonight. I can't give you much news. The divisional route march has been cancelled. I'll try to get leave next week, very likely.

Our machine guns are turning out frightfully shoddy. Some vital spring has been made of the very worst material, and apparently snaps like a dry twig, putting the gun out of action. We shall, of course, take out a number of extra springs, but they can hardly be fitted in a moment. The gun was made in Belgium by an American firm, I think, the 'Lewis'.[17] Of course you mustn't tell anyone about that, or that I told you. I fancy it's an offence under the Army Act.

Bye-bye – dearest love. Ged.

---

16 After being forced to resign from the Admiralty in May, following setbacks to his plans for the Dardanelles, Churchill became Chancellor of the Duchy of Lancaster. This was a lowly, non-departmental office, but it allowed him to retain his seat in the Cabinet and the war council. As his daughter Mary Soames later remarked: 'He was determined to see through events for which he bore a large responsibility, and strategic policies in which he believed wholeheartedly' (Mary Soames (ed.), *Speaking for Themselves: The Personal Letters of Winston and Clemetine Churchill*, London, 1998, p. 110).

17 The standard British machine gun was the belt-fed, water-cooled Vickers, but in the summer of 1914 the lighter, magazine-fed American Lewis .303 was being developed under a European patent.

Wednesday 7th July
Jellalabad Barracks, Tidworth, Hants.

Dearest Mummy

I'm just writing a word for you and Dad. I fear we may go as early as next Tuesday, but the Thursday or Friday seem probable. I'm sending back all my extra kit, and keeping only what I intend to take abroad. Two things I should like got for me, if anyone has time, a mackintosh ground sheet and a Bellow's French dictionary. Stuart's people are coming over to Eastbourne, where his brothers are camped.

I hear rumours of a big attack on the German lines. The men are in transports of joy at the idea of going to the front. Arrangements are proceeding now. No news else.

Don't fret, for God's sake; try to get better. I'll come to see you as early as I possibly can, if we get leave.

All the love I can send you, in the meantime, and Dad and Granny and the Kiddies. Ged.

Wednesday 7th July
9 Greville Place, London NW

Our son

Well, even what one has been expecting every day is a bit of a twist when it comes, but Mummy bears up bravely, far better than at the first alarm, and you may rely upon me to do all in great things and little that a man can . . . All your recent manoeuvres there suggested finishing off training and nearing the day of going out, but we are on tenterhooks now to know whether it is to be Flanders or Dardanelles. Dearest boy of ours, I can only say 'God bless you' again and again a thousand times . . .

It is so good to get a word which brings what you are doing nearer to us. Always will you get a daily letter from me. No more now. This is from Mummy too and carries all her heart. Dad.

Thursday 8th July
Jellalabad Barracks, Tidworth, Hants.

Dear Mummy

Please pass on to Dad my deepest thanks for his letter. I haven't anything to say, except to wish that you were alright and to beg you and Dad not to fret. We are going to France, almost certainly. We shall get twelve hours' leave exactly before then. Unless I hear to the contrary (by wire) I'll apply for Saturday. It'll just give me time to come up and say good-bye. The 15th Division are going out today; most of them are gone already. Very dearest love to you and Dad. Ged

Friday 9th July
9 Greville Place, London NW

Our Dearest Son

It is everything to us that there is a chance of seeing you tomorrow . . . I suppose there's no chance of being allowed to see you off at the port of embarkation, or even meeting you at the station there? Find out these things for me if you can, but don't let it be a worry to you when you have so much to do. Mummy I think you will find much better . . .

You need not tell me not to fret: your father is I suppose as full of faults as a human creature can be, but he has the heart of a lion (though I say it) and strength enough under God for himself and all around him when strength is needed. Though a certain stoppage in all decent souls makes full speech impossible on things too dear and deep to be expressed between father and son (being menfolk and denied emotional relief), yet there never was in the world a son dearer to a father nor a better son. So, my boy, in this great crisis of the world we both, in different ways, stake our all and nothing less. But you would no more have me weak, than I would have you. So now for Mummy's sake we shall have that best thing – a complete and cheerful courage – both knowing the immeasurable love that lies behind it. Mummy will speak to you for herself, and I will bless you and ask God every waking hour to bless you, and dare pray that you may come back to us. No more until tomorrow. I am trying to get all the work I can done today. Dad

2

The Lys Front

The 19th Division left England for France on 17 July 1915, the 7th South Lancs on board the SS Onward. *When it arrived in France the division was assigned to the Indian Corps, which was holding the line on the Lys front, and whose headquarters were at Norrent Fontes, about ten miles from St Omer. The battalion began marching inland from Boulogne on 19 July, and Ged's first communiqué home was a hurriedly written field card. This was followed by a two-part letter, begun in Boulogne on Sunday 18th and finished near St Omer on Wednesday 21st.*

❖

Sunday 18th July 1915
[Boulogne, Pas-de-Calais]

[Dear Mummy and Dad]

I'll write you snatches now and again and post it when I can; at present all letters are forbidden.

. . . We crossed the Channel in the dark, with all lights out. Three hundred yards or so to the right a destroyer escorted us, a swift thing rather blacker than the environing sea. We marched up through a dark town and settled down in this rest camp about three this morning.

The day has been like other days in camp, conferences on one thing and another, parades for inspection, and issue of emergency ration. If I come home wounded I shall bring you all some army biscuits; they fill no more space than a locket, and will certainly outlive the family . . . [*half a page cut out by censor*] . . . I went out at five o'clock this morning. I wish you could have seen the town as it looked then, in the early brilliance of the sun. On the ridge to the left, between me and the water, the white walls shone and the red roofs of the houses. On the right, the older quarter climbed in the shadow of the hill, a grey church tower standing forth like Goliath coming out from the ranks of the Philistines.

I'm going down the town in a little while. I'll write you more tomorrow (perhaps).

Monday 19th July
9 Greville Place, London NW

Little Son

Your card came this morning and even its compulsory laconics were dear to us but we understood better why Oliver wanted much more, though the cook should hit him with a spoon. After this drop of skilly we want a whole porridge bowl of your whereabouts. You are in France now and we can scarcely believe it, and you are taking a hand in the biggest business since the world was, and a father like me feels superannuated and wonders what use he is after all, though pegging away in his fashion. We are longing to know or guess in what part of the *charmant pays* (*et pays heroique*) your tent is pitched, and where your route lies, and what you and Stuart think of it all, and how it strikes the men – very like the fellows, except for clothes and style of fighting gear, that went with Harry the Fifth on an opposite errand.

But this is the diffuse drivel of a wandering mind and soldiermen on service want solid news from home. I suppose there isn't any. Mummy seems braced and better every day and has written letters in all directions this weekend – a score of them at least. It's always a good sign when letters are polished off like that. She will speak for herself, but I confess it was the pinch of my existence to part with you on Friday amid the Noah's deluge on Tidworth – a surprising twinge for this old bosom, that ought to have been so well prepared, and for the first seven minutes in the motor I wondered whether the stronger sex was not going to be for a moment the mere woman of the two. But, Lord bless you, that passed in the right way and the rest was rain and philosophy – about an equal quantity of both.

Andover station, and the train packed with khaki – wet, but jolly, and taking to hymns with a tone of Rabelaisian cheer when they had exhausted the music-hall ditties. We loved them all and in the hustle to get into the train I hoisted your green bag on my shoulder in thorough sympathy with them. Mummy and I then dined on the train and were also cheerful, and faith came to us, and we also loved our lad more than ever before, and we got home exceedingly late and the work went better for Saturday than might have been expected . . . Everybody at Cliveden wished you good luck – so did the *Observer* and *PMG* people, especially the sturdy master printer of the *Observer* . . . who takes enormous interest in the son of his real friend, the editor. 'Nearly everybody has somebody out there you know,' said the railway porter at Andover, 'and it seems to bring you together like. There ain't no class now!'

God bless you and guard you – Dad

Monday 19th July
9 Greville Place, London NW

My dearest tall Son

Your silly card arrived this morning and was satisfactory (even to the xxx's) as far as it went, but it wouldn't go far to quench hunger or thirst – and now, being a greedy mother, I'm looking for letters. I wonder where you are and what you want and how soon before I should start sending out the little extras which you will like to have. Let me know – always – if there is anything you want specially. I've told the office to send you and Stuart your *Observer* each, and ordered a number, I think a dozen or so, to go to Major Winser.[1]

After we left you . . . Dad and I looked out of the opposite window

---

1 Major Peter Winser was Ged's commanding officer: see the Biographical Notes below; all nicknames and Christian names are cross-referenced to surnames in the Index.

occasionally. I talked frivolities, but we got through all right. We really could have taken you all to Andover and fed you there if we'd had an ounce of common sense, which seems to have deserted these prime parents of yours. We waited on the platform at Andover for one and a half hours and saw numerous Tommies going on leave and going to the front . . . In the meantime give my love to Stuart and say I'll write to him tomorrow. Dearest love my dearest lad. Prayers and blessings and God Speed to you – Your Mummy.

Wednesday 21st July
[*en route* to St Omer]

[Dear Mummy and Dad]

As a matter of fact, I haven't had time to go on since Sunday. On Monday we came up here to billets about twenty miles from the battle front. I dwell alone in a wee inn where we all get three meals a day extremely cheap . . .

So far we do very little: inspect the men daily, and today a short but rather tiring march over a road or lane that may have been paved by Henry of Navarre – I wouldn't be certain. The spirit of the officers is excellent. They can march quite a few miles without turning a hair. The country rolls gently, hiding red hamlets in the folds. The roads twist (unhedged for the most part) between fields of waving corn, sometimes dipping and rising again to a forest, but generally undulating, dotted with odd windmills and lines of high trees like columns. It's the land of Victor Hugo . . .

Love to you, Granny, Vi, Noonie, Kitty and Bunny. Remembrances to the maids. I'm sorry I missed Edith coming away. Ged . . .

Friday 23rd July
9 Greville Place, London NW

Dear Old Son

. . . These have been two curious days – dark and raving, with heavy rain and a few thunderclaps this morning. We all confess that this tense atmosphere sets every nerve jigging. Thunder and rain always make me want to go out and walk . . .

We are all well but there is still no news of you. I accordingly extend my theories and imagine you (no doubt erroneously) stationed to relieve the Belgians on the Yser instead of Frenchmen near Arras. I had a delightful talk with AJB yesterday. Submarine affairs going on very well. We can never know quite how many we dispose of, for a submarine disappears when you miss it as well as when you hit. We have undoubtedly got a good many and the latest list shows the pirates did not sink a single vessel of any kind last week, though they have been over five months at work. It really looks as though all the much-boasted Teutonic scares – submarines, Zeppelins, poison gas . . . guns and the rest – were going bust one after the other. Jellicoe in his deprecating sailor-like way feels pretty confident to say the least of smashing the Germans if they ever come out. My own strong impression is that the sea affair is all right, and no great power holding the sea was ever beaten yet . . .

God bless you my boy. Dad . . .

Saturday 24th July
[between St Omer and Hazebrouck]

Dearest One

I'm awfully sorry I couldn't send you a note yesterday, but I was up half past five and after a long day's marching had scarcely a moment to myself till bedtime at half past ten . . .

I rose at 4.30 this morning, after sleeping very cosy in the garret loft, amazingly clean and nice, of a tiny wing in an uninhabited manor-house far from anywhere. We have now marched seven or eight weary miles over a road fit only for steamrollers and penitential friars. You would scarcely credit the difficulty of marching for a day (even with this long two-and-half-hour halt) in full equipment, pack, haversack, water flask, pistol, field glasses and so on. Two or three dusky horsemen have just ridden past us . . . Some of the men march very pluckily. I fear a good many are faint-hearted when inglorious drudgery calls to be done. How you would laugh if you could hear me chattering

French – with a fluency which sometimes startles myself – to the country folk, bargaining for straw last night for instance, with an old lady who screeched a vile dialect, and deaf old man, silver-haired, who told me chatting by a straw rick under the harvest moon that he had been a soldier in 'soixante dix'.

Here we marched off again. I adore these Flemish countrysides, the open road, the sea of wheat – 'ceres ripe for harvest waving' – and the frieze of dull trees below a rainy heaven . . .[2] We have just lunched off a mess of beautifully cooked eggs (half omelette and half scramble), French bread and butter from a wheel loaf, apple jelly, all home-made at a farm where all our men (B Company) are billeted in barns round a four-cornered yard with a castle gate like a picture from *Don Quixote* . . .

My shoulder feels as though it would crack off; how these pack straps tug. We have covered about twenty-five miles in two days. It doesn't sound much, but you will know now what it can be. Still, I might be shouldering an eighteen-foot pike, like my fore-runners, or heaving a gross targe along. I have had two and a half small tumblers of Bordeaux wine (ten years old) with the sourness mellowed off, a light admirable red wine. I sip your brandy now and again, so does Stuart. I have to censor my men, so bye-bye for now.

All the love of my heart to you . . . Ged.

Saturday 24th July
9 Greville Place, London NW

My dearest Laddie

I expect Dad, being a better correspondent and letter writer than ever I was or could be, has given you any news there was to give. Also I've been very tired since I wrote last. I managed to write twenty-two letters and seventeen cheques on Monday and had otherwise a rather

---

2 From John Milton, *Paradise Lost*, Book IV, lines 980–2 (Oxford World Classics edition, 2004): 'With ported spears, as thick as when a field / Of ceres ripe for harvest waving bends / Her bearded grove of ears, which way the wind / Sways them'.

lazy day, being a day when rest was fairly essential . . .

I've had your other coat relined and cleaned. Say when and where I am to send it . . . I wish we knew where you were or what doing. Those postcards are a boon, but still unsatisfactory . . . With my love to Stuart, whom I shall try to send a word to, and my dearest love, thoughts and prayers for you, my dearest one. Mammy.

Sunday 25th July
[between Aire-sur-la-Lys and St Venant]

Dear Dad

. . . The package reached me just before lunch. The veriest of Chinese paragons would not deserve all the attention that has gone to its selection and arrangements. We are sucking the acid-drops at the moment. Five of us lay last night under an orchard pear tree, our beds – valises – radiating from the base of the trunk.

I believe the cows ate our straw in the night, but I slept magnificently and woke up as fit as a fiddle . . . Madame here feeds us on the fat of the land and cooks amazingly. I forgot to tell you that we occupy the chief room . . . of the farmhouse which forms one side of our billet. We bath in the river or canal as often as possible, instance this morning. Stuart keeps well, but I see little of him. Our hostess's brother-in-law has come in on leave till tomorrow. He handles a heavy gun near Rheims and says nothing has happened near him for months. We heard the guns at our first billet – a nerve-shaking sound, though muffled, like the reverberation of an organ, very soft. No more news. Love to you and Mummy. Please give full details as to how you all are. I wish I could kiss Mummy once for every acid-drop. If I see anything to send, it shall come. Love to the girls and Granny. Remember me to the maids. Ged

Tuesday 27th July
9 Greville Place, London NW

Dearest of dear lads

Your first letter arrived yesterday morning, with three sheets, rather cut-about. I suppose you'd said something that the idiotic censor disapproved of and so he simply chopped it off. I hope he had some brains or intelligence to guide him and didn't just do it for cussedness, 'cos I know I'm as safe as houses . . . Your second letter arrived as we were dining – the Morants were here – so I read it out. Dear lad, if I could have shouldered that burden for you it would have been a joy to me. Dad seems to think he knows where you are at the moment . . .

As usual, in the last week, we are inundated with people lunching and dining. Last night Sir Robert and Lady Morant. Today lunch Bishop of Pretoria – Mike Furse and Julie Heynemann; tonight Sir Edward and Gerty and Katharine Furse, then the MP for Calgary, Bennet, dines here Monday Bank Holiday, so we are more or less busy. I believe Dad dines with Haldane on Thursday, and I go to the theatre with Gerald McKay. He has phoned to borrow one of your toppers . . .

Dad is out, I believe to help in the transfer of the *PMG* to some unknown individual, but I'm not certain. All I do know is we shall be poor next year and I wish the girls will do something to help in the house. Una says her brains are too good to go to housekeeping. Dearest love . . . Mummy.

Tuesday 27th July
9 Greville Place, London NW

Dearest Old Son

When your second letter came it was unclipped by the abhorred scissors of the censor and it was a splendid one with the features of things and their atmosphere. The family were happy and it so touched this parent's idiosyncrasy, perhaps because we have so many kinks in common, that I felt myself beside you all the way and wanted to put something on my shoulder, were it but a broomstick, and go marching . . .

You will ask me of news of my own. There's not much. The *Observer* really seems to be becoming a moral mainstay for all staunch people, and thanks come from all parts of the world. I really expect to finish with the *PMG* in the next few days and it is practically certain that I shall . . .

Wiffles and I had a great game in the garden when the weather lifted yesterday afternoon. I bought him a red ball and he went mad with excitement. The said Wiffles is quite invaluable to me. Well, the girls are done with school for the time. Don't know yet whether Viva is through her matric. – and don't feel as though she would get through. Una has got second prize for swimming and is first in mathematics and high in science as usual. Kitty is top at everything and head of her form. Jimmy is the proud possessor of a report which shows her coming up quite well among the babies.

Alas! the pack is the soldier's sorrow, and ten miles with it is always as much as twenty without. You and your men must have had some gruelling days – and getting the straps off at night a blessing under the stars. We are all well. This . . . carries love exceeding, 'Good night and God bless him' – Dad

Thursday 29th July
9 Greville Place, London NW

Dear Old Boy

No further budget from you so the longer it is delayed the more keenly we wait for it. You were marching on the sound of the guns, so I suppose you have heard them by now, or at least the big ones overbooming the rest . . . Mummy – who is brighter, and going out with Gerty and Gerald to the theatre tonight – will have told you about Viva. I was delighted the plucky little thing did it after all. Now she has got through her matric. she can concentrate on the things she likes . . . It is a pleasure to see all your sisters released from the shackles of learning . . .

In the evening I dined with Winston at his mother's and walked home with him afterwards to Arlington Street, and didn't leave him until after one. Of course we talked war, war, war, chiefly the Russians, and agreeing on most points. How the Russians contrive not only to fight as they do, but to keep a line at all, is a mystery to us . . . One must believe them to know their own, but it keeps one's heart in one's mouth that they are holding on to Warsaw while all their communications are threatened two hundred miles in rear . . .[3]

The Government here don't know quite what to do yet about National Service – Asquith and K. of K. still rather wanting to do without 'compulsion' (absurd word) when full organisation is essential, and direction of the whole people by its Government is the thing required. Still, though we shall want a million more men, we have three million now and are getting on far better with the munitions. France expects us to have about a million and a quarter men out there to hold at least a hundred miles of line, and, by Christmas, that is what we shall be doing. What a magnificent speech Lloyd George made to the miners today.[4] He has faults, but he has a trumpet voice and a winged spirit and he is our real national leader in the war . . .

Our very love to you. God bless you. Dad

Tuesday 3rd August
[near Merville]

Dear Mummy

Since I last wrote you a long screed, I haven't had much to say. This time I can give you something better than the card bulletin . . . Congratulate Vi for me on passing matric., and Noonie and Kitty for doing so well. I hear unofficially that I have been gazetted a full lieutenant – goodness knows why. Can you send me four little bronze enamel stars, like those on my British Warm, only brown? Burberry keeps them – but I don't know what other shop . . .

---

3 German armies were advancing to the north and south of Warsaw, but, according to a Russian communiqué, the Russian forces on the Lublin front were 'repulsing the enemy's onset with valour and tenacity': *The Times*, 20 July 1915, p. 6.

4 At a conference of mine owners and mine workers in London, Thursday 29 July, Lloyd George pointedly made a rousing appeal for a spirit of self-sacrifice. The war, he said, would decide 'the fate of freedom for ages to come' and 'he poured righteous scorn upon the men and women who think that freedom implies the right to shirk, that it implies "the right for you to expect to enjoy, and for others to defend"': *The Times*, 30 July 1915.

I can't give you much news of the front. Very often we hear cannon buffeting the air in the distance, and dim lights flicker in the east of nights. An aeroplane passed the town the other evening, and the guns fired at it. You see a sharp flash, then a puff of thick smoke, and a second or two later the thud comes to you, muffled and dull. Motor cars tear along the high road every now and then – that horrible cobbled road.

A wild desire came upon me last night to ride along that highway till I couldn't go further. The road runs on straight into the sunset and the gorgeous flame yesterday might have draped the sky behind the death of Agamemnon, a deep gold, almost alive, like coral. Rain fell in the dusk; I think that at the right moment, rain brings one nearer than anything else to the heart of nature.

All young officers are learning to handle machine guns more or less. I like the toll, but a bayonet, or still better a sword, pleases me better – all in imagination of course. I forget whether I told you that I'm learning a bit about bombs and grenades, things almost as deadly as machine guns. And that, I think, is all that I have to say for the time . . .

Bye-bye, dearest love to you and Dad, Granny, Viva, Noonie, Kitty and Bunny. Enjoy your holiday and remember me to the maids.
Ged . . .

Wednesday 4th August
[near Merville]

Dear Mummy

Life today has proceeded as life did yesterday. The rain and extreme cold have passed; massive clouds fill the sky and the air, as so often in this region, silvers all the low country . . .

I ate today for lunch a new dish, an ear of Indian corn, broiled from the field by the farm. You butter the hot ear thickly, and nibble off the grains like picking a bone. It's not worse than eating asparagus, and the corn is very good. I honestly don't like asking you for things too much, but will you put in a tin of corn on your list as a possible element in parcels? . . .

I was chatting with 'Madame' just now in her orchard, where, like Granny, she was walking about watching the fruit ripen. She's a nice old thing, very gentle, with mouse hair and a face unused to anger. She says the soldiers – Scotch especially – have taken 150 francs worth from her. But the residue reddens in great clumps and looks very good.

No more gossip today. Bye-bye. Dearest love . . . Ged

Saturday 7th August
'Shootlands', near Dorking, Surrey

Dearest and dearest Lad o' mine

I know I haven't written for a very long time, but I know also that you will understand that I must have been fairly busy . . .

Your letters, even when wee bits, give the liveliest joy. Hume's mother gives me Hume's to read . . . Stuart writes occasionally, and now we're getting settled I shall send you all a parcel of some sort this week. Tell me if the jam from Tiptree comes – because Hume hasn't mentioned it and I am not going to pay for things you don't get . . . I've written to Mrs Saull to cut the stars off your British Warm and will send one to Burberry to send out as soon as they arrive . . .

How your wish to walk through the sunset brought back the years – when I hadn't so much housekeeping and felt just so . . . when a wild wet windy day at Tynemouth tore my hat from my head and my hair down and splashed me all over, so that I had to go to a shop to be made slightly presentable. Those days were worth it. I'm glad you're learning machine-gunnery – most important I think. How I wish you were here . . .

By the way, did Dad tell you that you're on the Christ Church Oxford Roll of Honour? The list has come, but as Dad has taken it and I don't interfere with his letters or papers I can't send it, but will ask him to if you like.

I sent today £1.00 of Woodbine cigarettes for your men and a little toffee to fill the box. Tell me if they like them and tell me how often you want them. Dearest dearest love . . . Your Mammy.

Thursday 12th August
[*en route* to Vieille Chapelle]

Dear Dad

. . . Will you tell Mummy that, up to date, no jam has come. Jam is a very sticky thing: it may have clung to some subordinate in the Post Office. I think Granny sent me a cake yesterday; I sampled a slice and found it admirable, but as we were moving and I couldn't take it, the servants had to eat the rest. My servant, by the way, is an awfully nice boy, a miner, but very clean and tidy.

For heavy troops, infantry to wit, all marching is very troublesome; night marches fret one especially. Everything you pass glides by like a shadow; you keep no idea of distance, merely plodding along with the rest of the machine. You can't see before your feet, and every tiny inequality in the road jars you through and through. Don't think I'm enduring the faintest atom of hardship; roads last night proved pretty even, and there are always glimpses of things transfigured by the night. As we passed a cottage garden in the dark a breath of some flower – stock I think – crossed the way for a second, just like a scene in a novel. One's blood goes quicker, though, tramping along a deserted street – the houses faintly luminous and a big church tower looming at the far end; or to come suddenly round a corner upon the gaunt wreck of a village church . . .

Aug 13th . . . They called for letters unexpectedly at noon yesterday, so I left this to be finished and despatched a field postcard. Yesterday afternoon a parcel arrived – Mummy is a veritable witch; the towel came just right . . .

I fear some particular censor at the base gets your letters, reads the tit-bits to his fellows and decides that the information is far too dangerous to be allowed near the firing line. I got no word yesterday; perhaps it was merely a delay in the post.[5]

5 Although outgoing mail to the BEF, and other areas served by the Army Post Office, was liable to be examined at base it was seldom opened. A proportion of the mail was, however, checked to ensure that only the recipient's name, rank and unit (i.e. and *not* their location) were on the envelope; if the sender gave too much information it would be forwarded with a warning slip attached.

The Germans visited this house in October and a bit of a scrap followed because the English came along. The people are very nice and glad to do anything for us. We sleep – the officers – in a reaped cornfield, five in a row, each at the foot of his own wheat stock. I should like to see Wiffles. Let him smell the blank sheet I have put in . . .

Now for mendicity, as usual: could Mummy send a bottle of 'Pond's Extract', and would you mind sending me one of Molière's plays – a school edition will do, perhaps be best. When that is finished I'll plague you for more, I daresay . . .

Do you know, there's a great deal in what some paper said, that the Germans have secured – and were within an ace of winning by – a kind of moral ascendancy. We are convinced – naturally we don't care two figs for it – that they are acquainted through spies with every movement of every unit; and in other ways one has to make an effort to shake off the spell of their astounding efficiency and preparedness . . .

Please censor don't mutilate this (I expect you've already done so) more than your King and Country really need.

Bye-bye Dad, love . . . Ged . . .

❖

During August the four battalions of the 56th Brigade each spent a week on the Lys front under the direction of the Lahore and Meerut Divisions of the Indian Corps, which held the line from just north of Festubert to Givenchy-lès-la-Bassée to the south. There they learned the basics of trench warfare. The 7th South Lancs were based in billets at Vieille Chapelle, where training concentrated on the use of weapons and munitions, and was interspersed with bouts of physical exercise.

❖

Monday 16th August
[trenches, Festubert–Givenchy front]

Dear Mummy

I'm writing this on the floor of a bomb-proof shelter, built of sandbags, eked out with old doors and boxes. It's very cosy – even at night – and comparatively roomy. These trenches expose one to hardly a vestige of risk; once in a month, perhaps, the Germans fire a light shell at the parapet, and yesterday at breakfast they pitched half a dozen shells round the pump. Nobody was hurt. Then at tea-time a gun from somewhere east put a few shells into a wrecked house just behind here, where they expected an artillery observer I should think.

The night was noisy, but nothing disquieting appeared. I nearly fell asleep while walking about. I don't know what fatigued me. One has to expect little sleep except by day here. Stuart comes in tonight and my company goes back.

The line here takes in a bit of a village, a shapeless mangled wreck – wilderness, with here a gable-end and there two partition walls or a chimney stack. I send you two roses gathered yesterday morning in the garden, riven and forlorn, of what was a chateau with charming grounds – smashed now like a doll's house under a crowbar.

I think Dad knows where I am now, but he does not give me any clue. His letter came extraordinarily welcome when the ration party brought it in about eleven o'clock last night. I'll just write a bit of a note to Una Christina who sent me a very nice letter perhaps eight days gone. So bye-bye now, with dearest love to you, Daddy, Viva, Kitty and Bunny and of course Granny . . . Ged . . .

Monday 16th August
'Shootlands', near Dorking, Surrey

Dear Old Lieutenant

The card made me think you were in the firing line and you may think indeed how we are waiting to know more, and what unexpressed things are within us . . .

Your letter recalled for me certain things in that wonderful book by Clausewitz, *On War*. Its spiritual insight is even more remarkable than its technical thought. Washington's men, Wellington's, and all who fought for years against Napoleon (or against Hannibal for that matter) had to be wrought to immeasurable patience, obstinacy and fortitude by their officers. I know the Germans well – very few in this Country know them so well. They are very good, thorough, *gründlich*, well-instructed, well-equipped, and to wear quite down their advantage of forty years of preparation has to take more than one year, and perhaps more than two years. But there is no supermanship in the Germans – less than in us really. Where we prepare, as in the case of the Navy, we excel . . . Slowly we are getting our tackle and our hour will come. Meanwhile, the 'three o'clock in the morning courage' – ruling the long chill hours – is what we have to depend on . . .

Mummy will get all you want in the way of Pond's Extract and I will get you from town small pocket editions of Molière. It is a pleasure to be able to do something personal. That's where I envy Mummy . . .

God bless you dear son, with whom I commune deeply in mind many an hour. Dad.

Wednesday 18th August
[billets, Vieille Chapelle]

Dear Mummy

We arrived at our billet yesterday in the pale of daybreak, tired to death. It rained on Monday afternoon and the trenches became a mere glutinous mass underfoot. You plod and slide for literally two miles – as near as I could judge – through the mere communication trench to get out, let alone slipping in the front line, as you move painfully up and down collecting your men.

I came out in a fog that muffled the darkness like a cloak, trailing voluminous folds round the trees that still rise in the midst of desolation. 'Yes,' says you, 'but what about the war?' Really, very few shots came from the Germans all night. I've seen – but not handled – a lot of new bombs. Otherwise I haven't anything to tell you. I hope they won't censor my roses. Hitherto I have rarely needed my medicines, and then only aspirin and tonic; I expect it will prove invaluable later. Do you know I felt sorely tempted to drink the iodine before I left the trenches, owing to finishing my water bottle?

We've invented a grand new savoury. Fry sardines in oil, sprinkle Quaker oats . . . and break up the sardines. Eventually you get a thick paste, extraordinarily good. I've left out the condiments. Sardine oil replaces butter. Don't fry too lightly . . .

Are my stars on the way? . . . Bye-bye. Dearest love . . . Ged.

Wednesday 18th August
'Shootlands', near Dorking, Surrey

Dear old Son

So you are more or less in the thick of what there is, and I suppose will have nearly a week of it. We are only hoping you will have time for another long letter and will tell us, if nothing particular has happened, some details of nothing particular. Somehow I fancied that on Sunday begins the week you would be beginning to expostulate personally with the Boche, about the same time as I am accustomed to wrestle with the printers – who, by the way, unlike the Huns are good chaps and are greatly interested, to my surprise, in the young warrior, their editor's son. Old Conibeare, the master printer, always talks as though he had quite a prominent share in bringing you up by hand.

Well this has been a great day, for Chidson has filled it from morn to early eve and we have just come back late after seeing him off at Dorking. He was the same unspoiled hilarious honest person, and after you and with McClinton there's no boy I love anywhere near as much as this same Hume. He is cropped so close as to look shaven like a monk and his upper lip struggles to conform to the King's Regulations[6] – and he is a trifle pale in spite of being weathered brown a bit by campaigning, and his eyes, when you look into them,

6 A moustache, sometimes called a 'Charlie Chaplin', was favoured by British army officers; by an unwritten law it was forbidden to other ranks.

have already the set scrutinising look that soldiers in war get . . . but otherwise it was touching to see him so unchanged. He was full of a splendid confidence, despite the beastly trying character of the present . . .

He smoked a few cigarettes with comic deprecation of that mature habit, and Wiffles, though taken aback on his first appearance, soon became exceedingly friendly to him . . . He goes back tomorrow night after his five days' leave, and was pleased and joyous in his nice way that we had made so much of him, and he said that often – and more than ever on coming back for an interval to civilisation – it seemed all like a dream.

Amusing [it] was that after dinner we had in the old soldier who does agricultural labour and whom we let sleep in the barn . . . He served eleven years or more – nearly twelve in the army (1868–1879 inclusive) chiefly in India. Isaac Deedman . . . now a forlorn old figure, but a fine man of his hands in his day; so in honour of you and Hume and the King's uniform I gave the veteran twelve shillings, one for every year he has been in the army. He was full of quaint blessings and incited Chidson to valour saying 'Never be affeared to go right for 'em, Sir, it all do come well then.' Finally he prophesied with almost Biblical conviction that Hume would be 'a King' – it was just like a page out of Thomas Hardy's novels. I won't write any more as it waxes late . . .

Good night and God bless you, best beloved son. Dad.

Monday 23rd August
[trenches, Festubert–Givenchy front]

Dear Mummy

Here I am again, sent up to the line with one or two others, but no men, to learn more. One doesn't gather much. The days pass very quietly, just a rifle snapping now and then; the night is a bit noisier, the Germans in this part shooting a good deal. Ours lie low and the Boches don't like it one little bit. They fired a machine gun a bit last night, not at anything in particular; the bullets crackle overhead – quite out of reach – like a pair of steel castanets. The parapet of the trench here is growing like the wall of Heidelberg. It's common knowledge that both parties are building ramparts against one another now, in lieu of the old deep trench.

This life is unendurably tiresome. Hardly anything happens; you feel no excitement; the danger exists barely enough to vex one without inspiring . . .

By the way, I forgot to tell you that I am somewhere in France about two miles in front of somewhere else in France. Ain't you thrilled? We saw the German guns bring down an aeroplane last night. A high explosive hit it full and it twirled down; I think the shell must have killed the pilot and observer. I hope so. The Germans cheered immensely . . . The day passes very slowly. I brought a novel which I gulped in no time. I've been killing time with a couple of rotten magazines all day . . .

Returning to our begging as usual: can you put in the date-and-nut parcel, a pot of shrimp paste or potted meat and a novel of Meredith – cheapest pocket edition – (would Dad mind choosing, but not *Diana*)? Also a box of lemon squash tablets made by Fortnum's . . .

Bye-bye and dearest love to you . . . Ged . . .

Sunday 29th August
[billets, Vieille Chapelle]

Dear Mummy

Here you have at last a full length epistle, properly buckled and periwigged. Yesterday nothing of military importance occurred. In the afternoon a parcel arrived containing many good things. I see you addressed it yourself . . .

Last night B Coy gave a concert: we formed a ring in the stubble field, and borrowed a piano from the nurses in the hospital opposite. One of them came and sang herself. Stuart sang a delightful song of Denis O'Sullivan's – *The Stuttering Lovers*; afterwards we provided sandwiches and drinks for the officers . . .

On Friday evening we 'proceeded' as they say in orders 'on a short route march'. We moved about four miles and halted for tea in a big forest, a place of thin-stemmed glades and aromatic herbs, traversed by a road of trodden clay. And so we halted, as it might have been the army of Agincourt, with the chimneys of the field kitchens figuring monstrous engines; whence home through the twilight.

Other news, good, bad, or unimportant, I have no atom of. Wherefore good-bye for the present; with dearest love to you and Dad and Granny, Viva, Noonie, Kitty and Bunny. Ged.

PS I think they'll coffer us in the cellar yet awhile. Cheer up and keep well.

Monday 30th August
'Shootlands', near Dorking, Surrey

My dear old boy

Having had two good nights' sleep and Mummy being far better than ever so long – may it last – I feel ready for anything reasonable this morning. The bracken has gone in a few days into brown patches, and scattered stooks are left among the new stubble in the cornfields that were moving high a week ago, and autumn sang already in our trees . . .

Over there I see that you are all very busy with *malice prépensé*, or with intent as we say. All the wrinkles and practice you get at the schools will stand to you on the day of wealth, whenever that may be. Dullness is never to be counted on as a permanency in this war: it is too big and too grim and too fully stuffed with issues of everlasting import . . .

I'm glad you have got the Molières. If you want any more or any other French stuff let me know. You shall have anything you want. I see the German soldiers are said to carry *Faust* in their knapsacks more often than any other books. I wonder if part two? I mean to read it thoroughly while we are down here, but have not taken it up for a week past . . .

Mummy and I walked together for two hours last night until we scrambled through pitch-dark woods. It was like old times. This is a paper Argosy freighted down with precious loves – Dad

❖

At the end of August the 57th and 58th Brigades of the 19th Division went into the front line between Festubert and Givenchy-lès-la-Bassée: the 56th Brigade was held in Army Reserve near Lestrem, where the 7th South Lancs continued its training, and provided working parties for the front.

❖

Friday 3rd September
[Army Reserve near Lestrem]

Dear Mummy

I'm not sending you much. I've just written a note to Dad. We went last night to work on one of the long serpentine trenches that feed the line. It was just by a long-captured and abandoned German trench. Flares went up steadily; once or twice big searchlights conned the heavens and went out; once a burst of rapid fire at a company next to us. One officer – a delightful fellow – hit, but I fancy not gravely. I found a skull in the grass and had it buried. Browsing in the German trench I picked up an old, unused bomb, took it to pieces and brought home the explosive as a souvenir. I may send it. Much rain since yesterday evening. Mud and greasy roads.

Dearest love to all. Ged.

PS I was a long way behind the firing line.

Saturday 4th September
'Shootlands', near Dorking, Surrey

Dearest of Lads

Your letter this morning was better than a bathe off Trevose Head – it freshened and I know where you are – sure and bedad. Dad always knows, but your mother, my son, wasn't blessed with brains or a head for maps, unless on a huge scale, nor can she follow the intricacies of her boy's quotations, but what would you? If Dad and

Mum both had these qualities, why your head would bulge in quite unexpected places . . .

The house is empty today, so nice; no noisy babes, no untidiness . . . You'll see the *PMG* is over, so the lid is lifted, but how it will matter financially I don't know. Badly perhaps . . .

I suppose no chance of leave for you yet? I'll order that jam this very instant, but unless you give me hints (or more) how can I tell what or when you want things – soap and such things; socks and so on. Dearest love, blessings and prayers ever for my dearest one. Mummy.

Monday 6th September
[Army Reserve near Lestrem]

Dear Mummy . . .

I can write you a bit more today. I think very few people outside France can ever have seen so much of her humbler life as we are now meeting. Billeted ourselves in these little cottages, and negotiating with those who own the men's barns, we see the peasantry intimately. Most that I have come across have proved kind and nice. The dame (or rather bevy of dames) who harbours my platoon now has behaved churlishly, rather. Perhaps one can't blame her. Horses have been tethered to her orchard trees, a number of rich old apples, and have gnawed off all the bark. The trees will never bear again, and whether this year's crop, chubby already, will ripen, I shouldn't like to say. That is not war, but some unneeded carelessness on some soldier's part. Then the men – I hear – have several times emptied slops in her pump sink. We bridle our troops strictly, but they can (and many others before) like pilfering fruit.

. . . They live a very frugal life – perhaps a heritage from the tax-ridden days of the Old Monarchy; for instance my hostess here, an old lady, gaunt, vigorous, grey-haired, was eating for tea the other day a pear and a slice of bread. Meat I've scarcely seen among them since landing; coffee, vegetable broth, bread without jam and not always butter, constitute the staple of their diet. I wish I spoke their tongue better. I can't converse freely; my tongue drags often and the ear is always slow.

I went into a house yesterday, mainly out of curiosity: the gate had a written notice that various English needs could be satisfied within. Every house now adds a little to the stocking by selling bread – generally beer too – to the troops, and postcards. Anyhow, I found a woman of unusual type, rather refined, pale, sitting by the stove with a shawl over her shoulders. I bought a bit of chocolate and chatted awhile. Her husband's a prisoner in Germany, well treated I gathered, but working at something (I didn't catch what). She had her grandfather's medals over the mantel, in a little case – the *Medaille Militaire*, the Legion of Honour, two Crimea medals, and one for saving life. I think he fought in 1870 . . .

The censorship threatens to be more strict in future. Never mind. Give my love to Dad, Granny, Viva, John, Kitty and Bunny. Dearest love to yourself. Ged.

PS . . . We had one of the other company captains to dine in our mess last night. What do you think we gave him? 1) Tomatoes. Potted ham of French manufacture from the grocery store in the village. Toast. 2) Curry, admirably cooked, and potatoes boiled in their skins. 3) Pineapple (fresh) and Cream. 4) Dates. Nuts. Shortbread.

White wine and Lemon Squash to drink. B Company so far has completely outdone all others in its mess. Have you tried my sardine and Quaker oats recipe? . . .

By the way I daren't send the German explosive for fear of accidents. It's only two hardish blocks (about 2½ inch square) of red stuff in red wrapping with various remarks and directions. It's made by the A.-Carbonit (ask Dad what that means – I think the Carbonite Coy.), is called apparently CONARIT-SPRENGKORPER, and smells pungent, like asphalt but sharper. I kept the detonator too, a wee copper tube filled with chemical of great blasting power and irritability. That I'll send you if I can – I'll ask Williams, our bomb expert. Stuart seems fit; I saw him last night. I miss him terribly.

Will you get me a canvas bucket (pay by cheque on me) from any outfitter – Harrods, the Stores, Selfridges perhaps the best? And when you order it will you ask them to paint my initials on: 'R. G. G. 7 S. L.'

Poor censor: Bye bye again and dearest love to all of you. Ged.

PPS Again I think of something I meant to say and forgot before – about the South Wales miners: I think every soldier at the front would be glad to hear that they were blotted out and their places sown with salt . . .[7]

Bye bye again. I forgot to say that the brandy is going.

Tuesday 7th September
Old Buckhurst, Withyham, East Sussex

My dearest old boy

No chance to send you a single word yesterday. Important business letters to do in the morning: then trains to catch in breathless haste: just did it. Three changes at cross-country stations and the third train brought us in lumbering and late . . .

We feel being out of your news, so that we can't get your letters until we get back tomorrow. Mummy is delighted that you write to her so much for her very own self and of course I see the letters just the same. I'm afraid, no I'm sure, that you are often and often dog tired. I know that digging is man's proper employment since Adam and Eve made that silly mistake, but the human back was designed before the Fall and in my opinion was not meant by its Creator to take kindly to the shovel. Heaven bless you at the end of the day after such delivery. Don't be worried if the tone of the *Observer* is a little grim and stern. I never doubt the issue of the war, though feeling that only a long and tremendous conflict can lead to a clean issue . . .

Jimmy had a jolly little birthday and marched round with a Union

---

7 The root cause of the unrest in the South Wales coalfield in 1915 was the miners' belief that the need for increased war output was being exploited by the mine owners; but their willingness to strike, in defiance of union leaders, led to the imputation of unpatriotic behaviour, and stories even circulated that they were acting at the behest of German agents: *The Times*, 3 September, 8 September 1915.

Jack, three times as big as herself, which was one of the presents she asked for, moved I think by childish military sympathy with her big brother whom she adores. More tomorrow. You know how hard it is to write when on visits. All the very love to you. Dad

Thursday 9th September
'Shootlands', near Dorking, Surrey

Dearest of Lads

What an interesting letter about the peasantry and how splendid for you to see things as they are, but don't let them depress you. The French peasantry have always been frugal and good cooks. The English, except in rare cases, always thriftless. It's the middle classes – upper and lower of England – who know and try to know how to manage, but even the poorer classes are getting better. Not in towns, where these horrible picture palaces abound and where they'd rather spend their money and go without food. The whole system needs reorganising. Just as, although the Tommies get well paid and their wives looked after by charitable and other sources, only in rare cases do they attempt to save. I suppose it will come to them all, being directly taxed: and they should be, even the servant class, who really don't realise the war in the slightest.[8] They are fed, housed and looked after generally – apart from pay by their employers – and even if they have people at the front they don't realise. A want of imagination seems to have something to do with it. It does seem unnecessary to ruin the orchard and I don't wonder any old dame is cross about it. If you practise your French as much as possible you'll soon get used to it – it isn't as though you'd never learned.

---

8 At the outbreak of war ordinary wage-earners were exempt from income tax, which began at 9d in the pound for salaries over £160 p.a., but in a supplementary budget in September 1915 the threshold was significantly lowered, affecting working men earning more than £2 10s per week: Arthur Marwick, *The Deluge: British Society and the First World War*, Boston, 1965, p. 129.

Why is the censorship to become more strict? Have any of you been indiscreet? It can't be you, because I never know where you are and you tell us nothing . . . And, dear lad, get rid of that explosive thing. Such awful accidents can happen – I know of one or two – and unnecessary risks of that sort aren't worthwhile. I do wish they'd put Stuart back with you; of course you miss him.

I've sent to Selfridges about the canvas bucket, also to Maud to send you out a flask of brandy . . .

Don't, dearest lad, hesitate even to just hint, if you don't like asking, for any single thing you'd like. You know it is Dad's and my delight, now you are not with us, to know we can give you something you'd like. Deepest love, prayers and blessings. Mummy

Friday 10th September
[Army Reserve near Lestrem]

Dear Mummy

I really forgot [to] whom I wrote yesterday – I could write you a long letter today, were there matter for one. Truly there isn't. I'm exactly where I was yesterday, waiting for the post. The country shines as usual under a breezy sky . . .

Various oddments suggest themselves. I saw a 60-pounder gun this morning. At a rough glance it looks just like the old cannons that travelled from siege to other siege with the armies of our ancestors – a long-barrelled, heavy thing, on a carriage with four great wheels and a team of horses . . .

Last night a hay-rick in the district caught fire. Huge excitement. We went to see. The wind blew it away from a barn which otherwise would have been in flames in no time, having a thatched roof. Some French were there gesticulating, banging at it with poles, ramming it with a ladder as if they were charging the walls of Saguntum – all to help it burn quicker. The phlegmatic English said 'Why not let it burn black, when in a few hours it would be smouldering harmlessly, instead of spangling the orchard with flames and the countryside with sparks?' That seems reasonable, but I must confess I didn't think of it till I was told. However 'Les Français', who had a sensible enough idea of their own – to get the fire thoroughly over quickly – banged and poked and tilted as though they were razing an operatic Jericho to the accompaniment of at least one orchestra.

Tonight I go up on another working party, perfectly secure. This time transport is being provided to convey us. Think of it, rattling up to the trenches in motor-lorries. Unquestionably we are much thought of by the authorities. I shall be jolly grateful, because the walk up to our working point takes two hours each way. No joke with four hours work in between.

. . . No more today. Bye bye. Dearest love . . . Ged.

❖

On Tuesday 14 September the 7th South Lancs took over a sector of the line for the first time, occupying trenches north of Festubert. For the next seven months the battalion remained on the Lys front, alternating time in the front-line trenches with periods in reserve billets and reserve trenches.

❖

Tuesday 14th September
[trenches, front line north of Festubert]

Dearest Mummy

I guess you saw from the card that I'm in the firing line: Lord bless you – firing isn't the word; only a few shells high up and an occasional shot. I wish I could show you my whereabouts on the map but that must wait. Your Ronsard beguiles the time.[9] Up all last night but slept a bit this morning. Water scarce.

I can see, away south, a long wall of heights, faint and grey between a luminous sky and dark trees nearer to hand. At this moment an

9 Ged's allusion to the poet Ronsard appears to be a hint as to his location, in the vicinity of Richebourg. See above, pp. 24–6.

artillery duel is proceeding; we drop two shells on a German ruin, then they do as much for us. Proceedings then [for] ten minutes, amid the admiration and applause of the Infantry. Please send parcel as soon as you can with some boots and vermin powder. Love to you and Dad. Ged.

Tuesday 14th September
9 Greville Place, London NW

Dearest laddie of mine

I couldn't write to you on Sunday because Dad had his first gastric attack since Cumberland and spent a glorious sunny day in bed with a doctor in charge. Of course Edward says it is smoking too much and now that the biliousness is nearly over he is smoking as hard as ever – 50–60 [cigars] a week . . .[10]

The weekend was really a thing of peace and the weather glorious. We picnicked on the river daily, had wonderful sunsets, and quite interesting people. Kitty allowed to stay up each night for dinner and very proud in consequence was the small person. I'm glad you've heard from Stepmother. Vi and Una seem to have had a good time and only arrived home in time for a late tea . . . I've already ordered the things you want sent on Friday and will despatch as soon as they arrive . . . Say if you want anything besides luxuries and food. What about socks and vermin powder and eau-de-Cologne?

No more Zeppelins yet, and I hope they won't come . . .[11]

Dearest love and blessings and prayers for my boy always and ever.
Your Mammy

Selfridges write they will despatch a bucket as soon as possible.

---

10 Edward Goulding, later Lord Wargrave, a particularly close friend of J. L. Garvin: see Biographical Notes.

11 On the night of 8 September, according to *The Times*, 'Hostile aircraft visited the Eastern Counties and the London District and dropped incendiary and explosive bombs' (*The Times*, 9 September 1915). The press did not reveal precise details of the damage caused by an air-raid, especially the location.

Thursday 16th September
9 Greville Place, London NW

My Dearest boy

What an interval – four whole days missed for the first time since you went out – indeed, it seems an age since I wrote last. You will have marvelled as to the cause and speculated as on my being wholly or partially zapped . . .

General Long, the head of the transport department at the War Office, came over yesterday and of course we confabbed for hours. I had heard much of him and took a great liking to him . . .

I would give almost anything to write to you fully; but it is better to err on the side of reticence, for there is far far too much blabbing in our incautious society, and even yet the enemy learns far too much from London itself of what goes on at the front or is projected. Very sharp measures ought to be taken when these conversational leakages recur in ways that would make your hair stand on end considering the persons concerned . . .[12]

I may not say much about the Zepps: it is forbidden. They came over the house you know that is opposite the Marchesis';[13] bombs fell between the road inhabited by Clack and the railway station by which I go to Edward's; far more mischief on the other side of Babylon – Vi and Una and Maud were by themselves and heard about fifty bombs exploding at one time, crashing nearer and nearer: they were very plucky indeed and night after night London has been grimly

12 Maurice Hankey, secretary to the war council, regarded 'society gossip' as one of the most dangerous sources of information to the enemy, and one example of a 'conversational leakage' might be given: on 9 February 1915 the Prime Minister wrote to his confidante, Venetia Stanley, that the Royal Navy would shortly bombard the Turkish forts at the Dardanelles, adding: 'This as I said is supposed to be a secret, and indeed I believe it isn't known to some members of the Cabinet, though Violet [his daughter] heard Louis Mallet talking about it most indiscreetly at dinner one night': Michael and Eleanor Brock (eds), *H. H. Asquith: Letters to Venetia Stanley*, Oxford, 1982, pp. 419, 423.

13 The Marchesi family lived on the opposite side of Greville Place: the 'house that you know' must refer to the Garvin family home.

composed. Most of the dead and maimed are women and children, as innocent as your mother and sisters of military action. The Huns can get no imaginable aim of war by it, God curse the beasts and their demented system. All our inmost loves and blessings on you. Dad.

Thursday 16th September
[trenches, front line north of Festubert]

Dear Mummy

And Dad, who really ought to get a letter for himself this time – all is well with me. I have done nothing glorious, not even gone in front of our wire in the dark. I haven't really tickled any sniper, although I duck as a matter of form whenever a bullet goes over the top of the trench. I'm well fed and can't eat the whole of my ration. My servant, by the way, cooks excellent bacon and eggs for me. German and British guns provide a free Aunt Sally entertainment daily on one another's reserve trenches. All of which is allowed me by a benevolent democracy – on condition that I keep thirty men moderately disciplined, much against their will, and do every day four hours of duty – tonight eight hours – walking up and down the labyrinth supervising sentries and occasionally peeping over the parapet. The Huns are a clear Danube-breadth away from us and very peaceful. Stuart I saw for a moment yesterday, fit and healthy. Williams passed – inspecting bombs – and telling us lurid tales about another section where the men can get three hours' rest only if a rude and heavy howitzer jostles Wilhelm severely. He works very hard but appears well. On his advice I threw away my German detonator – the thing that starts a bomb – because he feared trouble if I should keep it.

So much for the war. The country is bare; a few rows of tall skeleton trees diversify to the north a wide stretch of flat, with a line of wrecked cottages. Southward I see far off ranks of sombre woodland, hedging the long range of a plateau, grey even to field glasses. Sunset and sunrise beautiful and fresh. Jupiter all this month – I think he is the one – has lanterned brilliantly in the east . . .

I think that must do for today as far as news goes. Now for the begging, as usual . . . Lots of wants: two spare pocket-lamp batteries – 'Ever Ready' No. 121 B. S. (Harrods). Another body belt – very useful at night. Can one get in London 'Trench Candles' – thick stumpy ones that last a long time? I should like two or three if they can be got. Will you send me about once a fortnight some kind of tinned pudding. I think Harrods make them. Puddings are terribly scarce in France, but really they're only a luxury.

Now I apologise for the gross sensuality of the last part. Bye bye – Dearest love . . . Ged.

PS I hope everyone feels alright now after the Zeppelins. xxx

Friday 17th September
[trenches, front line north of Festubert]

Dear Dad

. . . Last night in the small hours, I went on a great derring-do, namely a short patrol. Five of us went, crawling through the wire and grass most uncomfortably, but heard and met nothing. We didn't go dangerously far, as we had nothing to learn, but to hear whether the Germans were working. So far the weather has continued excellent. The only discomforts are: 1. The impossibility of bathing and the difficulty of washing even one's feet. Water is scarce and accommodation also. 2. I hate being unable to stand up and look freely at the country around me, especially as all the prettiest landscape clothes the low hills on the German side. 3. I live in perpetual dread of vermin. Already this morning I've sprinkled the most part of a tin of Keating's over my dug-out. I wait in tense anxiety for the advent of that vermin powder.

Will you ask Mummy to send me a clean towel, and a bottle of hair-wash (cheap and in a small bottle because that will be easier to carry and a breakage won't matter).

I've breakfasted today on an excellent omelette, my servant's first attempt – and the first chapter of *Harry Richmond* . . . After that what more have I to say to you? Nothing – but that I send my deepest love . . . xxx Ged . . .

Saturday 18th September
[trenches, front line north of Festubert]

Sweetest Mummy

When your letter arrived last night I was just enduring a 'hate'.[14] We had men repairing our parapet from the front as usual. The Germans got wind and sent over six shells, followed by heavy rifle fire. The working party lay flat in a ditch and got off unhurt; the rest of us stood to arms under the parapet. When the Germans had done that twice our artillery gave them a few rounds and we in our turn fired rapid, thoroughly enjoying it. Then to bed, except the sentries and me. I was on duty the first half of the night and took another fellow's watch from midnight to dawn. I read your letter the first moment I could. You seem tired. I wish Dad and you would take a thorough rest for a week or two. Saw Stuart this morning – very fit. I've got a souvenir for you, a bit of steel picked up hot after a shell burst on our parapet yesterday. Dearest love to you and Dad. xx

PS We've had no shells except light noisy harmless ones. Ged.

Sunday 19th September
[trenches, front line north of Festubert]

Dear Dad

I can't tell you much today. After a comparatively quiet night, only marked by a rather short sleep, we've had nothing to disturb us all day except snipers. Three opposite us are especially active and dangerous. One got my servant this morning with a bullet through the mouth and cheek that narrowly missed killing him. Poor boy, I was awfully proud of him. Fortunately the wound isn't serious, but I want the blood of that sniper. I'm writing to his mother now. I'd give anything it hadn't happened, but we had good luck otherwise.

Dearest love to all. Write Mummy tomorrow. Ged.

---

14 A German artillery bombardment: see Glossary.

Sunday 19th September; evening
9 Greville Place, London NW

Dear old son

Last night the 'phone thing jangled at my elbow as the editor was finishing his proofs – always a close job . . . The 'phone voice was Viva with 'When are you coming home? And there are three letters from Ged.' There had been none for days so the news helped the paternal mind into its taxi the sooner, and it came home to read you to its supper, and was made very cheerful to find you brisk and blithe. I suppose you have been having an exceptional dose in the way of ditch duty. Digging and troglodyting ought to be the original employment and natural use of the sons of Adam, but how that first parent would rub eyes and newly lament the Fall to see some millions of his remote offspring in ditches and dug-outs all across this ancient continent . . .

I had a good talk with Lloyd George on Friday – found him at half past five at the Ministry of Munitions lying on his back on a couch. Whatever else he is, he has the large imagination and the temperament of vigour and promptitude. We must get bigger things done, and all things done sooner. There I am entirely with him, as you will see in the *Observer* this week . . .[15]

I suppose you will need all your training before so very long. God bless you – our dearest inmost love – Dad

Sunday 19th September
9 Greville Place, London NW

Dearest dearest lad

It would give you joy to know how pleased I was to get your two cards and one letter last night – so that I got Vi to 'phone to Dad, whom I knew worried a bit, that you were still in the trenches. Of course I

---

15 In the *Observer*, 19 September 1915, Garvin called for more vigorous leadership from the Government, and particularly over the question of conscription: 'If Mr Asquith's miniature mob is to decide against National Service it will take upon itself heavy and even terrible responsibility.'

knew you were there when your card came, but when nothing else came I worried a bit, though not much. You can and may tell Williams that I'm glad he got you to destroy the detonator . . .

I am sorry the water is scarce and I don't know how to get over that difficulty. In the parcel today I have sent: 1 Boots vermin powder – 1 set silk undies – 1 pair socks – 1 Virol toffee – 1 Slade toffee – 1 packet Brom. and some scent for smells . . .

I'm going to Harrods tomorrow morning to try and get all you mention on your list – and will make a note of the puddings. Is there anything you specially want – and what about your birthday – no chance of being home on leave I suppose? . . .[16]

All servants leaving on November 1st owing to constant friction downstairs, so I think Vi and John should learn some kind of housework or keeping before I get too broken up to give a hand.

With dearest love and prayers and blessings, laddie mine. Mummy

Monday 20th September
[trenches, front line north of Festubert]

Dear Mummy

Will you thank Dad for a letter which came last night – more than welcome since no mail came through the day before. A pair of boots came too, and my bucket. Thank you very much for all. I'm sending back today my watch for repair and the big brandy flask. Please don't think I'm not fond of your gift, but the little flask weighs lighter in a full pocket. By the way, I'll only send the watch today. I'll keep the brandy flask a bit to fill my other phial in the billet. I don't drink it much, but it's useful to rouse one on stumbling dead with fatigue out of a dug-out into the cold of a very dark winter morning before daybreak.

I feel half lost without my servant. Perhaps it's selfish. I knew when I saw his wound I should have been glad to hurt that sniper. But since we've been in the trenches I've been alone very much, and losing him I feel cut off. My new servant is nice and looks after me very well,

---

16 Ged would turn twenty on 12 October.

better in some ways, but the other is such a nice boy, and I'm grown used to him; perhaps I'm sentimental – I find myself more so than usual out here – but I was pleased when he caught my hand; I came up just after he was hit, from the next traverse . . .

Well, for today, Madonna mia carissima, bye bye. Ged.

Wednesday 22nd September
9 Greville Place, London NW

My dear old son

Two letters to myself, a big and little one, made me quite conceited and I felt magnanimous to let them be read by the rest of the family – this is a joke: all your letters are at least temporarily in common – but felt quite disturbed by the sad news. *Gott strafe* the sniper that shot your servant. Poor boy; and I know you will feel it as I would. Do send me his mother's address and tell me whether one might send her a pound or what. I would very much like to do that or whatever else might be suitable, and at least to send her a line as from one parent to another. As the railway porter said to your mother and me in the train the day you left: 'There ain't no class now' . . .

I wonder when you will be relieved and have a spell behind. Here it is golden September weather by day and luminous by night, so that people remark the parks with fresh feeling and talk of the beauty of London moonlight above the darkened streets. The girls went back to school yesterday and Viva and Kitty to the dentist yesterday – a pleasant preface. They all four look blithe, sew hard for soldiers, and I need not say are entirely devoted to the one brother of them all . . .

God bless and keep you, our beloved. Dad.

Thursday 23rd September
[trenches, front line north of Festubert]

Dear Dad

Henceforth look to be in the dark as to my whereabouts and what we are doing. Renewed orders have come round enjoining absolute secrecy. Personally I find myself at this moment where I was when I last wrote. I've a longish letter waiting which I'll send off probably tomorrow. It's delayed by having it not yet finished.

Nothing else to say: I'm storing fine tales for you – that's what the men always say – but you mayn't have them yet . . . I'm awfully sorry you should have worried by that erratic mail, but I fear you must look to have that occur more often now. Will you thank Mummy for a parcel which will be awfully useful and is very nice.

Dearest love . . . Ged.

❖

The Battle of Loos, 25 September–4 November

At the end of August J. L. Garvin learned from well-placed friends of a coming offensive and he wrote to his wife on Friday 27th:

> *I cannot help thinking, and have some reason for thinking, that Geddy may shortly be in one of the most terrible struggles yet fought in the west, perhaps may be in it at any moment. I am longing for a word from him, whether to you or me doesn't matter . . . I find it hard indeed to tackle work in the old high-hearted tone, and never imagined a fortnight ago that one's whole soul could be so sorrowfully changed. Pray, pray for Geddy.*

In fact the offensive did not come for another month, but it fully justified Garvin's fears about its ferocity. On Saturday 25 September the British First Army attacked along the front between Cuinchy and Grenay, aiming at Loos-en-Gohelle. Ged's brigade was immediately to the left of the fighting and was not directly involved, but he had expected to be in the thick of it and sent home an envelope marked 'Don't open – Keep SECRET till I say'. Inside was a short goodbye note. The 56th Brigade escaped the carnage of the first day at Loos, which was proportionately not much less bloody than the first day of the Somme, and the battle dragged on until 4 November with little prospect of a breakthrough.

❖

Sunday 26th September
[reserve trenches, Festubert–Givenchy front]

Carissima Mia

I'm awfully sorry if you worried at my not writing yesterday. I hadn't a moment. I can't say all that happened, but practically from noon we hadn't a spare settled moment until dark and most of the morning I had to keep on the run.

We moved from the front line to the reserve trenches; my company that is. You may tell Dad that this in no way affects the prospect on the Western Front. Anyway, before we had come far, the heavens opened and the rain descended on us. Gideon wouldn't have been in it with all the pitchers. We waded – literally – ankle deep in splashing water collected in the long yards of trench made rainproof by trampling on the clay. I came in better than most of the men, but with drenched boots, puttees crusted with slime, and – to show you what it is – my feet inside the sock slippery with mud. I wrung real dripping water from my socks when I put them on again in the morning, after sleeping with my feet wrapped in a rejected pair of pants. Which all proves what one can do with words: now wouldn't that do for an attack on the War Office like Burke's denunciation of Hastings?

Today I'm perfectly dry after sunning myself in an orchard, and I secured a thorough good wash in your bucket. Fervour weakly describes our feeling towards clean water out here . . . Must stop. More tomorrow. Dearest love to you, Dad, Granny, Viva, Noonie, Kitty and Bunny. Ged

Monday 27th September
9 Greville Place, London NW

My boy

Your letter as thick as a packet came this morning and I do all your wishes. The cryptic little paper shall not be opened until you say 'Sesame' . . .[17]

---

17 Ged's goodbye note, with instructions on how to dispose of his belongings.

We read at home of the great push at last. After Saturday's and Sunday's sweep how will it continue? I wait breathless for the communiqués of this afternoon and night. I had thought it would start about three weeks ago and was not surprised when the first intimation came out yesterday in the late editions of the *Observer*. What would I not give to know where the 7th South Lancs have been, and how it has gone with them and our son. The Lancashire Battalions, both West and East, have done greatly – just as in recruiting, contributing and organising; no county has come out better. Well, since Mummy and I must wait we must wait. I feel as though the whole map of that region was known to me on a scale almost as large as nature. Will science ever give distant vision as it now carries distant sound? I think that must come and wish we were so far, though the censor would no doubt try to stop the sight rays . . .

God keep and guard you. God bless the great cause in this tremendous struggle where you are. Dad.

Tuesday 28th September
[reserve trenches, Festubert–Givenchy front]

Dear Mummy

. . . After a day's relaxation, we rose in the small hours again today, under a frosty moon, alert as we always are and ready for any dawn-prowling Hun who might come so far. The dawn glimmered through the orchard, pearl-lustred behind the ebony fret of the branches. I admired and shivered, murmuring poetry in ecstasy between the tooth-chatterings; a most ludicrous Captain Fracasse, I assure you. Really, I wasn't cold at all by that time; still, one must exaggerate a bit to show one's on service; instance the men, who growl at the rain and paint, for their unhappy relations, a very *Inferno* . . .

We've had very little rain, although a certain quantity of toil. Some people are like the girl in the fairy tale: toads jump out whenever they open their mouths.[18] Withal, I admit they have grievances; but when

---

18 In *The Fairies*, by the seventeenth-century French author, Charles Perrault, toads fall from the mouth of the ill-mannered and proud girl, while jewels are

it's part of the game we ought to keep our grumbles to ourselves. Bye bye. Dearest love to yourself always. Love to Stepmother, Curtis and the kiddies. Ged.

Wednesday 29th September
7 Lansdowne Road, W

My most dear laddie

Your letter of Sunday's date came to me this morning and gave me very much joy, in spite of the squelchiness of the mud in your boots and socks. I've ordered that two pairs of socks go out immediately and I think you'd better wear two pairs at once – or keep one pair in your pocket.

You seem to be having a lively time out there just now – but in spite of all the beloveds' worry about all their own special beloveds, everyone is looking very cheerful, which is a blessing just when the bitter cold and wet have set in, even in London. I suppose sending puttees or clothes is no good and I won't till you say – even woolly undies.

I'm glad to hear of you ripening, as well as drying, in an orchard; and I am revelling in an absence from routine and seeing exactly the same face daily.[19] When you do come back, I expect that you'll want to live in a bath with piles and piles of hot water and towels. Leave, I suppose you know nothing of at the moment . . .

Of course Dad's study is even more hopeless than ever – books three layers deep on the settle and three rows on the floor and where there are no books there are papers – all the foreign and English papers since the war are piled in the conservatory and the bound copies of the *Observer*, so it is no longer to be got into and is only an annexe to the dumping ground. What's to be done I know not . . .

Now no more – as there is no more – except dearest heart's love and blessings and prayers ever for my laddie. Mammy.

---

scattered when the sweet and courteous maiden speaks.

19 Christina was then staying with the O'Sullivans at Lansdowne Road, enjoying a lengthy break from the rigours of home life at 9 Greville Place.

Wednesday 29th September
The *Observer*, Newton Street, High Holborn WC

My dearest lad

Mummy called me up on the 'phone when I was at breakfast this morning and read me your letter, from which I gathered that you were in the reserve trenches with the 7th South Lancs and that the weather was abominable. Pray Heaven that the Boche be not too much helped by either of these facts! It has been icy cold here and pouring. All night the storms raved with wind and rain over London. We thought of you fellows as we used to think on stormy nights of men at sea . . .

Dear son, I wish I were wet and you dry – vain wishes. The news of the push has bucked us all up in an extraordinary way and we are full of pride in Kitchener's armies. The division engaged must have given the overweening Hun as unpleasant a surprise as his conceit ever got in the war . . . Of course we don't expect too much as regards gaining ground and realise the price to be paid against such mazes of thick and bristling wire as you are faced with, but the moral effect of one successful go in the eye against the Boche is enormous and so no doubt you feel it. There will be fierce work now up and down the long line and we snatch at your letters . . .

Endless love from Vi, John, Kitty, Jimmy, Granny, the Maids, Wiffles, and I had almost said from the walls and dumb things of the house as well as – Dad

Saturday 2nd October
[reserve trenches, Festubert-Givenchy front]

Dearest Mummy

After all those scribbles, as unsatisfying as captain's biscuit or unleavened bread, here I send you a long letter about all things, except war. Even after the official notification I hint only with the greatest diffidence that a battle has been going on somewhere on the British front. I'm perfectly safe. The cold and wet have yielded this morning to a bright cordial sun. Our trenches, already pretty dried by yesterday's frost, are nearly free from slime today, and everyone expands again from their depressions.

In a part of our trench we have found a long layer of green sand – a geological product of whose significance I'm ignorant, though Dad can enlighten you. Anyway, the rain filters through and leaves a good footing, as it does not on the clay bottom. That apart, the sand gratifies the sight as very few things do in the trenches – a beautiful blue-green or brown and green like a cat's eye, occasionally filling me with a wish to bottom so an ornamental pool in a jolly garden. I fear I can't send you any, though did you keep goldfish I'd try . . .

Well that's no news for you, and information of my own is scanty enough. I shall be able to supplement, impressionally, the war correspondents when I get back, though very slightly. Still, I mayn't say anything to you at present.

I am still in the reserve trenches, contemplating the world. Here, I'm glad to say, I can look around me without snipers competing for my brain. That privilege you can hardly estimate until after a few days' residence among the sandbags. I find I must be busy all afternoon, so I can't go on . . .

Will you send me a pair of the thickest socks, nice and long? That's all the clothing I need, but parcels from time to time of odd things like chocolate or biscuits or puddings always cheer a soldier's heart.

I'm glad Vi is learning to keep house; it'll do her a lot of good, especially if she makes mistakes. Perhaps the household will not relish her mistakes. I can't write to Dad today. He may see this before you. If not, pass on my love to him. I send my dearest love to you both as always . . . Ged

Monday 4th October
[billets, near Festubert–Givenchy front]

Dearest One

I tell you at once that in the small hours of this morning I arrived in a wayside inn to collapse promptly over tea, a slice of Lumley's birthday cake and above all, base gratifications, your letter. I don't want to exaggerate, and as I tell the men – to their disgust I fancy – it's all part of the game, but I wore my pack ten hours, working a part of the time and marching. I threw it off in the end with a will you may imagine . . .

After tea: *ma foi*, how cold. Past bombardment I suppose has broken the windows and a chill winter drives needles to our marrow. How lovely this countryside appeared today, green and blue and grey disclosing the tenderest hues, and a fresh wind – something frosty – hawking the clouds like wild swans. I adore this country . . .

All my love to you . . . Ged

Tuesday 5th October
9 Greville Place, London NW

Dear old son

I read your letter this morning as arranged before sending it on to Mummy. Then I took it to her myself and paid my own missus an afternoon call. Really she looks years younger – very young and very sweet and I sighed at not being able to persuade her to take the change long since. But far better late than never. I wish she would take a few weeks longer, and so do your sisters, which is very self-sacrificing of us. Mummy and I were very cheerful together and walked quite a long way through Kensington Gardens and back to Church Street, looking in all the old furniture shops, before she dropped in to tea at Lady Colvin's. I need not say that a certain young gentleman in khaki was very much the staple of our conversation as usual, and that the little walk in the Holland Park neighbourhood recalled how many associations – from the little boy in a red jersey who . . . rolled gardener's lawn-mowers into kitchen areas – a Hunnish noise that was – to the time when you and Curtis walked from Westminster together in absurd tail coats and top hats . . .[20]

Mummy and I feel easier that the weather is better and Cording's boots of some utility . . . I wish that Flanders were made all of green sand, more than anyone ever wished that the moon were made of green cheese. It is very trying that we have to be almost mum to each other about the events that the whole world is talking about, and you

---

20 When Ged was young his parents had rented a house in Elsham Road, close to Holland Park.

may imagine how from hour to hour I wonder what is happening and where you are now . . . Give my love to Stuart and say that though I don't write to him – or to anyone but you – I keep him constantly in mind and affection . . .

All the girls but Una have colds, but all like Granny and this writer send their dearest love to you. Here Wiffles comes pattering in, now that fires with the turn of autumn are lit in my study again, and I shake my fist at him because he is drier and warmer o'nights than my son does. Blessings on the said son. Dad.

Wednesday 6th October
[billets, near Festubert–Givenchy front]

Dear Mummy

I didn't write yesterday because I thought Dad should really have a letter. I find time too short to write to both of you as a rule these days. I've just read a letter from you and one from Dad, both seeming cheerful. I only discovered from Stuart's letter, which he lent me, that you were worrying so much. I've been so secure that I confess I forgot how much you must have been worrying. This confounded censorship won't allow even the faintest indication as to whether we're in a healthy place or not. You needn't worry for a few days anyhow . . .

I think I may become a smoker before the end of the war, to keep my jaws busy for want of other exercise. Meantime I'm eating far too much. The want of exercise, vigorous and untrammelled, combines with a walled-in feeling to nibble at your nerves and cloud your capacities, though slightly. I hate it, that sense of being shut in. Nobody can conceive the deadening influence of those sandbag walls, eternal, monotonous – or the joy and uplifting at getting clear and feeling the space unbroken round every limb. That's the only inconvenience, beyond a certain amount of mud. I had a marvellous night when we came out of the trenches, hauling men out of sticky mud rather like molasses. With heavy equipment they stuck – several of them – like Norman chivalry hunting cairns in the Tipperary bogs.

About my birthday. Stewarts in the Strand have an excellent electric lamp. I've already asked Dad to give me a pocket Wordsworth or some prose-writer (say a good translation of one of the great classical historians), but a cheap one, because it may be soused in many kinds of mud; besides, you two really give me so many things. Don't send a hamper . . . Dearest love to you and all. Ged.

Sunday 10th October
7 Lansdowne Road, W

My very dearest laddie

I was so rushed yesterday that I hadn't a moment to write to you. Firstly, when I got your letter first thing, I took it over to Dad at Greville Place – settled the house books – and saw the wonderful Xenophon he has bought you. Folio I – a lovely myrtle-green leather binding with gold tooling round the edges . . . Quite delicious and to be kept in your room for you. I went down to Stewarts and got the special electric lamp and left them to send it to you, after [they] had written your name on it . . .

Dear heart, I'm not worrying about you. I should like to know where you are, but as that cannot be, I'm very patient and everyone thinks you are wonderfully good to write so often and your letters are always a joy. Of course no mother or wife, or any womankind, can feel exactly happy not knowing what her boy is doing or where he is.

I don't believe you'll like smoking when you do start. I hope you'll never smoke as much as Dad, whose teeth are getting quite brown with it. I think your sandbag walls must be atrocious things, although I suppose fairly warm. I'm sorry for you there . . .

Now no more as I've nothing more to say, except the usual – that I send my dearest love, that nearly all my waking thoughts and prayers are for you, and some for the other two boys in whom I'm interested, and that I wish you many happy returns – Mammy. Do say if you want any more Tiptree.

Thursday 14th October
[trenches, Festubert–Givenchy front]

Herzgeliebte

For so sweet a letter as you and Dad only can write, I thank you with all the joy it gave me when my servant brought it last night. Much thanks too for the telegram. The Wordsworth sonnets have delighted me . . .

I came here on Monday evening from a so-called rest billet, where you do parades as at Tidworth, and furnish working parties from time to time to accomplish odd jobs in the dark. One thing: I got my first hot bath since I've been out, a thorough wash in a big tub of beautiful hot water, installed in a cleaned-out stall in the back of a farm. How I luxuriated in it, soaping myself all over with your coal-tar tablet . . .

I spent the queerest birthday. Most of the morning, except for breakfast and a look through my presents after, was occupied in going away to far-away company headquarters and coming back . . . Then on duty in the front line, teasing sentries, that is, and generally holding myself in readiness to meet trouble in the form of vexed colonels or enquiring sappers or gunners. Then back to high tea, pressed-beef-and-potato stew, before standing to arms at dusk.

Then – thrilling moment – at half past twelve, I clambered over the front-line parapet, a loaded revolver belted on me, and a little bomb in either hand, on patrol. I had three others with me. Two stuck in the wire and came on later. The third wriggled with me to a point that seemed about fifty yards in front of our wire and then found himself totally unable to control – though he muffled it – a violent fit of coughing. Then we wriggled back. It's a nervy job because you never know whether you may meet a prowling Hun; and to one crawling, stomach on earth, with one wriggle about every ten minutes, even a molehill or a thistle strikes suddenly out of the darkness as though a man lay there attending you.

When I came in at half past two I found my pistol missing. Nothing more maddening could well happen. Will you order me another (to be paid for by my own account) of the same kind (Smith and Wesson .45 revolver) to be engraved with my name and regiment and sent out as early as possible? I fear Dad's must rust in the grass, maybe only ten yards from our parapet. I can't spot it with my periscope.

Lest you should worry, this is only the second time I've been on patrol, and I've since discovered to my downfall that my 'fifty' yards can't be above twenty from our wire. With which comfort I bid you farewell Madonna, till tomorrow . . .

Bye bye. Ged.

Friday 15th October
[reserve trenches, Festubert–Givenchy front]

Dear Dad

. . . I hope neither of you worried at receiving no word or token. I've no news since yesterday except that I am in the reserve trenches now, very comfortable, warm and dry. Last night, though no letter – perhaps mislaid in the post – came to harbour a big box of Turkish Delight from Selfridges . . . I had a quiet morning with dank mist hanging around trees and a big wrecked house behind us, dew bright on the grass and rushes. All my men have been taken for odd jobs, so after looking around generally I picked up one of my Wordsworths and read . . .

How strange in these trenches to see a road running straight back out of the parapet, like a ride in the park. One never thinks anything of living in a ditch in the fields, but when, from one's end-of-the-world, the track suddenly springs into the unknown and untrammelled – it seems symbolic.

No more now. I must write to the kiddies and Granny for birthday presents. Tell Mummy the knitted puttees are excellent, and the plum pudding crowned our lunch just now right imperially. Bye bye. Ged.

Friday 15th October
Royal York Hotel, Brighton

Dearest old boy

By first post this morning nothing from you, the third morning without news, and in consequence even breakfast in this comfortable hostelry seemed less attractive than usual, while we said of the cloudy weather it was certainly not so good as the day before. Then lo! and behold – by another post before lunch there came your note done on your birthday, amid a profusion of all the military joys that the mud of Flanders affords. But when we got it the prospect of lunch became more taking, and we said of the weather: 'How excellent after all is a grey atmosphere by the Channel, when sea and land melt together in the mist' . . . So you can see how your parents have become reeds for your piping . . .

I can tell there has been heavy work in the zone north of Loos and the censor is good enough to allow us to know what every German journal proclaims, that our gas attack covered a large area. The German air-raid on Wednesday night did not touch our part of the world in London . . .

This day we have spent very quietly here. We sauntered. I bought your Mummy a new coat and skirt of smart corded dove-coloured stuff, in which I think she will look very bonny (it is almost impossible to believe that next Tuesday we shall have been married twenty-one years) . . . We go back to town in a couple of hours after dinner, but the three days have done us good and have been full of you . . .

God bless you. Mummy bids me send tenderised love. Mine is as you know, Dad . . .

Wednesday 20th October
[billets, Festubert–Givenchy front]

Dear Dad

. . . I still have no news. I can impart only that I've run no personal risk exceeding the common danger of this trench-fighting. Of course accidents will happen, but I don't think I am made to be the victim of accidents. I feel quite confident of coming to no harm. One's only difficulty is in all circumstances to act up to such a conviction. The spinning bomb and the whizzing – or snapping – bullet startles one from time to time, the more on account of the rarity.

I couldn't post the letter written for Mummy yesterday because we were moving. We came back to billets after dusk. I proceeded in advance and had a delightful walk towards the end of the afternoon. Curiously sad I find this landscape these days: the grey trees appear never to colour. Here and there the poplars are yellowing, and close at hand I see an occasional apple tree crimson. Puccini, not a man of exceeding merit, seems to have caught a part of the spirit in those wistful melodies of *La Bohème*, which I hope to hear with you before many weeks are out. This is merely hope, however.

About the enterprising Hun I can indicate nothing. I feel that whatever public opinion may think, England has not yet either physically or in conception girded her loins. The sooner everybody puts away himself, and shoulders his pannier for the common weal, the fewer will be the lives wasted in affairs like Neuve Chapelle, which, however they may promise well for the future, are in themselves, as far as I can see, bloody without being in any way decisive . . .

At this moment entered the farmer's wife, furious because my company are bathing – the first time in two months – in a shed where a copper gives them a chance to have a hot bath. Apparently she doesn't want the copper used – she's a grasping old body and wants money I fancy – so dashed in and emptied a cold bucket on the fire while the men were in their tubs, nearly scalding and suffocating them. When she tried to repeat it, the man in charge – a very civil fellow and ordinarily well-behaved – kicked her bucket on to the dung heap. She swears he caught her by the throat, but all the men say he didn't. I didn't know which to believe, but as the men must be got clean, I told her they would continue to use the bath. She said the farm would burn, and showed me half a hundred-weight of coal at least six feet away through the wall, and said the heat from the copper fire would turn it into coke. I disagreed. Then her wood was being taken, so I said if it was her wood (the man at the fire said it wasn't) we'd pay her. Anyway the men had to use the bath. Then she said we were like the Germans (I fancy he must have caught her by the throat, though not seriously; or perhaps merely she worked herself up to fancy?). I got rather angry then, and perhaps unwisely told her we were in the trenches for her sake, that I had seen my men killed for her, and eventually that she was a disgrace to her Country. All this (it's extremely comic) in very broken French, but of necessity subdued and quiet. An impartial Frenchman would have split his sides laughing at us I think. Well – Bye bye Ged.

Wednesday 20th October
9 Greville Place, London NW

My most dear laddie

I have three of your letters now to answer . . . Your hot bath must have been the most wonderful experience, which I hope will soon be repeated. Do you want more soap or towels – socks – hankies – and what about undies?

I'm hoping you're keeping a strict diary about all your doings. They give me the keenest feelings to hear of, and I only wish I could crawl too, even losing a revolver. That, by the way, was why I didn't write yesterday. I thought it so awful that when we got to town at 5.00 I went to the Army and Navy Stores to get one but couldn't. They said not for a month. Then home and hunted for receipts to get the name of the man where Solano got yours. They had none, but I got one this morning and after engraving your name am sending it at once. I pray it gets to you very soon[21] . . .

Was that torch the right kind and do you want any more stumpy candles 'cos I've got lots of them? Stuart wrote and said he'd seen you on Sunday and that you were fit. I was so glad to get his letter because I believe you don't tell me when you're tired. I also heard from your servant – very grateful for what I sent and saying he hoped he'd be your servant when he went out again and that you were good to him . . .

You must be having a pretty bad bit of it, but as long as you are safe I don't mind. You are not sorry to have had Hume's letter are you? Dad and I thought you'd like it even if it was terrible and I suppose was just

21 Christina later discovered that the store could not supply the weapon; she 'saw red' and renewed her search: after visiting 'no less than seventeen shops and stores' and 'walking till I was so tired I was prepared to sit on the curb', she thought of using one of her husband's contacts at the War Office, and by this means she quickly supplied Ged with another pistol. It cost £3 11s 6d.

what you saw yourself[22] . . .

. . . What joy to get you back, even for a short leave. We look forward so to it, you'd hardly believe how much and how we love you, our boy. Dearest love . . . Mammy.

Friday 22nd October
9 Greville Place, London NW

Dear old boy

A pressed evening as usual now on Fridays, but a word if only a short one shall go. Your letter last Wednesday *pour moi moimême* has just come by after-dinner post and makes the paternal peacock expand his moral tail. If indeed you could get leave before many weeks are over what a joy. I wish there were some certainty on the point, as otherwise I would go over there by favour of the authorities who are good enough to think me not a dangerous person, and I would probably contrive to see you. Over your Hogarthian account of the old lady with the copper and no thanks I laughed and sighed . . .

As for what you say about England girding the loins and taking the sterner conception once for all, I cannot say how much I agree with it or what good reasons I have. That is why my references to the war have been almost as scanty and guarded as might be. You will have gathered the same from the tone of the *Observer*. My job is exceedingly difficult. If one speaks out, it is unpleasant and thankless business, apt to be misunderstood by the blissfully ignorant; nor can one speak out plain enough without risk of causing more disquiet than understanding. If one is reassuring and talks like Pangloss whatever happens, one simply encourages fatheads in delusion and even statesmen in inadequacy. To hit the point of stimulating without disorganising, and getting action forward without shaking nerve and disordering imagination, is an extraordinary tax on judgement . . .

Whether the friend who wrote the 'bulldog' passage in your autograph book remains here or joins the army as a brigadier will

22 Hume Chidson had been involved in the battle of Loos. He occasionally wrote to the Garvins, who sent his letters to Ged.

probably be determined within a week or so – perhaps at any moment after you get this.[23] Others, though more patient, are just as strong for a man and above all for a plan. So we shall probably get at more unity and vigour and foresight within the Government, but only after unpleasant things have happened or become inevitable in the Balkans.[24] But *sursum corde* my son. England saw far far worse times in former wars before she came to victory . . .

I feel ever in increasing companionship with you. God bless you. Dad.

Saturday 23rd October
[trenches, Festubert–Givenchy front]

Dear Mummy

I hadn't time yesterday to tell you much. On Thursday evening I saw a little battle-plane, a fine sight. You remember those stories about pirates; and Dad can't have forgotten *Long Tom*; it reminded me of all that, gliding slowly over and then with a flash and a puff from its bow gun circling to pursue swiftly a German aeroplane which I'm told it brought down. The big biplane queened it incomparably, like a frigate above the sunset. How ill all this picturesqueness compares with that grim letter of Hume's. Still, my experiences of battle have not yet passed the blank-cartridge and sheathed-bayonet stage . . .

I may see you during the next four weeks, but the prospect is too problematical to count on; so don't hope too much, though I'm longing to see you . . . Bye Bye. Dearest love always . . . Ged.

---

23 A reference to Churchill, who tendered his resignation as Chancellor of the Duchy of Lancaster on 11 November. He left for France a week later, reporting for service to his yeomanry regiment, the Queen's Own Oxfordshire Hussars.

24 British strategists were gravely concerned that any success for the Central Powers in the Balkans would have serious ramifications on other fronts, and once Bulgaria joined the enemy and declared war on Serbia (14 October) Allied prospects in the region looked bleak. Finding a solution to the 'Balkan business' became a pressing concern.

Monday 25th October
9 Greville Place, London NW

My dear old lad

It is grey and clammy and late autumn begins to bite. When it is cold and raining we at home think of all you good men in your holes and ditches, or weltering in the slush unspeakable, and we feel deeply ashamed of ourselves, as though we were doing something wrong in having a roof over our heads, and had stolen our clothes and fuel. But it doesn't help you all for us to be very thoughtful by day and wakeful at nights. Surely in all the chapters of human experience there never was anything so entirely extraordinary as what you are all going through on the Western Front . . .

On Friday I had a weird day. I lunched with Lloyd George in Downing Street. Winston Churchill and his wife came in. We talked very long and full about the Balkan business. Afterwards I walked with Winston to the offices of his present job – Chancellor of the Duchy of Lancaster. Two rooms – a back and a front – beyond the Abbey and Victoria Tower, and looking across gardens to the Thames. Tin boxes, bare walls, maps, papers – all neat, but Good Heavens! – after the mighty and majestic Admiralty, with its endless corridors and countless rooms, this sort of small lodging is an incredible come-down, and I realised more than before how Winston feels it. Besides, he has no real executive work to do and I can no longer be surprised that he would rather go back to the army if he cannot get more scope at home, nor shall I again advise him to stay. What a world of strange experiences, strange triumphs and joys, strange sorrows and thwartings. Fiction is nothing to it.

Afterwards I went to see Mr Balfour at the Admiralty. Infinitely courteous, we had a good discussion as always and I spoke my mind about certain matters – not the Navy. We at home have been very loyal, restrained, patient – keeping our heads, impeccably British and all that – but we are just getting a bit tired of correct demeanour and don't want to be betrayed by our virtues! The fact is a Cabinet of twenty-one gentlemen of utterly different minds, temperaments, affinities, capacities and antecedents cannot direct a war properly, but can only jabber to the crack of doom without coming to a decision. We must have more unity – vigorous and decisive – at any price. I won't say any more but these words are mild and faint by comparison with the facts and the need . . .

We long to know when you are likely to have a chance of getting leave. God bless you. Dad.

3

Winter in the Trenches

At the end of October Ged was given leave, and he probably left for London on or around Wednesday 27th, returning to France on Tuesday 2 November 'after the five precious days that meant so much to us' (JLG). He rejoined his battalion on the inundated Lys front.

❖

Friday 5th November 1915
[billets, Festubert–Givenchy front]

Dear Mummy

I'll just send a line before going to bed. I've spent the day with a working party in some very dirty trenches, whence I return to find your woolly boots a great comfort . . .

We work aimlessly and, in comparison to the labour spent, profitlessly, an immense amount of needless labour is used owing to the fact that apparently out here it's no man's job to supervise general improvement in the comfort of the trenches. Nothing is ever undertaken till everybody can see the need for it, and very few jobs are finished thoroughly and thoughtfully. We infantry are wearied and badgered about three times more than we need to be because the sappers won't make up their minds which of their jobs they want to do most, and let us do it once for all. Secondly, no one organises draining and cleaning work, and apparently nobody thinks, except hurriedly on the spot. The trenches could have been made by now – without extra labour or expense – twice as habitable as they are.

Read how school books moralise about the Crimea. No, we run no faintest present risk of becoming a military nation, though we may be war-like . . .

Bye bye; dearest love to you and Dad, Granny, Vi, Noonie, Kitty and Bunny. Ged

Friday 5th November
9 Greville Place, London NW

Dear old Laddie

Guy Fawkes Day, with no creature taking any notice of it whatever, and at this blessed hour of writing not even a Zepp raid in place of bonfires and fireworks . . .

The speech came off last night – the Constitutional Club packed from end to end as it had never been. To my surprise I spoke for an hour and a half . . . and to my amazement held my audience to the end . . . It was F. E. Smith's first public appearance as Attorney General – the youngest on record. He made a fine chivalrous courageous defence of Winston Churchill, like the warm loyal friend he always is, and it was nice of him – on his first appearance as a Cabinet minister at any meeting – to take the chair for me. Lastly one of Edward's strange freaks of management, Horatio Bottomley, spoke. I had never heard him before and wouldn't have missed it for worlds. There was the real thing – the demagogue with an irresistible yet composed flow of really glorious humbug – shallow, absurd, irresponsible, yet full of apt humour and ingenious terms, with a peroration that was really fine in movement and appeal. I watched and watched, liking as you know to add human types to my mental portfolio, and convinced more than ever that the living world is very very like Balzac! Home after midnight . . .

[This] afternoon I was interviewed at length for the *New York Times* and told the Americans again something of what we are really doing in the war. Our friends there tend to be 'rattled' and stampeded because the Germans make the most effective display at the moment . . .

For a couple of days after your departure Wiffles nosed your trail all over the house. He doesn't understand why you stop coming in to eat and sleep in the regular way that dogs prefer. All the dearest loves and God bless you, my boy. Dad

Monday 8th November
[billets, Festubert–Givenchy front]

Dearest Mummy

We move tomorrow into the line, though not into the actual trenches. Since I came back the actual rain has been suspended and the cold, though intense, is ameliorated by comparative dryness. Hard frost ends as swiftly slush or bog – the sure result of rain – as the best pumps. Pumps of course don't necessitate one's being frozen to the marrow as dry frost does . . .

Don't be alarmed – I had another slight bilious attack last night; over now except for a bit of shivering. That'll go in bed. I've taken some hot lemon made with your tablets. Will you send out my British Warm? And some soup tablets now and then . . .

I live on your letters. Nothing else to tell you. Bye bye. Dearest love . . . Ged.

Monday 8th November
9 Greville Place, London NW

My son

Perhaps you miss us more than the first time, as we miss you. It is usually so, on going back to the ditches after the first visit home . . . When you were home we talked about hardly anything we meant to talk about. I had intended to ask you all sorts of questions about your old letters: what you had meant by this and that, but it was a rush . . .

[Yesterday] evening I went to Lady Randolph Churchill's – the usual family bevy of beautiful women there, really beautiful, but only one other man – Winston, and with him I had the best talk I ever had. As prompt and warm as ever to learn about you. Rather than keep a political sinecure, in spite of the big pay, and being an irrepressible man of action, I think he means to join the army somehow and see service somewhere, but instead of going to Flanders and losing himself in the crowd of brigadiers he may do a brilliantly adventurous and unexpected thing.[1] Let that pique your curiosity, but I can say no more yet, and cannot even to anyone at home. I never liked him better . . .

John is fencing away outside, Kitty and Jimmy adore your little presents and Mummy is well, though tired because much of the work of the house falls on her since Maud left . . . Granny frail but loving you as we all do. Bless you. Dad

Monday 8th November
9 Greville Place, London NW

Dearest of dear lads

Your two letters, one in the morning – as a prayer for the day – and another as my blessed goodnight . . . were wonderful to get, but made me ashamed that I had not written oftener; but there seemed so little to say and so much to do . . .

Yesterday we lunched at Lady Robert Cecil's and it was quite charming, although she, dear woman, is very very deaf and one has to speak into a mouthpiece while she holds an ear trumpet . . . Dad dined out with Lady Randolph Churchill, and I tried to tidy the study and did tidy every portion of the floor, then went to the pantry and finished that. Only one maid in, and the usual things to be done. Today Maud's usual morning work – washing and seeing to, and orders given . . .

I've sent a parcel today, with over-socks, waistcoat, British Warm, socks and some eatables. I've also received boots which shall be repaired. Tell me if there is a thing you want and you shall have it . . .

Dearest love – my blessings and prayers ever. Mummy.

---

1 Churchill had asked the Prime Minister to make him governor-general and British commander-in-chief in British East Africa; he had devised a scheme for attacking the Germans there with armoured cars: Martin Gilbert, *Winston S. Churchill, Volume III: 1914–1916, The Challenge of War*, London, 1971, p. 563.

Wednesday 10th November
[billets, Festubert–Givenchy front]

Dear Mummy

I hoped to have a quiet evening to make up for yesterday. We were moving and busy all day, and today, having left my letter till evening, I must go off with a working party at an hour's notice. The trenches are flooded. Stuart could find no sleeping place last night except his mess table. I'm in a dilapidated farmhouse behind the line, in a little room undamaged by shells and quite cosy . . .

Will you send me a box of iodine tubes? Mine bent and crushed . . . in my pocket (send Burroughs and Wellcome, not Boots). The vermin pad seems good on the face of it. We've all rubbed our feet with whale-oil to keep heat in and damp more or less out . . . No more time now. I'll write long when I can. Bye-bye. Dearest love to you and Dad, Granny, Vi, Noonie, Kitty and Bunny. Ged

Thursday 11th November
[reserve trenches, Festubert–Givenchy front]

Dear Dad

. . . I'm still behind the line, though well within range of little shells. Fortunately I'm [a] kind of grass-widower, and wander in my pleasaunce heedless of Hun 'pip-squeaks' chirping and fluting to wretched people a quarter of a mile to my flank. I have a redoubt to look after that requires a daily visit, half an hour of tramping and paddling down a communication trench, then a visit to Stuart on the way and a further half hour of dancing the greasy foot-board. Then the same back. It gives one quite healthy morning's exercise.

I'm glad to say our artillery pounds the Hun considerably, which compensates for the wet trenches. Really the fen district can't hold a bulrush to this area for water. With Cording boots I stood up to the knee today in a one-time communication trench, now a picturesque irrigation canal. The said boots keep [out] much evil and I sleep dry in my cubby-hole in the farm at night. The stockings Granny sent are grand . . .

Bye-bye. Dearest love to you, Mummy, Granny, Vi, Noonie, Kitty and Bunny. Ged.

P.S. Stuart's only middling, but I think is shifting to a better billet. Bye-bye.

Thursday 11th November
9 Greville Place, London NW

Dear old lad

We were concerned to know that one of those wretched little attacks of land sickness had sent you to your bunk, and we much want to know that you are better . . .

I am dining with Winston tonight, but hear from a private source that he has definitely resigned. I don't yet know the details. Last Sunday I made up my mind not to battle further against his desire to be out of it. Well, he has made his mistakes like all prompt, buoyant, daring people, but in his grasp of the whole war he has been bigger than any other minister. But he has never had power in proportion to his ideas – execution by other people has marred what he has conceived. He concentrated the fleet, grasped sea power at once, and when he ceased to be First Lord of the Admiralty (where you saw him) he left this Country with a more absolute naval supremacy than we possessed after Trafalgar. Now he falls to that worst influence – the malignant unreasoning vendetta of mob-ignorance. There's a lesson in history for you, let his faults and mistakes be put as high as you like, but his time will come again . . .

Viva in sad pain with her neuralgia, but serene. The others well, Granny better. Mummy well but herself hard-worked for want of servants. Dearest love and blessings to our boy. Dad

Thursday 11th November
9 Greville Place, London NW

Dearest of dear lads and best of sons

I think I should really start with your letter of the 5th . . . I suppose there are brains and organising ability which could be put to the base use of draining and cleaning trenches – but I also suppose, as long as no real row is made, it goes [on] and most things come through somehow – and hang the expense and discomfort, as long as the millions are spent and the people who do the spending are quite comfortable in London. I do hear such tales of the trenches, but hope yours are not so bad. I think my idea – mooted to Lord Robert Cecil – of asking for a cessation of hostilities on both sides for one week and letting the wives and mothers go to those same trenches – would be quite good all round . . .

I hope the flageolet is successful and helps to pass dull hours.[2] The over-socks have gone – also the waistcoat . . . and I'm getting a rug for you and a 'Tommy's Cooker'; about a yard and a half or more of twist has gone, but tell me if it's the right sort. I don't know, and it looks pretty black stuff. Also some apples, bananas, chocolates, soup cubes, Indian corn, and the remains of port left from dinner which I thought you'd like to share . . .

Dearest laddie, good night and God keep you and bless you and bring you back well and happy to us . . . Mummy

Tuesday night, 16th–17th November
[reserve trenches, Festubert–Givenchy front]

Dear Dad

I guess you'd like to know what the firing line is like now. Anyway I want to tell you. First of all, I've seen several Huns, mostly clambering about or mending a very dilapidated trench about daybreak. I think we shot some. In one place, where their trench was bad, a spot where four crimson sandbags [lie] in the parapet, I saw them bailing and scoops going all day.

Our own line is terrible. For two days and nights I had men standing

2 In October Ged had requested that 'a flute or pipe of the tin-whistle description' be sent out to him, with instructions and some suitable music, 'say a book of "famous operatic melodies"'. Shortly afterwards Christina sent 'two whistle affairs' and the only book of music she could find during a visit to Brighton.

in water. When I took the rum round at daybreak, my knees broke the ice on the water. Dirt and damp even penetrated my big fisherman's waders, which we've all been supplied. Fortunately we had two warm days and frosty nights. Rain has come again this evening, though, and we go back – only for twenty-four hours though – tomorrow. Dirt gets on everything. For three days I was too tired and later too busy; today I haven't washed or shaved. Mummy's 'Tommy's Cooker' and tinned macaroni made me a glorious breakfast yesterday morning and most of yesterday I revelled in Thucydides who fascinates me.

My cape has come and a parcel of food. Thank you all and Mummy especially. I've met Williams and seen Stuart, both pretty well. In these reserve trenches we're very dry and comfy with excellent dug-outs. I've made a hot-water bottle tonight from an empty rum jar, so with the port – how nice of you to think of sending it – I'll sleep very cosy. Nothing else to tell you I think. I read the *Malade Imaginaire* before coming in, but missed parts of it through feeling rather dull that afternoon. I'm fit as a fiddle and standing out against the cold like any polar bear . . .

Bye bye. Dearest love . . . Ged xxx

Thursday 18th November
9 Greville Place, London NW

My dearest one

It was good to get a card from you this morning – although it breathed of wet trenches and waders. How sorry I am for you all in that cold . . . I didn't write yesterday because all the morning I was busy and not very well, so rested most of the afternoon with hot-water bottles for company and dozing. I dreamed of you – worried that your toes might be more than ordinarily cold and wondering what I could do . . .

Last night I had to go out to dinner, much against the grain . . . Home not very late and freezing to bed. Viola, good girl, has at last tidied her room and I'm to give her 20/– for doing so, still hoping that once tidy she will keep it so . . .

Tell me the latest date parcels should be sent to reach you for Christmas and what special things you'd like . . . I hate the very idea of Christmas here – in fact it won't be Christmas without you and it seems a farce . . .

Dearest love to you, lad o'mine and heart o'mine. Prayers and blessings for always for you. Mummy.

Monday 22nd November
[billets, Festubert–Givenchy front]

Dearest One

I do hope you've thrown off that cough. How does Vi feel now? . . . Tell her not to overwork, and subdue, as much as possible, the inclination to be dictated to by mistresses as to what she should read. She knows better than they what she wants.

Yesterday I had a long ride . . . visiting redoubts all over the country. I loved the ride in the failing afternoon. Awfully funny, I got caught by the dark and grew very impatient, riding about over ploughed fields, hunting up one place. Seeing a light, I hailed it and, getting no satisfactory answer, trotted over. There was a fellow in middle of that sticky waste holding a lantern. 'Who are you?' I asked him. 'I am the meteorological observer for this district.' I nearly fell off the horse with laughter.

Today, starting early through a country glistening with rime, we marched back to this town where we stayed in August, well behind. With luck we stay here until about Christmas. I thoroughly enjoyed the march; Stuart and I were together and we chatted. The exercise braced us all up too. No other news . . . Bye bye. Dearest love to you and Dad (I hope the speech went well), Granny and the babies. Ged.

Monday 22nd November
9 Greville Place, London NW

My dearest son

Was it Thursday I wrote to you or when? It seems a long time – longer than any interval since you went out . . .

I envied Winston going off in his plain khaki having filled so great a place in the State. Before the war, my age – forty-seven – seemed almost young, and now it seems decrepit. Oh my boy, would I were beside you. I would be very cheerful then, whatever the weather. I much fear that the pumps cannot do all we hoped from them this winter, not because there are not enough pumps, but because the lie of the land is such that no machinery can give good drainage. That is the opinion I get from other quarters; and I was very interested in your account of the methodical Hun exposing himself to laudable marksmanship in his desire to scoop and bale. To their temperament, so sentimental and brutal alternately, and delighting in extremes, the situation is more trying than to ours. They are going to propose a bad peace presently, but we mustn't agree!![3] . . .

All well except Mummy's cold trying . . . all love you still more, which seemed impossible. God bless you. Dad.

Tuesday 23rd November
[billets, Merville–Lestrem area]

Dear Mummy

. . . I'm rather tired and have a busy day tomorrow. By an extremely unjust order we have to march eighteen miles (there and back) to clean out some billets left not perfectly tidy. I know myself they were as clean as could reasonably be asked when we only spent two nights and a day in them.[4] What's more, most of the complaint is due to the regiment there before us. The general of the division has a feud with us, which I fancy causes this arrangement. As for the regiment that complained about us, their complaint – I've heard it in detail – disgraces themselves.

---

3 In November 1915 German envoys made known through informal channels the terms on which Germany might agree to peace. In Britain this was seen as an attempt to divide the Allies, taking advantage of the recent change of government in France.

4 The 7th South Lancs came out of the line on the night of 19–20 November and stayed in billets near the front until the 22nd, when it moved further back, mostly likely to army reserve near Lestrem.

Never mind. The day after tomorrow I'll manage a decent letter for you. Bye bye. Dearest love to you and Dad, Granny, Viva, Noonie, Gipsy and Bunny. Ged.

Thursday 25th November
9 Greville Place, London NW

Dearest and most beloved of sons

. . . I didn't write yesterday because I was busy almost all day and only got to rest late in the afternoon, and had only been resting one quarter of an hour when Bess and Biddy turned up.[5] It seems incredible that the loss of one maid should make so much difference, and the worst is no one seems able to supply the maids. In the evening we went to dine with Mrs Robert Grosvenor and there met Madame Moncheni – Mrs Grosvenor's cousin – [and] a Baron Monchen, who was Belgian Minister at Constantinople till war broke out . . . The poor old Baron had lost every farthing he possessed, and had seen his grandchild mutilated at the beginning in the streets of Belgium.[6]

Dad is reading the *History of the World* alternately with Thucydides and comes to bed at about 1.00 a.m., talks of war economics, but says he can't economise on cigars, and taxis aren't extravagant because his time is worth 5/– every 10 minutes, but he will do with two meals a day. Isn't it amusing?

Your letter this morning, saying you'd had a ride . . . a march and a proper talk with Stuart was splendid, and that you may be behind the lines and safe until Christmas gives me a much easier mind. I hope the splits, cream and jam arrived well and safe – and were liked.

Dearest lad, God bless you – goodnight – our dearest love and prayers and blessings are ever for you. Mammy

---

5 'Bess' was Christina Garvin's close friend Elisabeth O'Sullivan, sometimes also called 'Step' or 'Stepmother': see Biographical Notes and Index.

6 Fearing a guerrilla resistance to its invasion of Belgium, the German army carried out summary executions, and stories of atrocities soon circulated: the German army killed 5,521 civilians in Belgium, and another 896 in France: Strachan, *First World War, A New Illustrated History*, p. 50.

Friday 26th November
9 Greville Place, London NW

My dear old boy

We were full of indignation at the episode of the billets. Such things are disgusting to decent minds and it is the hardest part of a soldier's discipline to bear it. We are anxious to get your next letter and to know what happened . . . The German army used to be full of petty tyrannies and brutalities, but our own service has, for the most part, been very creditably freer from them, and they ought to be most scrupulously avoided in connection with the new armies . . .

I wonder how you are having the weather there. We are so cold that we are nigh withered and my hand scarce can shape letters. I dined at Lady Randolph Churchill's last night – the usual bevy of bird-like society women, very bright in colours and smiles . . .

It always gives me a quite odd satisfaction when I hear of you riding. Ride as much as you can my son, and don't read so much. Here come Viva and John going to bed – [they] look over my shoulder and immediately charge me with heaps of love for you . . . Good night my very dearest old son and all love a letter can carry from home and blessings on you indeed. Dad.

Saturday 27th November
[billets, Merville–Lestrem area]

Dear Mummy

This is really the longest spell since I came out when I haven't sent a satisfactory letter. Partly it's my own fault, partly I've been very tired and busy . . .

Well, I saw a fifteen-inch gun fired. I missed part of it as the gun was behind a hedge, but I saw the shell being hoisted by a little crane. Then the team elevates the gun barrel (a short solid barrel on a very high carriage), a fellow waves a handkerchief, everybody gets well back, and then a second wave. Then – I didn't see how – the gun goes off. A huge flame leaps out; a heavy bang makes all neighbouring tiles clatter to the ground and many windows fly in sunder and lo! a little black thing flying away very fast through the sky. All very exciting. The report really is quite mild; one can stand within a few yards of the breech without stopping one's ears.

On Thursday I was orderly officer, a duty which keeps you up late to visit guards, but is otherwise very little irksome. We held ordinary parades, made inquisition on the losing of kit (most men had lost something) and paid the company . . . On Friday we held ordinary parades, but a heavy snowstorm checked us in the middle of the morning. Today the brigadier inspected, when, although far from perfect, B Coy – mine – was the best turned out and cleanest.

Next week we have a full training programme, which will leave very short space for writing letters. Even this week I've had very little leisure. I admit I've been down town twice. You can't think how nice it is to get back to a little town and sit dry in a warm room for dinner, or have tea at the pastry-cook's with a big cup of chocolate . . . By the way, I drink crème de menthe now. Harvey got a bottle and sipping it I liked it, so have a liqueur glass sometimes. If you'd rather I didn't drink it, say so. I'm not – lest you feel alarmed – consuming Edward's Cognac very fast . . .

Today the ground was pied with unthawed snow in the furrows, and the sky blue with clouds folded like galley sails. Yesterday was kaleidoscopic in its changes. A golden sunrise and frost melted into sunshine, followed by darkening and heavy blue with ominous sharpness in the lines of a far-away wood; then hail, rain and eventually snow. I saw cottages across the field wrapped in a haze and suddenly the enveloping storm descended on my part of the high road. The snow whitened all the fields and branches in a few minutes, but continued to fall softly for about half an hour. I can't remember having watched a snowstorm before. How magically it falls, almost as though one were passing from one world into another. Ben Jonson occurs to one: 'Have you marked but the fall of the snow / Before rude earth hath smutched it?'[7] – delicious lyric.

---

7 Ged misquotes from Ben Jonson's play *The Devil is an Ass* (acted 1616, printed 1631): 'Have you mark'd but the fall of the snow / Before the soil hath smutch'd it?' Act II, Scene ii.

Afterwards the sun shone again and the sky sent more clouds, like galleys across the blue . . .

I think parcels for Christmas ought to leave about the 12th, but one can't say, even vaguely; battalions have been warned to get ready for swollen mails . . .

I've just finished an excellent dinner: soup, joint, cake and coffee in the offing . . . Bye bye and dearest love to you always, Granny, Vi, Noonie, Kitty and Bunny. Ged. xxxxx

Sunday 28th November
[billets, Merville–Lestrem area]

Dear Dad

I projected a letter to you last night that would satisfy all your longings to hear tales of action . . . I can't really tell you much because one does so little. You know already how, during that last spell, I broke ice with my knees in carrying round the big rum jar at daybreak. I forget whether I told you about the man of mine who was shot, standing on the parapet first thing in the morning, trying to put a pump hose out. We had to leave him on the parados (the top of the trench behind) all day due to the impossibility of moving the body back. That was horrible. Next morning I think we paid for his death – of course one can rarely affirm with certainty that the German vanishes because he is dead. My men claimed four Germans.

I very much enjoy hearing the slow travel of a howitzer shell and watching the heavy smoke of its explosion and the spouted sandbags or wreckage. The Huns dropped some heavy stuff on us one morning, not near me. I think he didn't do very much damage. Our guns of every calibre . . . punch him steadily and succulently – if I may divert that word from its proper use – while the little 18-pounders slap him in the eye and knock holes in his parapet.

When I first went into those trenches – a bright moonlit night – I liked the look of them so little that to keep the men as dry as possible I took them three at a time along the parapet in front. That was exciting if you like, crouching along, lowering three men in and waiting for the next group, hoping no German machine gun would fire a random burst. Luckily the Huns kept very quiet that night. When I was relieved I guided – or piloted – the relief myself in the trench; lance-corporals and such-like make bad guides from a habit of exaggerating.

Coming out the last time was bad. The men, relieved late, took literally hours to concentrate along the flooded trench, their kit weighing them down, although we went in as light as we could. When we set out at last along a muddy track, one man stuck. I dragged him along. Then another stuck and it took three of us a good twenty minutes to put his foot back into a loose jack boot. Then I led him awhile by the hand – he stuck again for a minute or two before that – on the grass: in the place where we had to cross a mud hole he took root another time. Heaving, pushing, pulling – all failed. At last another officer came up, and we two grabbed one leg and dragged it out, so that we could push him along without leaving him time to adhere to anything again. 'Exasperation' hardly does my feelings justice. The man whined all the time about the size of his boot. He's a confirmed nuisance, a smug tradesman I think, assiduous at chapel and thoroughly faint-hearted . . .

Your letters always nourish me for the next day or two. Mummy's too, drop 'like the gentle rain from Heaven' (our good Will never trailed a pike in the Low Countries, pretty clearly) . . . Dearest love to you, Mummy, Granny, Vi, John, Gipsy and Bunny. Ged.

PS Remember me to the maids and let Wiffles smell this piece of paper. Will Mummy send my Sam Browne and some 'Bromo'?

Tuesday 30th November
[billets, Merville–Lestrem area]

Dear Mummy

I'm awfully sorry letters get so uneven now. I couldn't write last night because I was kept busy so late. It's midnight now and I've just finished arranging and preparing work for tomorrow . . .

I've been given a class of men at a day's notice to train as snipers and observers, very responsible jobs. I have to think out (mostly after previous thinking in) all sorts of lectures on map reading, telescopes, German habits and so on – to occupy, if you please, four hours and a half daily. Add half an hour physical training before breakfast and two hours, or really ninety minutes, after breakfast; a sandwich lunch today; last night and tomorrow, hour lectures for all officers on irrelevant subjects: how does that strike you as a cure for exhaustion? All officers nearly have taken, or gone to, special battalion classes – Major Winser's notion – in various things like machine guns and bombs and scouting. If I get much more efficient, guess I'll transfer to the Huns . . .

Bye bye. Dearest love to you and Dad, Granny, Vi, Noonie, Kitty and Bunny. Ged.

P.S. . . . Stuart seems terribly worn and dull. He needs a full fortnight's rest, but will never get it I suppose.

Tuesday 30th November
9 Greville Place, London NW

My very dearest Laddie

Your letter this morning was so delightful and breathed of all the wonders so much – that I knew you were as happy now as you could be out there and in the circumstances. It really was a joy to have such a letter and I heard Dad chuckling as he read it . . .

Dad has settled that we economise by having one day a week 'meatless' – so we are doing so – and I'm going to do without another servant for some time and so save something. This is all because the nation is living on its capital to provide for this war.

About Christmas things – as soon as I can find what the girls want I will get theirs . . . For the maids, I will give them 2/6 each from you – but remember to mention it in your letter because that will please them more than the money.

I have been making up your Christmas lists of food today, for seven of you – and something for your men. Can you give me hints . . .

crème de menthe – I'm sending you a small bottle with the Xmas things, but I greatly fear that you can't have turkey . . .

Don't forget you've a forty-year-old mother this Xmas day – not fair, but fat and forty – but still your mother. I think I'll get a pink dressing jacket, from you to me – you were so funny when I was young enough to wear one.

Dearest heart – good night and God bless you – and guard you – and bring you back to me safely. Mammy.

Wednesday 1st December
[billets, Merville–Lestrem area]

Dearest One

I'm writing this after dinner in almost my only moment of genuine leisure since yesterday's letter. I not only have to work out, instantly after stopping in the afternoon, the morrow's programme, but having worked it out have to learn myself most of what I teach the men next day. What makes it hard however is that in the morning, right up to the time of starting special work, I must work with the company as usual. In the evening an hour's lecture tonight by Williams, and on Friday night operations, for which Lumley and I have just concocted a most ingenious scheme. Add to that letters to censor – to tell the truth I've had to hand them over mostly – and you'll see what amateur military schoolmastering really means. I owe you much thanks, Madonna, for three big parcels. We all smacked lips over the splits and cream for tea . . . Thank you very much indeed for the towel and for the foodstuffs, I feel absolutely pampered. I'm deluged with bounties (I've just found the green sweets). You make the whole winter Christmas . . .

Lumley has a miserable cold, but curiously this healthy life seems to have made me proof against germs. I've had no colds to speak of. I mourn to think of you and Dad shivering at home. I hope war economy isn't cutting down on fuel, especially when I, who in fullest faith need them less, am deluged with warm comforts . . .

Turenne is of necessity on the shelf for the present, like the 'little tin soldier', put back in the box[8] . . . Bye bye. Dearest love to you and Dad, Granny, Vi, Noonie, Gipsy and Bunny. Ged. Remember me to the maids . . .

Thursday 2nd December
9 Greville Place, London NW

My dearest lad

Imagine our delight to get a fat envelope with many sheaves and one of the best of all your letters. We don't know yet exactly what you are doing or for how long or why, but in spirit we emerge with you from the great slough wherein whole armies wallow . . . As for crème de menthe my dear boy, who are we your parents to order your conduct now that you are passing through that last test of manhood – which your father was much inclined unto but never knew? Neither asceticism, nor indulgence, but controlled enjoyment – even with a whimsical and riotous gaiety when the mood takes us: that is a right part of happiness and full being. Crème de menthe is a pleasant liqueur for your years, as old brandy would still be for mine were I in khaki. As a rule, one glass held up for colour and then appreciated in taste is good both for liqueurs and port, and two glasses maybe sometimes, but it is best never to go beyond the latter for one's senses should be like one's brain, finely receptive yet robust . . .

Upon discussion in family assembled, we have agreed with merriment that our duty in wartime as an aid to national economy is to go without meat one day a week. We started yesterday and we all protested against the delightful arrangements whereby Mummy took all the penance out of it and made it a luxury. Capital macaroni with tomato sauce and grated parmigiano, lentils with rice and chutney, potatoes mashed under a lovely brown crust and that delicious dainty cauliflower *aux gratins* . . .

---

8 Ged was in the process of writing an essay on the great seventeenth-century French general, Marshal Turenne (1611–75); he began researching the essay in England and continued at the Western Front.

At Bess's on Monday night we met a Roy Martin, representing the vast institute of the American Associated Press – which telegraphs interminably to heaven knows how many newspapers – very positive, very superficial, yet a very nice man. More and more I am driven to the conclusion, though with regret, that Americans are more taken by casual, momentary impressions than any of us Europeans, so old, yet so fresh, and that there is more shallowness in their life than with life of any other civilised people. That is what they have to correct. They are very provincial, yet assertive. They don't know what they don't know. Of course the exceptions in mind, as well as in heart, are the salt of the earth, but when they live here they want to stay here.

All your sisters are working very hard and are well . . . Blessings on you. Dad.

Friday 3rd December
[billets, Merville–Lestrem area]

[Dear Dad]

'The rain it raineth every day.'[9] I'm sitting watching it in a farm kitchen, after a few breathless hours.

I slept on the ground floor at company headquarters. This morning, about half past four, knocking on my window awakened me to receive a message from the adjutant.

A move before noon. Slip on boots and Burberry and out – pyjamas and all – along the muddy highway to rouse Lumley. We couldn't do much, but I roused the company sergeant major and we gave him a few instructions. Then back to bed for an hour's sleep. First news in the morning was that the old man, on whose stove the servants had cooked for us, was dead suddenly in the night. Worry and distraction, delay in getting breakfast (I'm afraid I was notably unfeeling). We packed and waited. No definite orders as to place, time, or what to do with kits.

---

9 The famous refrain from the clown's song that concludes *Twelfth Night* (Act V, Scene i).

Suddenly, after several hours' waiting, and surmising, a message to parade at once. We got out, leaving men to fetch kit on, and behold – here we are, in a village three miles south of the last billet. I think tomorrow we move again. We're very comfy here. I'm afraid this move may delay the afternoon post – that's the only serious inconvenience. Don't imagine anything to be impending. The whole front is remarkably quiet. I don't know why we've moved, but it's not for any reason that need worry you . . .

Bye bye. Dearest love to you and Mummy, Granny, Vi, Noonie, Gipsy and Bunny. I hope you're all throwing off colds. Ged xxx

Friday 3rd December
9 Greville Place, London NW

My dear old boy

There came another long letter, a splendid one, all for myself . . . You have had a grim moment or two and, though we laughed at the nonconformist feebleness who stuck in the slough at every moment, the lurching through the communication trenches must be horrible. Isn't John Bunyan infallible in his sense of the primitive things – 'the Slough of Despond'? Altogether it was just the letter I wanted and after sixteen months of war, hard as I have tried to understand, it made me understand just a little more . . .

Yesterday a long day's stretch at the office, dictating endless letters. Edmund Davis and his wife and Roderick Jones came to dinner and we were all animated, so it was midnight before we broke up. As we were sitting down, who came in but Solano – [in] khaki, but with an astonishing coat contrary to all King's Regulations – a British Warm with a sort of tippet of Astrakhan fur round the collar. This sable sort of ruff increased his already exaggerated air of seriousness and mystery: very important – dead secret – 'Only I could! Would I?' Of course. As a result I went to the War Office tonight – strange to say the first time I ever had set foot in the place, familiar as I have been with the Admiralty over the road – and had an hour's talk with Sir Archibald Murray, the new Chief of Staff. It was a remarkable conversation, absolutely frank, straight and unconventional on both sides. I was asked to give the benefit of my twenty years' study of German thought, methods and designs, and I gave it – perhaps not quite uselessly as regards one or two points. I liked Murray. Yet how the unreasonable longing for a Marlborough besets one, and how one begins to realise the stature of Marlborough in combined military and diplomatic genius. Without diplomatic genius an alliance is hard to work . . .

The shafts of the searchlights from different points crossed like swords over the darkness of Whitehall, and high up a bright red point like a scudding star went away to cross the Thames, the searchlights hunting it. It was for them to practise by, but what sort of mechanism impelled it I don't know. How I hope that some artist amongst us, preferably some new man and of genius, is trying to keep some record in etchings or otherwise of these night scenes, which make London seem so vast, mighty and obscure . . . It is so late, I must close. Dad

Saturday 4th December
[billets, Merville–Lestrem area]

Dear Mummy

After all I am not in the trenches tonight, nor shall I be for several days, all being well . . . Don't worry about Christmas things for me. Parcels mayn't exceed seven pounds and you mustn't inundate me. I shan't be able to appreciate your presents if I have to over-eat to taste them all. A few sweet biscuits and crystallised fruits would be as good as anything for parcels. I think (for the men) sweet things are good; they'll all get cigarettes and tobacco from other people . . .

Don't spend too much though; everybody'll be sending something. All the men have fur coats now, a sort of British Warm of sheepskin or goat's hair. Also they've been given two blankets. They keep fit . . . No more news; dearest love to you, Dad, Granny, Viva, Noonie, Gipsy and Bunny. Ged . . .

P.S. Let the maids have something from me at Christmas. Thank you for reminding me . . .

Sunday 5th December
[billets, Merville–Lestrem area[?]]

Dear Dad

I continue Mummy's letter from last night. We are once more in a destitute cottage . . . We came across today over roads flooded in places knee-deep. I rode on in front, setting off in a bright tranquil dawn about half past seven. A keen wind had dried the yard and freshened the air. But for a huge pack which made me bump and jog till I was sore, I should have enjoyed putting my horse at the flooded lanes, which he much disliked, backing now and again, till I feared a collapse into the hidden ditches either side. The Huns dropped shells near us – a daily habit, I hear – as we came in, most of them blind and failing to burst. No damage came near to being caused . . .

By the way, nothing represents a great part of the war better than Captain Bairnsfather's *Bystander* cartoons. You should watch them. To us out here they seem absolutely faithful to truth.

Bye bye. Dearest love to you, Mummy and all. I hope your 'flu improves. Ged.

II 'Dear _____, At present we are staying at a farm.........'
Cartoon by Captain Bruce Bairnsfather, first published *c.*1916

Monday 6th December
[billets, Merville-Lestrem area[?]]

Dear Mummy

No mail has come in today yet. I'm hoping for a letter from you, and the *Observer*. I've no news. We spent the morning – a blue, windy, sunny morning – improving our billets. This afternoon we rested. This evening it rains hugely, notwithstanding which we sent a working party to the trenches. I hear these trenches are not so bad as the last. I'm not wanted tonight, so I shall get a hot bath . . .

Stuart, I'm sorry to say, has been sent to hospital. He's run down and harassed. We all agree he needs a thorough rest and change of association. I'd have told you before, except that he was afraid of your worrying his mother by letting her know. Leave him to tell his people himself. He'll be far better off getting a rest a way back.

I hope he'll be kept some time. Delay any letters or parcels for a while. I can't give you his address at this moment. That's all. Bye bye. Dearest love to you . . . Ged . . .

Monday 6th December
9 Greville Place, London NW

Dearest son

Rain, mugginess and mist, and Mummy gone out in it to begin Christmas shopping, which as you know is the most solemn function to which womankind can address itself. Another letter of yours came this morning to our contentment . . . It sounds an iron grind and we wonder you ever have time to send us a line at all. Never break into your sleeping time to do it. A wise soldier sleeps when he can . . . We are very sorry and concerned to hear that Stuart is out of sorts. Give him our love and if there is anything in the world we might be able to do, only let us know and we will try . . .

I did on Saturday as important a page as I ever wrote[10] . . . For our

10 In the *Observer* of 5 December Garvin asked: 'Shall our army be raised to higher standards or kept at a lower level as some statesmen prefer? Public opinion must be stirred.'

work at all points we want more men, more men, more men. We can't break up into parties, yet this damned voluntary system – rooted deep in our insularity and moistened by our incorrigible sentimentality – means still slowness, doubt, delay. We ought to keep up our strength at the Western Front . . . We ought to hold the Dardanelles . . . We want more men, my son, more men, more men. The politicians still boggle at finance, not seeing that any method to make a clean job, and shorten by the speedier employment of maximum forces war costing £5,000,000 a day (nearly £3,500 a minute), would be by far the cheapest. Well, we get forward – slowly, but we do . . .

Yesterday the usual reflective and recuperative Sunday . . . God bless you my boy. Dad.

Saturday 11th December
Linghem, Pas-de-Calais

Dear Dad

Again the wheel has spun me. Behold, the night before last I got a note from the adjutant: 'You are to go to L— on a course of instruction on "trench warfare"'. So here I am – transported from the trenches a foot deep in mud, where from toe to waist I was a cake of sticky mould – and sharing a nice sitting room with Bell, a boy from C Coy, awfully nice (ask Stuart about him). We each have beds to sleep on and a wee bedroom apiece. I spent the morning listening to a lecture on sandbagging and trench-building. Then we took sandwiches and went out and did it. All the officer's class toiled with baskets of mud, spade and sandbag to build a trench, a redoubt behind the line. Quaintly enough a party of old fellows representing the press came along and saw us at it. None of your acquaintances I suppose . . .

Well, bye bye, dearest love to you, Mummy, Granny and the kiddies. Bid Vi not to overwork. Ged xxxx

Sunday 12th December
Linghem, Pas-de-Calais

Dear Mummy

I couldn't post yesterday evening the letter to Dad or a note scribbled for you . . . By a queer irony, the Tiptree came to me in the trenches, where I weltered in mud and slime in face of a big wood. I welcomed no whit differently. The strawberry I ate in the trenches, the cherry is still at hand. Bell and I think the peach preserve delicious. We mess together in a little parlour, rather cold and of course uncarpeted, that we rent for a franc a day from the lady of the house. We mess very well. Your golden pudding came up glistening and toothsome last night. Today we're eating the nuts – most excellent. I heard Mass in the church this morning . . .

We've just decided to postpone our jaunt owing to rain. For more than a week no day has been steadily dry, and most have been intermittently wet. You cannot conceive the horror of trench mud. When you are tired to death and weighted with pack and blanket, thick stretches of paste, knee-deep, grip your leg suddenly and overthrow you, or suddenly in the slime your foot catches and you slip and flounder and wish you were anywhere. The demoralising effect on the men is very serious, but wears off once they get rid of their burdens . . .

In the wire at this last trench one could still see German corpses left from ancient attacks, rotting jackboots and heaps of clothing. The Hun snipers were good, but caught no one while I was there, though they commanded a great part of our parapet during much of the day . . .

I found this afternoon an exquisite saraband of Leclair's in my flute music. It's really for a fiddle and I can only play a phrase or two . . . I can't think of anything else I want to tell you, except that you mustn't think of going out in the rain to shop for us. We'd far rather get no presents than think of you at home getting cold and wet to send them out. I'll try to send you a letter for Christmas Day, but mayn't be able to time it just right. Anyway do enjoy yourself with Dad and the kiddies and don't worry about not having me there.

Dearest love to you, Madonna, Dad, Granny, Vi, Noonie, Gipsy and Bunny. Ged.

Tuesday 14th December
9 Greville Place, London NW

My dear old son

I can scarcely believe that three days have passed since I wrote to you – the longest time since you went out. The reason is that I have been run clean off my legs . . . With Lloyd George and Carson until late on Friday night, talking over the possibilities of a more efficient political direction of the war. Saturday heavy. Then about eleven o'clock, as I was sitting at my dinner at home having had no Christian meal since early breakfast, who should turn up but C. P. Scott of the *Manchester Guardian* who . . . stayed until after midnight, talking politics while his taxi jigged up two-pences outside. Sunday, a molecular day of recovering . . . Monday, yesterday, the worst of days – unavoidable readings and writings in the morning, political lunch at Waldorf's from half past one to nearly five . . . then dressing with the haste of variety artistes for dinner at the Colefaxes . . . A rather pleasant night, but in all that day not a chink for letters. As for this day, I began by writing with care a public appeal to be issued by a committee which wants to save the Shakespeare Head Press from being broken up . . . then to the office for more writing, interviewing and dictation, until now which is half past six. And the Morants and one Colefax (Mrs) coming to dinner with us. And Wickham Stead of *The Times* coming to lunch and confab. tomorrow, and Raymond Recouly, once of the *Paris Figaro*, now of the French Foreign Office and [a] lieutenant after a year's service in the war, in London again for a few days and writing to me to fix interviews. So goes the whirligigging and amidst it all I must think, and think with my essential brain in an ice-box, but with vitality for expression . . .

As for Christmas things, I have not yet had a morning or afternoon to get them or think of them, but must give Thursday to the work. The girls are busy with exams, otherwise bright and Mummy is active too . . . Blessings on you. Dad

Tuesday 14th December
9 Greville Place, London NW

My very dearest one

What a horrid kind of mother you have got – not to have written a really proper letter for – it seems days. Saturday I really did intend to write, then your parcels – at least yours and all the others – took so long to pack up that it was late, before we knew where we were, then the children had to go to the junior games club party . . . C. P. Scott rang after nine and asked if he might come here right at once – and see Dad before seeing Ll. G. the following day – Dad had asked him to come down from Manchester for the purpose of meeting Waldorf and of seeing Ll. G. – Dad having dined quite late with Waldorf, Ll. G. and Carson on the Friday night. Well, Dad didn't get home till near midnight and his study was in the usual Saturday chaos and the drawing room had not been used, so the dining room had to be made warm and comfy. C. P. Scott arrived about midnight and stayed talking to Dad for quite a while . . .

Sunday, Dad didn't get up till two and when I left at 2.45 to go to a concert he was in his bath – the concert I'd promised Sybil [Colefax] I'd go to was got up to make funds for the arts people who have been so hard hit by the war. They made nearly £400.00 as all the songs and recitations and stories were given by the artistes, and Sybil had the idea of getting the same kind of thing done for the British Women's Hospital. It seems it is done once a month by the Palladium people.

Well, home about six and too tired to write – only had a boiling kind of bath, washed my head and got to bed. Yesterday putting clean chintzes on the drawing room and doing domesticities . . .

This morning the orders have just been given and I'm writing to you in case some totally unexpected thing steps in once more and stops me. All the children have their exams this week and are so busy that they won't appear at dinner. Sergeant [Melican] has had a cold for two Mondays, so hasn't turned up. I'm wondering is it worthwhile to have him on much longer – what think you? Tonight the Colefaxes and Morants dine here . . .

What is really wrong with Stuart – can't you tell me? I certainly won't say a word to his people. In fact I don't write to them unless they write to me. I expect they are all just as busy as we are. My cold is much better and if I can on some odd afternoons get a little rest I'm quite fit . . .

Dearest love and blessings and prayers – and hugs. Mammy

Wednesday 15th December
Linghem, Pas-de-Calais

Dear Mummy

I daresay that you'll have guessed that time for letter writing is short. Coming in for tea at about four we get the mail about five and must be in our places for a lecture at six. I'm afraid that when I first come in the flesh feels too weak to tackle letters; consequently I write this after tea . . .

Mrs McClinton writes about Stuart. You could tell her better than I that, above all, he needs a thorough rest and that at home. He says in all his ten days' leave your night was his only rest. His people rouse him and drag him round on visits when he needs hours of sleep. The strain chiefly, and insufficient rest, are to blame for his condition. I told you about Major Rogers, who has grown old among the blacks, is perfectly selfish and irresponsible, can do hardly anything himself, and makes everyone below him ineffectual. He drove me and the others out of our wits while we had him. You can judge how he'd affect Stuart. This is absolutely confidential, by the way. You can tell Mrs McClinton what you like about incompatible environment or anything else vague and expressive, but no more please . . .

Bye bye. Dearest love . . . Ged.

Thursday 16th December
9 Greville Place, London NW

Our dearest son

The posts are all awry and belated. Women bring them and the Christmas traffic is prodigious, so I suppose a general delay accounts for hearing nothing from you these four days. The time has seemed like a month . . .

Well, this I suppose must be your Christmas letter, if there is to be any fair chance of your getting it in time . . . It is perfectly idle for us to plan on making it a proper Christmas without Geddie. As for all the crowds in the street, you are not among 'em; and as for all the shops, you are not here to see them; and as for family feasts, when you are not here to share them they are shorn of their old glories – though not of quiet cheer. We wish that the 7th South Lancs, after having been such stout trenchmen through the bad weather, may have a chance of keeping a high old Christmas in rest billets. If you are doing it like that the family will keep high jinks too. But 'ware Boche. They don't want any more fraternising on Christmas Day and I shouldn't wonder much if they tried to give us a nasty knock . . .

Yesterday Wickham Stead and Madame Roze came to lunch and stayed as long, and appeared to enjoy themselves as much, as do all persons who come here to enjoy our unconventional hospitality. Of course we had a great talk on high politics and the necessity of making our affairs go better. 'WMGB' or the 'War Must Go Better' is a sort of motto which is the key of my mind just now; but I never realised before how intensely insular, that is to say limited and ignorant so far as the Continent is concerned, most of our people are. They know little of the history of Europe and even less of its geography . . . Today I have begun pipes as a war economy, but they go out so often that I don't like them at all.[11] The weather has been vile; your trenches must be appalling so a HAPPY XMAS *quand même*, our dearest of little sons. Dad.

Thursday 16th December
Linghem, Pas-de-Calais

Dear Mummy

I haven't had for long a nicer letter than the big one you wrote on Tuesday morning. I had it this evening after tea, and a word from Vi

---

11 J. L. Garvin habitually smoked cigars and never took to pipe tobacco.

for which please thank her. Likewise three parcels from you and one from Mrs Williams. How dear of her to send it – cake, sweets and a little book, Yeats's *Countess Cathleen*. Your bounty, Madonna, would provision a redoubt against the most vicious of Hunnish onslaughts. How shall I ever get through those bales of biscuit, pudding, sweets and fruit? As for Christmas things for the men, I was going to suggest towels. It sounds ridiculous, but for weeks now they've been using towels little short of black. A consignment of towels and scented soap would be more welcome than much pudding I fancy. The gloves you sent me are magnificent, but why spend money on two pairs Madonna? It's no good war-economising and then pouring away the saving in luxury for me. That British Warm, by the way, was as good a thing as ever we got I think.

Today I've been learning to build a wire entanglement. I'm no end of an engineer now. On Saturday we're to play about with explosive, just to get used to it. That'll be immense fun. The chief of the Divisional Staff [Lieutenant-Colonel A. S. Buckle] lectures us in a few minutes. We have the most excellent instructor here, a Captain Gompertz of the Royal Engineers who has served in India and out here for most of the war, has been sick or wounded for a time and now belongs to the division. He's a little man, keen, wide awake, confident, sure of his subject and exact in imparting it, and withal amusing and no how superior.

Bye bye. Dearest love . . . Ged.

Thursday 16th December
9 Greville Place, London NW

Most beloved of dear sons

I suppose you won't get this till quite near Christmas Day – so it brings with it very special Christmas blessings and love from Mammy, and all of us . . . Every time I wish, I wish for you and your safety, and your career, and just the you who are my own boy. So many Christmasses can I look back to – when you were so wee: and now the first one without you, so it will not be Christmas really till you come . . .

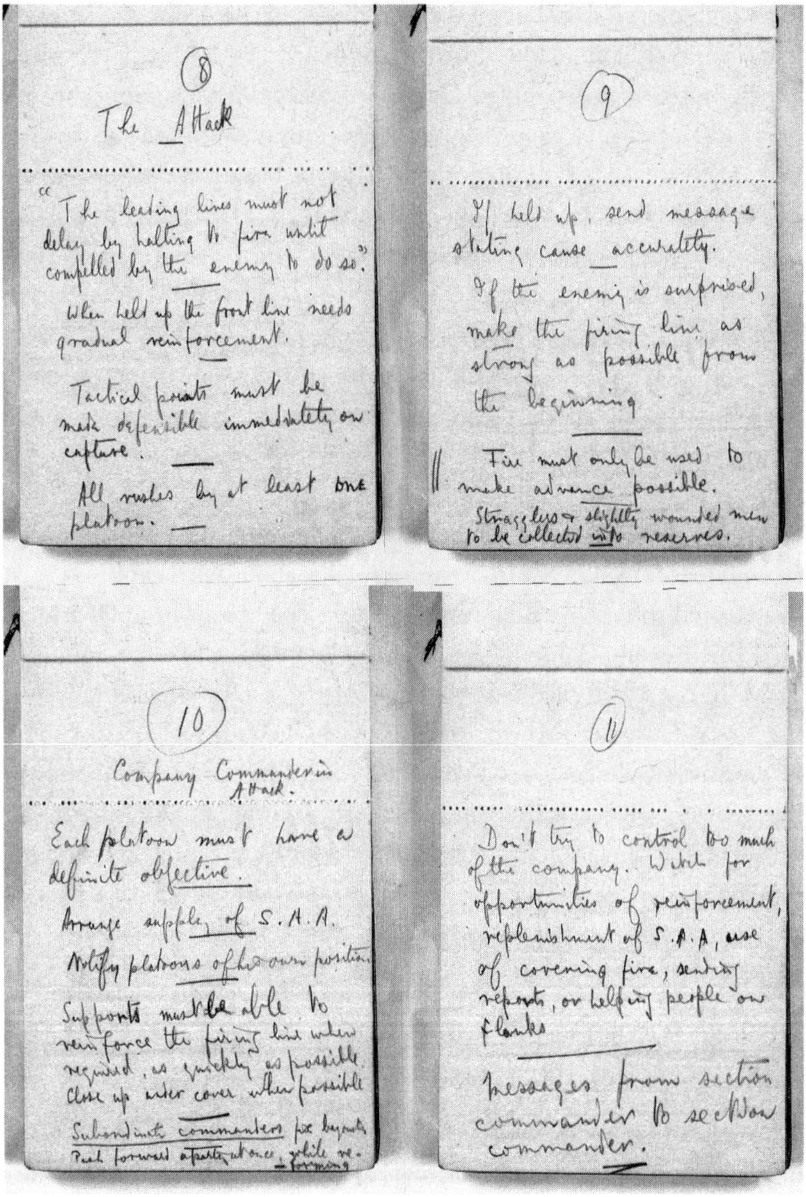
(8)

The Attack

"The leading lines must not delay by halting to fire until compelled by the enemy to do so."

When held up the front line needs gradual reinforcement.

Tactical points must be made defensible immediately on capture.

All rushes by at least one platoon.

(9)

If held up, send message stating cause accurately.

If the enemy is surprised, make the firing line as strong as possible from the beginning.

Fire must only be used to make advance possible.

Stragglers & slightly wounded men to be collected into reserves.

(10)

Company Commander in Attack.

Each platoon must have a definite objective.

Arrange supply of S.A.A.

Notify platoons of his own position.

Supports must be able to reinforce the firing line when required, as quickly as possible.

Close up under cover when possible.

Subordinate commanders fix bayonets

Push forward a party at once, while re-forming

(11)

Don't try to control too much of the company. Watch for opportunities of reinforcement, replenishment of S.A.A, use of covering fire, sending reports, or helping people on flanks

Messages from section commander to section commander.

III Ged's notes on 'The Attack' from his trench notebook.

© The British Library Board. Shelf mark 'Garvin 1'

Mrs Chidson wrote this morning . . . and she says she doesn't intend to wish anyone a happy Xmas because it's a farce: so it is, with all you dearly beloved things out there. When I wake, as I so often do at 4.00 a.m., I wonder how sleepy you are, how far the water comes up your legs – how cold you are – and how far one ear (you know you like your head covered) is open for Boche noises, and I hate the smug complacency with which I cuddle my hot-water bottle and turn over and try for sleep.

Dearest lad, God guard you and keep you, and I send kisses and love and blessings and prayers always to you. Mammy

Saturday 18th December
Linghem, Pas-de-Calais

Dearest Mummy

I hope you haven't been seriously unwell. Do please look after yourself and don't let Christmas overtire you. I can't send you anything but kisses and many happy returns of your birthday, but you've got the jars. I hope they're a really nice present.[12] I meant this to be a Christmas letter for you. As nearly as we can judge it should come either on Christmas Eve or Christmas Day. If it does come on Christmas Day I wish you many happy returns, Madonna. If not you must save them till then. I hope you'll all enjoy yourselves and have a really jolly time. Don't worry about me because by marvellous luck, the brigade comes back into billets tomorrow for a week. That'll just clear Christmas in comfort. I, Bell and a fellow from the North Lancs . . . ate your Christmas dinner last night. That galantine was excellent; Edith's plum pudding knocks the old ones into a cocked hat and the mince pies are fine.

I can't give you any news. The weather remains dull. We've spent a jolly day playing with guncotton. We exploded two pounds of it

12 For his mother's birthday on Christmas Day Ged had bought two small green antique Chinese ginger jars, 'Yung Chung or Ching period, 1723', a gift she had chosen on his behalf. They cost £3 8s 0d for the pair.

in a brook. It sent a fountain nearly as high as our house. Then we blasted a brick arch and some trees. I'll do anything you like now with guncotton . . .

I pipe every now and then on Granny's flageolet, and get lots of fun out of it. Really that's every single thing I can tell you. Happy Christmas and Many Happy Returns of the Day. Dearest love to you and the kiddies. Ged.

Monday 20th December
9 Greville Place, London NW

My dear old lad

Tomorrow a list shall be posted to you of all the books on order . . . I agree entirely about Stuart. We both thought here that he was suffering from sheer want of rest. We understand the other circumstances . . .

Today I am writing Christmas letters like fury, dozens of them, and the week will be just as full as it can hold . . . Yesterday's article in the *Observer* fluttered a lot of dovecots and I shall be somewhat abused again; but I am indifferent to that, serenely indifferent. The Government wants stirring up.[13] You will be interested to hear that the *New York Tribune* want to experiment with me for an article every Thursday – thousand words ('of's and 'the's not counted according to the queer custom of the trade) at £1,000 a year. I am taking it on; it will be a useful addition to influence as well as income . . .

Just as I write comes the great news that the great Dardanelles withdrawal from the Anzac and Suvla positions has been accomplished with <u>few casualties</u>. It is bitter to have to go and leave to the Turks again the ground won with immortal courage by the Australians. But if there have indeed been few casualties, the withdrawal is a masterpiece, for we were on sheer rock between the very devil, in

---

13 In his article that Sunday Garvin was directly critical of Asquith, calling for changes to the coalition and increased powers for the war council: 'Less dilly-dally in intent and far less shilly-shally in action': the *Observer*, 19 December 1915.

the shape of the Turks, and the deep sea[14] . . .

I had another letter from Winston. It was expected that he would get the command of a brigade, and if Sir John French had remained he probably would have done. I should think he will now have the handling of a battalion, and there will again be a 'Colonel Churchill' in Flanders after nearly two centuries and a half.[15] Everybody who grumbles says 'Why doesn't he come home and smash the Government?' – but politics look much easier than other things to those who are not experts in them, and amidst the multitude of tyros there is no wisdom. The Government will have to be remodelled by other means than smashing to begin with. Still, this service in the trenches that Winston is doing is an extraordinary episode in a statesman's career. At forty-one, he has crammed into his life enough experience to do for ten ordinary men. If he would only learn to wait his hour, but that is what he has always found difficult . . .

Without you, dear son, Christmas seems odder and odder. Deepest love to you and many blessings on your Christmas and on all your ways. Dad

---

14 This hazardous amphibious evacuation was completed in the early hours of Monday 20 December, just before bad weather broke, and the element of surprise was vital to its success: 'a great army vanished noiselessly from the shores of Gallipoli before the enemy were well aware that they were in sole possession of the field': *The Times*, 21 December 1915, p. 11. The evacuation of the remaining Allied forces at Cape Helles was successfully completed early in the morning of 9 January.

15 The earlier 'Colonel Churchill' was Winston's illustrious forebear, John, 1st Duke of Marlborough (1650–1722), who fought in Flanders during the Nine Years' War. Winston had been offered the command of a brigade by French on arrival in France, but had requested to serve as 'a regimental officer . . . before taking up such a senior appointment'. In the event his brigade was blocked: first by Asquith, whose conduct Churchill thought 'reached the limit of meanness and ungenerousness', and then effectively by Haig, who replaced French as commander-in-chief on 19 December. Churchill wrote to Clementine in January 1916: 'Haig tho' civil and I daresay friendly is quite out of my sphere: and I do not think he takes any active interest in my affairs one way or the other' (Soames, pp. 113, 137, 148).

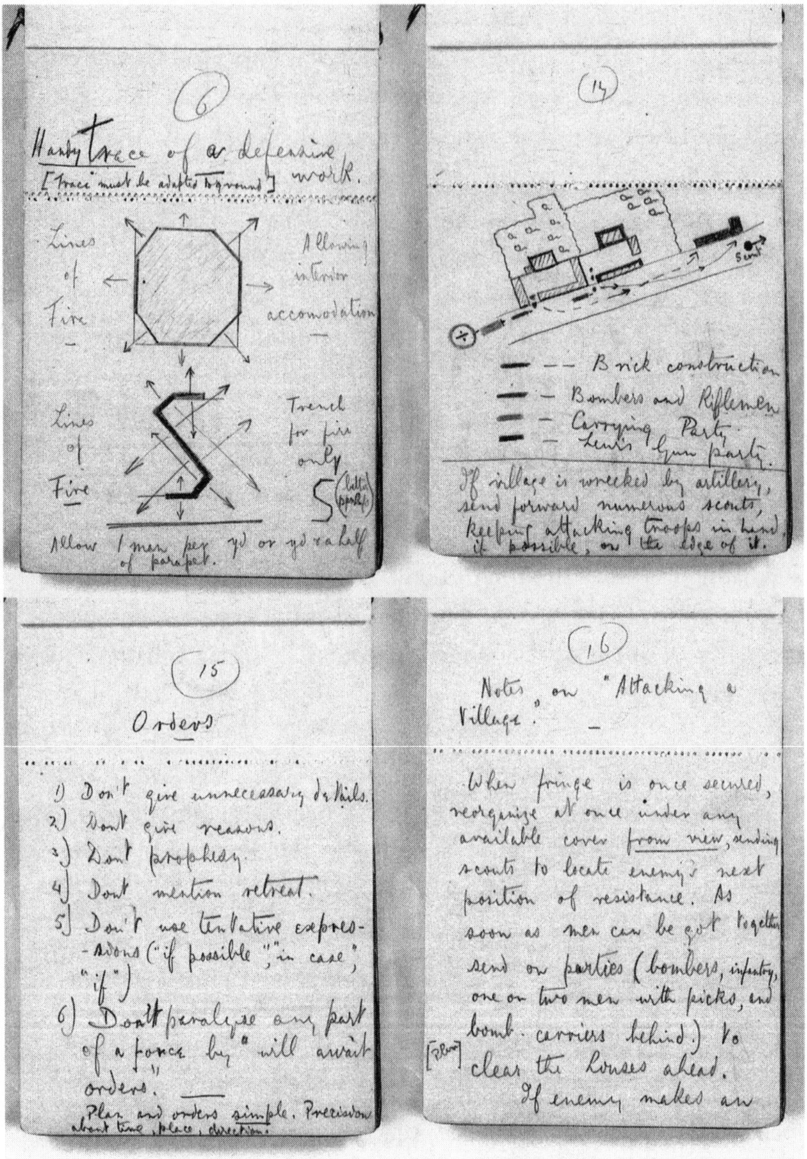

IV Diagrams and a list of 'Orders' from Ged's trench notebook.

© The British Library Board. Shelf mark 'Garvin 1'

Tuesday 21st December
9 Greville Place, London NW

My dearest boy

'But suppose he gets your Christmas letter too early!' says Vi.

'Write him another!' says John.

'Say Merry Christmas to him every day!' says Kitty.

'Yes, yes, every day!' says Jimmy.

So here's to wish you once more, like those cheers and a tiger, a Merry Christmas and a Happy New Year. It is getting to seem so long since I saw [you] that if you don't get leave soon I must get permission to visit the front, which I am bound to see anyhow during the next few months. A sudden telegram came from Mrs Winston today to say that Winston is coming home for just two days' leave and I'm dining with him on Thursday night. So that will be an interesting talk. Old Haldane sends me another cryptic epistle, wanting to dine tomorrow quite alone to talk over several things! So I'm going and we will see what he has to say. The broadside I fired into 'em last Sunday has shivered some of their timbers and shaken the whole ship, nor do I intend to stop gunning until the army and Navy and nation get a more adequate Government behind them . . .

I saw Ian Hamilton today – of course astounded, poor man, that our people have been taken off Gallipoli with only two casualties, I believe, in spite of his quite sincere prophecies of disaster; and many shared that view who did not agree with him in any other single thing. Every gun even is saved. It is the most astonishing re-embarkment in history, as the landings were the most wonderful landings . . . But the Australians go back knowing they have won immortal fame, and ready and longing to try elsewhere, after a real super Biblical go at the flesh-pots of Egypt.

. . . Your list of books with this. Blessings on you again. Dad.

Thursday 23rd December
Linghem, Pas-de-Calais

Dear Mummy

I'm afraid you're only getting the dregs of me tonight . . . We all sat up late last night making maps for the scheme today. In the end we didn't need them. We went to a bit of ground and there discussed an imaginary action with the Divisional Chief of Staff. For once the country was undulating with windmills on the ridges and as the day kept blue and breezy most of the time it was good fun.

If we get opportunity on return to keep our new knowledge in use we'll have got a deal of profit from the course. Unfortunately one learns as a rule [that] for want of practice one forgets, so that wisdom is rusted in the scabbard when it's needed. I shan't want any of Dad's books just yet. It's awfully decent of him to get them all, but he's being too extravagant . . . One good thing: the water level, if it hasn't already touched it, very soon reaches its highest point. We're quite halfway through the winter.

I hope you're all well. I'm afraid this is rather dull; I feel a bit tired and very naturally collywobbly tonight, which will pass off by morning. Dearest love to you, Dad, Vi, John (thank her for her letter), Gipsy and Bunny. Ged

Sunday 26th December
[billets, Festubert–Givenchy front]

Dear Mummy

I wrote the card to Dad yesterday, but couldn't post it. Hence two epistles today. This afternoon came a letter from you – ever so nice – and a dear one from Viva. I'm very sorry indeed if I've hurt her feelings. I try to thank everybody who sends things, letters, cards, Christmas things, especially letters. I'm writing her a bit of a note after this. Stuart sent me a card yesterday wishing me a Merry Christmas but [I] have no address. 'Eatables', as the men call it, is no bad place of temporary sojourn.[16]

. . . I begin to hate letter-writing again; so many people demand little half-formal notes of thanks, maddening little things, like wasps in your bonnet, stinging you to get out and very hard to get rid of. I love writing to you and Dad, but to most others – Urgh! . . .

16 Stuart was then at the military hospital at Etaples in the Pas-de-Calais.

I'll never spend a queerer Christmas. It was ordained we should move in the morning to rejoin the battalion. Horses and cart ordered for eleven o'clock. Packed everything. Kicked heels. Lunched on coffee and shortbread. Eventually sent servant. Transport forgotten. At three o'clock servant brought back wagon. Trundled along. Suddenly eyed familiar face, was greeted: in our divisional ammunition column I find a lad – Hawkins – who was up Homeboarders with me several years. I last saw him at school about three years ago, when I remember him as a funny perky little sparrow boy. I find him now a bit bigger and very pale. He came out to the division after me. I'm glad to know he's here and hope to have a good chat some time.

Reported to battalion – [or] such a '*bouleversement*' as there is. Williams has left bombing and become second-in-command to Hammill . . . Me shifted to D Coy and second-in-command to Sankey, also a captain now . . . I'm awfully sorry to leave my own men . . .

The gloves are fine; the refills for the torch came all right and the charm from the girls. Mrs Winser's things came for the men and she sent two excellent bottles of champagne to each company for the officers – a personal gift I think. Can you send a writing block to fit my pad as it's the only convenient way to get letters home. Love to all – Ged.

Tuesday 28th December
[billets, Festubert–Givenchy front]

Dear Mummy

I've no further news. I saw some anti-aircraft guns firing this morning. They're mounted on lorries just like the pictures, and station themselves on a road somewhere. Suddenly they spit out a perfect sheet of fire, very nice to see, and after waiting a second or two you hear the bang. They're quite an attractive sight, a couple firing rapidly, but I've never seen them hit an aeroplane. This morning I had to wander round many little cottages to find a billet for some officers we have with us for instruction. Always the same tale here, very voluble. At least two households are occupying every house . . .

Here's the corporal for letters. I've sent off two parcels of clothes and will send more as soon as possible. Bye-bye. Dearest love to you and Dad, Vi, Noonie, Gipsy and Bunny and Granny. Ged.

Tuesday 28th December
9 Greville Place, London NW

My dear lad

Well, no letter from you again which is not wonderful, considering how the traffic must have been choked both ways, and how the roaring gales must have been felt in the Channel. I'm writing this on my knee sitting in my reading chair in the study after dinner, so if the experiment makes my fist seem rocky, you will know why . . .

This afternoon I went down to St George's Hospital near Waterloo to give my promised address to wounded soldiers – odd function for Christmas pleasure. Of course I had no time to prepare any oration, but talked to them in their blue uniforms and all sorts of bandages in that theatre-like arena in the basement, where there were hundreds of them gathered, and at the end they cheered like anything again and again. Never did I value any applause like that . . .

Well, I am being adjured to go to bed early for once and hope to write more tomorrow when there is a word from you. Vi and John ask me to send their special love to you which is herewith transmitted. Kitty and Jimmy talk to each other and to Wiffles about you. Maima is trying to post you a parcel. Mummy has sent you New Year dainties and once more a Happy New Year and every blessing to our dearest son. Dad

Wednesday 29th December
[billets, Festubert–Givenchy front]

Dear Mummy

We go into the trenches tomorrow. I went down with that working party last night and saw them. Literally the country is a sheet of water divided by earth, little lengths of breastwork and strips of muddy soil. One goes up to the front line by a long plank path across country, winding about, crossing trenches often six feet deep in water.

When you get there you sit on your desert island all day and wave a handkerchief at the next island. With a tin of ration biscuits and your rum, it's quite like playing *Robinson Crusoe*. I don't know that a raft mightn't be made to ferry along the trenches. How the Huns would open their eyes.

Our guns are belching and pounding like very Etna. I think they're ours, but maybe it's the Germans. I don't know what it means. Somebody's getting his 'beaker-full' . . .

Dearest love to you . . . Ged . . .

Thursday 30th December
9 Greville Place, London NW

My dearest boy

The excellent [Dr] Blaber has just been to reassure us about Mummy, whose cold has been most hacking and wearing. So she went to bed and if we could only keep her there, but that is very difficult . . . It is a pity that you are parted from B Company, but I suppose your being second-in-command in D Company means recognised competence in your job, and when a soldier has that, increasing responsibility is always apt to change his circle somewhat . . .

Winston is back as you know and is certain to be colonel soon, though I don't know of what. A beginning has been made to break the ice between him and Jacky, but while the young man is more placable the old man feels that Winston 'punched him publicly' and is slower at making it up, but I am an obstinate reconciler between people who quarrel . . . and do not despair of bringing them together. The fact is that they all miss Winston's resource, originality and illuminating power in discussion and most of his late colleagues, including some who were not so sorry to get rid of him, think he should be back again on the war council.

I have been shaking things up a bit you see with the *Observer*, but for very good cause. It quite seemed the Cabinet might come to a clear split over compulsion; Lloyd George determined to resign if the laggard single men who have not come of themselves were not now to be fetched. So Asquith came round to a policy of prompt orders and the single men will have to roll up. The fact of drastic though limited compulsion being applied is a landmark in our history . . .

I had a pleasant chat with Bonar Law yesterday and breakfasted with Lloyd George this morning – almost a Barmecide breakfast, for London begins to be so bare of taxis in the mornings that I arrived almost too late for viands, but we had a capital talk. He is not perfect any more than the rest of them, but he is a stirring vital creature with a real touch of the man of genius and ready to do anything to get on with the war. My reading, Thucydides included, has simply stood stock-still for weeks. All the very loves to you. God bless your New Year and bless you, ever my dearest boy. Dad

Friday 31st December; New Year's Eve
9 Greville Place, London NW

My dearest laddie

Firstly, this is 7.30 p.m. on New Year's Eve and I write to you with all my heart's wish that the New Year coming in 1916 will bring you good fortune and happiness and any desire you may have. If it depended on either of these – your parents – there would be no desire unfulfilled. Secondly, you are not to worry or even think about me. I am having the time of my life in bed and not thinking about anything except resting and sleeping. My cough is not a bit troublesome and the haemorrhage has nearly stopped – so don't worry over it at all . . .[17]

I am so sorry about your having to leave your men; you have had them so long and must have been attached to some of them – and getting to know others is always a nuisance, but if it means a step up that is worth something. I heard from Stuart and he tells me he is run down badly, partly owing to have to overdo himself, partly to the kind

---

17 The fact that Christina was haemorrhaging suggests something more serious than ordinary bronchitis, and it may have been tuberculosis or, more likely, bronchiectasis – a disease of the bronchi, often caused by childhood measles, and more common in those days.

of life the trenches are, but he hopes to be back soon . . .

I wonder where your billet is, but am glad it is comfy – although being nearer the firing line isn't very comforting. How I wish I could get out to see you – I should so love it, son o'mine.

. . . Now my dearest son, I'm going to stop and send you just my fondest love, my prayers and blessings for your safety – and that your New Year may be a happy one, now that we're over the turn of the year. I hope you'll have glorious views and see some things worth seeing. Mammy.

4

New Year 1916

New Year's Day, 1916
[trenches, Festubert–Givenchy front]

Dear Mummy

I'm pencilling a note in a very cramped dug-out, horribly draughty on my island. These trenches aren't at all so bad; quite a lot of dry places. I've sat here all day with my boots off. Going out on patrol last night, I got them full of water, so they're being more or less dried. There are sheets of water over the ground between the lines . . . I went a bit out along one road just about midnight, walking in the edge at the side. I just missed several ditches, and went into one. I found nothing and only heard a distant word or two of German . . .

How is your cold? It ought to be gone now; I hope it is. I've had a nasty one, but it's going . . . Bye bye. Dearest love . . . Ged . . .

Monday 3rd January
9 Greville Place, London NW

My dear old boy

Your parents, Mr and Mrs Crock o'that ilk – the distaff side being the crockier of the two – were very much heartened by two or three notes from you coming together and in jolly high spirits. This was as good as medicine, though Blaber says Mummy is mending, but insists on keeping her in bed . . . Did we tell you that we are both very proud of our son being second-in-command of a company now and having, by all accounts we hear, the full making of a competent soldier in him? . . .

I sat up on Friday o'night, much to the general detriment and dilapidation of my body, to see in the New Year with proper spirit, and as the bells and hooters rang and blew, and while Wiffles upon the drawing room balcony barked loud to see his master below . . . my first thoughts and prayers, before and after crossing the threshold with the coal and salt, were for you . . .

I'm really going to have a long sleep tonight, and am sure that the prolonged rest in bed is doing your Mummy great good . . . Blessings on you. Dad

Thursday 6th January
[billets, Merville–Lestrem area[?]]

Dear Mummy

. . . Well, we went into the trenches on New Year's Eve, in a drizzle that eventually gave place to a chilly clearness with stars. About midnight, as you know, I with another officer and two men went out on patrol, stealing in single file along a yard of sedge grass between a flooded road and a sheet of water, both shining as far as you could see (only a short way by night). Next night another patrol. We crawled out, found old trenches full of water snaking between the lines, got quite close to the Huns, heard a shrill rasping screech – highly uncanny – like an alarm signal, and fearing capture retired in haste. The worst of patrolling is that you never know when you'll fall into a trap. I thoroughly enjoyed those two expeditions, all the same. That night was beastly. I had a little cramped dug-out with a door each end and the wind flapped the door curtain (somebody's abandoned mackintosh) and blew the candle out. I got awfully angry. Next night Lumley relieved us. We went back to reserve trenches where we had a mess and I had a cosy dug-out, the last night anyway. We started work the morning after we got in, feeling fit and merry in a sunny morning, blue and sparkling.

First the colonel came and put us on to another job. Then, just as I was gesticulating over a wall, bidding the men keep down and not expose themselves, a little shell . . . went into the wall six feet away if you please and nearly knocked me over. We had to lie low for about twenty minutes, because the Hun battery, with the light, caught us in the open and gave us about thirteen shots pretty quick. Nobody seriously hurt. One other burst about fifteen feet from me, just beyond a hedge. I've always wanted an experience with pip-squeaks. I got it that first shot. Good thing it didn't get me. Still, one never comes to any harm out here and I'm awfully careful. I've got two nose-caps, awfully nice . . . both from that battery. I'll bring them home when I come.

We were relieved in a heavy drizzle the night before last. Yesterday after late orders the previous night we marched back here. I thought the men went very well. The sun set rosy and lovely in a fresh evening. We all have beds with sheets, found by our own enterprise. I thoroughly enjoyed my sleep last night. Today furious clothes inspections and much indenting.

Last night I read *Un Coeur Simple*, one of the Flaubert tales, beautifully written and extraordinarily sad . . . I don't know if I thanked Granny, but her cake was excellent and the socks came just at the time when patrolling had soaked my other three pairs in the trenches. Hers are quite the best socks I get . . .

And I think, Madonna, that's all for tonight. Bye bye. Dearest love . . . Ged

Thursday 6th January
9 Greville Place, London NW

My dearest old son

Nothing from you these three days . . . You were going to have a spell in the reserve trenches – even that I should reckon a blessed relief at this season, when you must have had a blast or two of our wild storms. Mummy is up today . . . and receiving visitors. I think too soon, but it is hard to keep her in bed by any means short of having time to sit at her door with a gun . . .

I didn't write yesterday. Why? Because I spent eight mortal hours in the House of Commons from 2.45 to 10.45 listening to the conscription debate. There was I, if you please, in the front row of the Distinguished Strangers' Gallery next to Sir Robert Reid, the retiring

High Commissioner for Australia and Judge Darling, who turned off a four-line epigram while we listened – not one of his best, but as Dr Johnson said of the dog who dances on his hind legs, the wonder is not that he doesn't do it well, but that he does it at all. So with epigrams even passable, pencilled in a few moments in a crowd. As for the debate, I never disliked the House of Commons so much, nor felt more sympathy with Cromwell [or] understanding of what he did. What is more terrible, when great things are urgent, than the very clever unintelligence of the accomplished half-fanatical, half-scheming lawyer like Sir John Simon, quipping, quibbling, niggling and talking of his conscience amidst a conflagration like this? It was worse than the furious emotional prejudice of an eloquent half-educated labour leader like J. H. Thomas, talking of 'This 'ouse', and threatening strikes if single men are compelled; worse even than the echoing declamation of John Dillon, talking with that peculiar one-sidedness which always leaves me dead cold again towards Irish things . . . and all these were far worse than the mere talk of the stupids.

You would scarcely have thought there was any war going on to hear these people. On the right side Asquith was flat and weak; Bonar Law most excellent, acute, discriminating, really analytic and damaging, yet with perfect command of temper. He is much improved and will go further than I thought. Two excellent speeches in spirit made by men in khaki, General Seely and the Canadian Colonel Greenwood, both full of ringing sincerity and conveying to that mixed, haphazard mob of civilians left over from irrelevant elections of years ago, some sense of what the trenches mean. But no one stated the case for compulsion, for getting on with the war, for making an end of uncertainties and delays, as it might have been stated, and I left the House unusually heavy and condensing with wrath because there had not been more powerful searching scathing answers to so much mischievous sophistry. They were like men at a fire objecting to the use of fire-engines, first 'on principle'; and secondly . . . because the fire is such a little one that if you have patience with it you can probably put it out with buckets. A general election would be in itself a nuisance and a scandal, but I think it would sweep all these people away and give us a new majority with the sound power and energy of the Country itself.

This morning the *Tribune* cable done by one o'clock and then jumping out of a dressing gown, shaving and dressing in twelve minutes – good for me! – and to lunch at Prices with Waldorf and General Sir John Cowans, head of army transport and supply at the War Office, a jolly, shrewd, clever personage. Amusing talk about the sacred institution: 'We are always in the soup whatever we do,' said Cowans – 'Thick or clear!' said I with intent, as the waiter was about to say the same thing. He was full of joy as though I had brilliantly epitomised the soldier's monotonous alternative.

The loves many and dear to you, and all blessings. Dad.

Friday 7th January
[billets, Merville–Lestrem area[?]]

Dear Dad

Thanks ever so much for the two letters today. Being a company second-in-command appears to mean nothing. I daresay I shall get more to do when we settle down. My new platoon seem very good fellows and I've an excellent sergeant.

Today I'm orderly officer, which means inspecting five guards. Riding along the high road I got caught in a perfect tempest of sleet. It went off pretty quick, and left the evening fresh and sweet with an amber sunset behind the woods. Stuart sent me a longish letter last night. He doesn't sound exactly happy . . .

It's quite inconsequent, but may interest. The greatest feeling in the pitchy desolation of the trenches is the craving for light and warmth. One longs for bright light as for pieces of eight. Mainly one doesn't notice, but sometimes the tattered roofs and gaunt trees and the pervading chilly dark absolutely depress and disgust one.

I roared with laughter at a quaint spectacle today. We sent men to draw straw for billets. The trusses are huge and carried on a man's back. Suddenly, rounding a corner, I saw a great file of straw men, like giants, leading along the road and looking inexpressibly comic, as in a fairy tale, where the bad man witches his neighbour's sheaves to walk away in the night. Bye bye. Dearest love to you and Mummy, Granny, Vi, Noonie, Gipsy and Bunny. Ged. Remember me to the maids.

Monday 10th January
[billets, Merville–Lestrem area[?]]

Dear Mummy

I'm awfully sorry no letter went yesterday. I put it off till evening and then suddenly got orders to go on the range first thing this morning, sat up till late preparing butt registers and went off to fire before eight today. We lost the targets in an impenetrable forest and wasted all but a few minutes of our two hours recovering the bearers. I think our company was the only one to have proper registers though.

This afternoon, I've been throwing dummy bombs and supervising the issue (or 'dish-oot') of new clothes and kit to men needing them. That's my job now, to supervise interior economy and act as company housekeeper, while Sankey deals with higher problems of training and strategy. About 11.00 p.m. last night I nearly trod on a dark and groaning mass: 'Who are you?' 'Who's you?' 'Officer of the South Lancs.' 'Well, you mi' be, an' you mi' not.' This was reflective and rather aggressive. It was two men, drunk mightily and very incapable, who evidently thought, when I demanded their name and regiment, that I was a Hun spy.

. . . No other news. I hope all's well at home. As Bell and Coxon dine with us tonight, I'm just going down town to get some wine (not champagne). Dad told me you were getting up to see visitors; please don't – get your rest while you can. Bye bye. Dearest love . . . Ged.

Wednesday 12th January
9 Greville Place, London NW

Dearest, best beloved and preciousest of sons

I'm so ashamed, I hardly know how to write to you after this long silence and so many days in bed. You'll be glad to hear, firstly, that there is no trace of tubercular trouble in my silly lung – and so Dad is happier in consequence and the doctor much easier in his mind. There is no present chance of your having a stepmother yet – but I've been extraordinarily flat and slack so that to write, even to you which is such a joy, has been impossible. Even Dad has been slack, as always in January and February when he generally has to go away. He has been very sleepless and very cross . . .

. . . So that's all at the moment, dear lad. My first night out – I'm dining at Macmillan's tonight and must dress.

Dearest love – always prayers and blessings uncountable from Mummy.

Thursday 13th January
[billets, Merville–Lestrem area[?]]

Dear Dad

. . . I've not much time, but a bit of news. I'm actually in command of a company.[1] Sankey goes to the base tomorrow to instruct reinforcements, and however long I keep it up, I'm for the moment company commander. No easy job; I hope I'll do it alright . . .

I hope Mummy's still improving and you feeling fit again by the time this arrives. Bye bye. Dearest love . . . Ged xxx

Tuesday 18th January
9 Greville Place, London NW

Dear old Sahib

An acting commander of a company, no less, as they say in the Green Isle, and wondering whether his parent is ever going to write him a letter again. The truth is that I have been a proper slacker for a few days and had to get some store of sleep into my system before my elasticity would come, and I loathe sending you wooden letters when I am loggish. A couple of goodish nights with the aid of cachets has put some spring into one again. Mummy is so much better, though wisely

1 Ged was later gazetted temporary captain, dated 15 January.

keeping [to] her room until she gets even more, so that she writes you more letters now and in fine form. I was of course a parental peacock about you having the company to handle in Sankey's absence, but it must leave you so little time that I wonder you are able to keep us in touch as you do . . .

Last night at Edward's a few of the old guard of the Tariff movement gathered together . . . and among them was Henry Page Croft, MP, now a colonel, who has been out at the front for sixteen months and has been in most of the big actions – a fine fellow. Of course we talked of you, and he said you ought to be getting leave sometime in February. Can it be that such luck is possible?

Page Croft is having a fortnight this time, though he has never had more than five days before. He gave excellent accounts of the spirit of the men and it cheers me that you do the same. If only we had more force and grip in the Government – spineless sophists or purblind obstructives that for the most part they are. My patience with them's worn out, though it is difficult to make a change . . .

The many loves, the many blessings to you. Dad.

Wednesday 19th January
[billets, Merville–Lestrem area[?]]

Madonna mine

Lest I put it off for ever, here's a letter, something more satisfying than those lean postcards which I hate to send. I'm very busy and important these days. I'm as one having command, worried with returns and programmes of work, writing honeyed words of official pattern to adjutant and paymaster, and needless to say making mistakes, as when I forget until the last moment to assign to this platoon or that its dummy bombs or sandbags. One doesn't at once realise the importance of having everything ready beforehand. Before I retire tonight I must arrange . . . for tomorrow bombs, sandbags, instructor: when they're available, and where, and in what quantity . . .

The weather has promised spring for a week or two, with bright mild nights. This evening the moon came up like ivory, very early in a flushed sky. Curiously enough the west made no sign of sunset, shining white-barred and stormy. The whole day has been adorable . . .

May this find you and Dad much better, rested and stronger every way. Dearest love to you and Dad, Granny, Vi, Noonie, Gipsy and Bunny. Ged

Thursday 20th January
9 Greville Place, London NW

Dearest Laddie

It is exactly twelve weeks today since your leave and we hoped you may be coming again soon, but I suppose it is too much to expect from the Gods that be. It's always a better day when we get a letter from you, or a card; otherwise it's very glum . . .

By the way Edith is being married to a man in the 4th Dorset Yeomanry . . . We can't get any servants, so have taken Gladys Saull for odd things, and her mother helps us all she knows. The girls have gone back to school and are bewailing that one of their maids has left and they can't get anyone else. Everyone is in the same boat . . .

Your Sergeant Dee sent me such a nice note, thanking me for the towels and soap. I'm glad they were useful . . .

Dearest love, kisses – and blessings and prayers from my heart. Mammy.

Sunday 23rd January
[billets, Merville–Lestrem area[?]]

Dear Mummy

. . . Tomorrow we rise at six for a brigade route march. I shall prance mightily and most seigniorial on my steed. Also, I'm on a court martial – junior member of a very youthful court, in the afternoon. Next week's training as outlined looks hard and allows no leisure. I wish 'brass-hats' would recognise the strategical value of rest, instead of humming and horneting about the training of junior commanders. A little parcel, by the way, would fall on good ground, as perchance peppermint creams, cashew nuts (are they too

1. Christina Garvin, photographed around the time of the First World War

2. J. L. Garvin, photographed by J. Benjamin Stone, 1909.

3. 'The editor of the *Observer*': J. L. Garvin photographed by Hector Murchison, *c.*1914.

4. Christina Garvin and her daughters, *c.*1913–14: (left to right) Viola (behind), Katharine (in front), Ursula (on her mother's knee), Christina, Una. The girls were known by family nicknames: Viola was 'Vi' or 'Viva'; Katharine 'Kitty' or 'Gipsy'; Ursula 'Bunny' or 'Jimmy'; and Una 'Noonie' or 'John'.

5. A lesson at Westminster School, *c.*1910. The master is Mr Etheridge, who taught modern languages, and R. G. Garvin – 'Ged' – is the young man immediately to his right.

6. The 'Homeboarders', Westminster School, *c.*1913. Ged is the tall man with his hands in his pockets at the left of the picture.

7. Westminster representatives at the public schools sports competition at Aldershot in 1912, photographed in the school cloisters: (left to right) J. A. G. Cecil (gym; killed in action, 1918); Sergeant Melican (trainer); J. C. Ainsworth-Davis (gym); C. D. O'Sullivan (boxing); H. A. Wootton (science master); R. G. Garvin (foils; killed in action, 1916)

8. The 'Homeboarders', winners of the Westminster School Interhouse Combined Cadet Force Drill Competition, 1913.

From left to right, **back row**: Charles Robertson (*Scots Guards, 1916–18*); Michael Gonne (*RFC, 1916–18*); Miles Canning (*RE, 1914–18*); Ronald Howe (*Royal Sussex Regt, 1915–19*); Gerard Garvin (*South Lancs. Regt, 1914–16*); William Fisher (*London Regt & MGC*); Hubert Campion (*RVNR & RNAS, 1914–19*); Hume Chidson (*East Surreys & MGC, 1914–19*) **middle row**: John Ainsworth-Davis (*Rifle Brigade & RFC, 1914–18*); Alexander Forbes (*Seaforth Highlanders, 1914–16*); James Aitken (*Middlesex Regt & MGC, 1914–18*) **front row**: John Brookman (Indian Army, 1917–18); Courtenay Kitchin (*R.M.L.I., 1916–18*); William Aitken.

Of the fourteen, only William Aitken, at 12 the youngest, did not serve in the war; the eldest, Alexander Forbes, then aged 18, died of wounds on the Somme, 17 August 1916. Two others died between 1914 and 1918: Ged, killed in action on the Somme, 23 July 1916, and Michael Gonne, who was last seen at 2,000 feet over the Somme in August 1918 and is thought to have died in a German military hospital.

9. The officers of the 7th Battalion, South Lancashire Regiment, 1915 – (from left to right) **back row standing**: [unidentified], [unidentified], James, Hughes, Ridley, [unidentified], [unidentified]; **middle row standing**: [unidentified], Second-Lieutenant R. G. Garvin, [unidentified] . . . [unidentified], Milmas [extreme right]; **middle row seated**: Captain P. C. Vellacott, Captain E. C. Sewell, Captain C. M. Hewlett, Major C. R. P. Winser, Major Lewis, [unidentified], Captain Hamill, [unidentified]; **front row, sitting on ground**: [unidentified], [unidentified], Second-Lieutenant Hughes, Second-Lieutenant Bell.

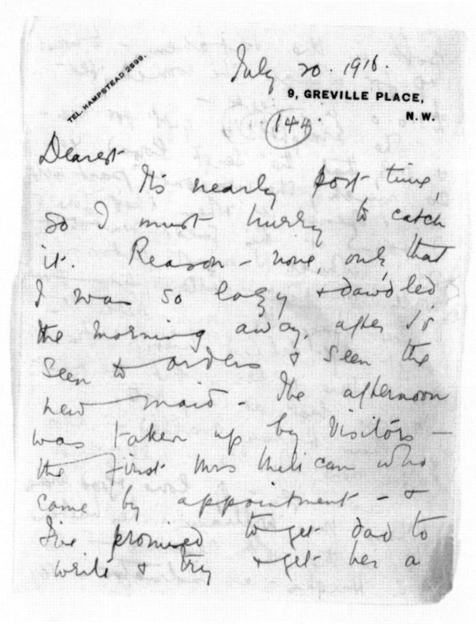

July 20. 1916.

TEL. HAMPSTEAD 2599.

9, GREVILLE PLACE,
N.W.

(144)

Dearest

It's nearly post time, so I must hurry to catch it. Reason – none, only that I was so lazy & dawdled the morning away, after I'd seen to orders & seen the new maid – the afternoon was taken up by visitors – the first Mrs Melican who came by appointment – & I've promised to get Dad to write & try & get her a

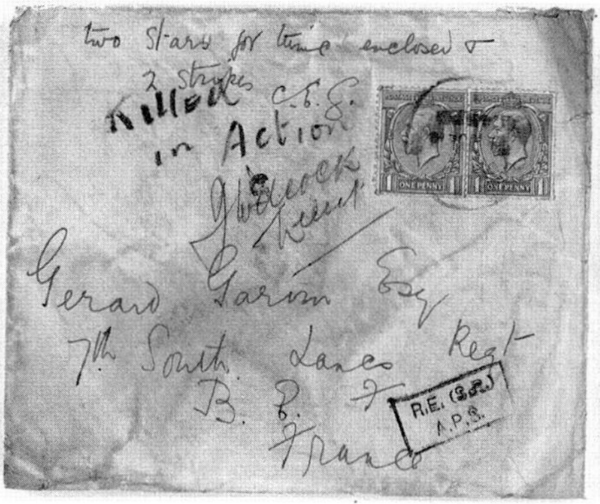

10. The first page and envelope of Christina Garvin's last letter to her son, 20 July 1916, which was returned unopened. She had enclosed 'two stars … and 2 stripes' for his tunic: Ged had been permitted to wear the rank of captain, though not yet gazetted.

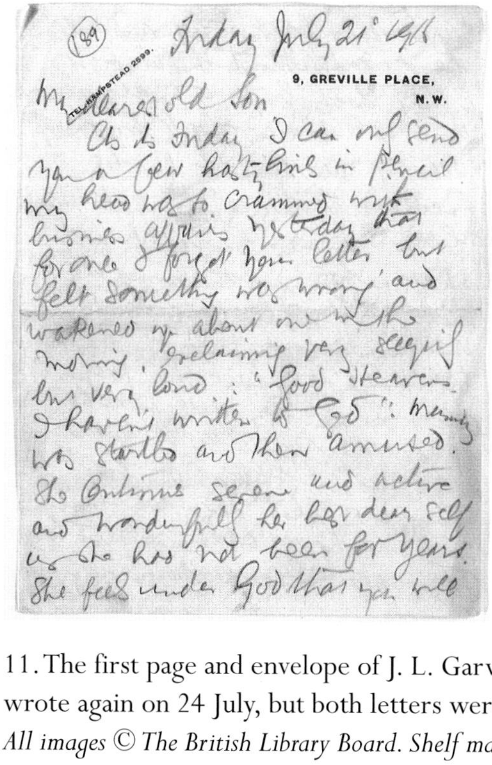

(189) Friday July 21st 1916

TEL. HAMPSTEAD 2599.

9, GREVILLE PLACE,
N.W.

My dearest old Son

As it is Friday I can only send you a few hasty lines in pencil. My head was so cramming with business affairs yesterday that for once I forgot your letter but felt something was wrong and wakened up about one in the morning exclaiming very sleepily but very loud: "Good Heavens I haven't written to Ged": Mummy was startled and then amused. She continues serene and active and wonderfully her best dear self as she has not been for years. She feels under God that you will

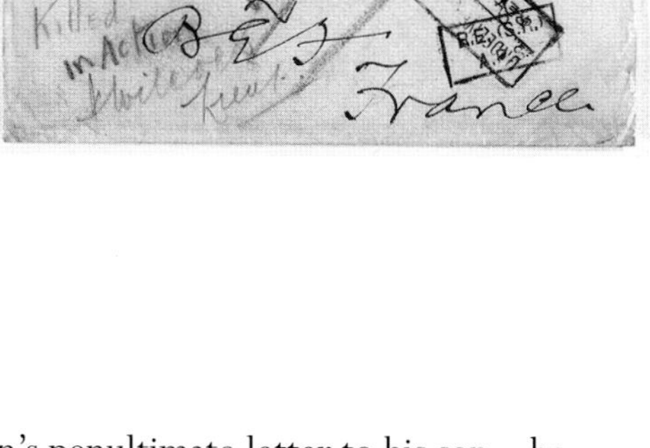

11. The first page and envelope of J. L. Garvin's penultimate letter to his son – he wrote again on 24 July, but both letters were returned unopened.

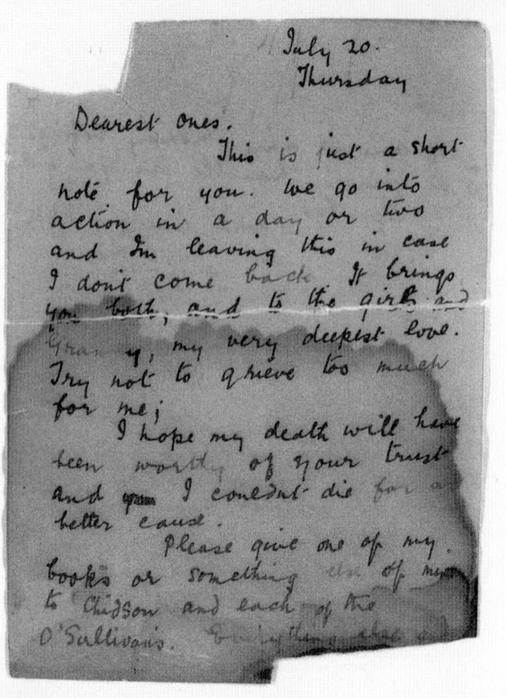

July 20.
Thursday

Dearest Ones.

This is just a short note for you. We go into action in a day or two and I'm leaving this in case I dont come back. It brings you both, and to the girls and Granny, my very deepest love. Try not to grieve too much for me;

I hope my death will have been worthy of your trust and I couldnt die for a better cause.

Please give one of my books or something else of mine to Chidson and each of the O'Sullivans. Everything

12. Ged's last letter home, dated 20 July 1916. It was written while the 7th South Lancs were dug in near Mametz Wood, sheltering from heavy German shelling, in advance of the night attack on the German 'switch line' north of Bazentin-le-Petit, 22–23 July 1916.

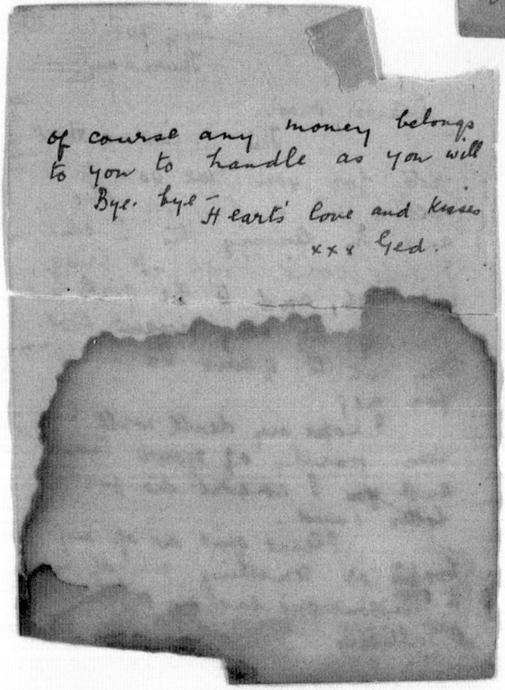

of course any money belongs to you to handle as you will

Bye. bye – Heart's love and kisses

xxx Ged.

July 20
Thursday

Dearest Ones

This is just a short note for you. We go into action in a day or two and I'm leaving this in case I don't come back. It brings you both, and to the girls and Granny, my very deepest love. Try not to grieve too much for me . . .

expensive?), shortbread, Imperial cheese and perhaps a little bottle of olives, if it stood no chance of breaking . . . Bye bye. Dearest love to you and Dad, Granny, Vi, Noonie, Gipsy and Bunny. Ged xxxx

Sunday 23rd January
9 Greville Place, London NW

Dearest of Lads

It was worth a week of crumbs to get a substantial feed by the end of the week – with many things satisfying, giving visions of glorious spring days and clear mornings and nights – and a gallant warrior riding through fields and villages and red roofs dotted about. Of course you're busy and important – all you young people are, and why shouldn't you be if at all in this life, but I like to think of you enjoying it all as well as the work. They all flourish, only that Vi got into Dad's special moods on Friday night because she shrugged her shoulders at him when he spoke to her about her music – she said he'd given her no peace and he over-worked, was over-wrought, over-worried, over-smoked (twelve in a day), over-stouted. He gave her one of those awful scenes that are as a general rule reserved for me, and anything John or I could say or do did no good. But we got him to bed at 1.15 a.m. and he came down to me again at 5.40 a.m. and started again. As he had to breakfast at 7 a.m. I stayed up and looked after him. So he had an awful day yesterday, but the work is quite good in spite of it. I spoke to Blaber and told him I thought he was going mad, but after he got home last night he asked me to read the *Legend of Montrose* for an hour. I did until John and Vi fell asleep. We got him to bed at 12.30 and I gave him a sleeping draught and he slept for nine and a half hours.

Today is better and he has forgiven Vi I think, because he took them both for a drive to Finchley. If he would only stop smoking so much – and now he's taking on lectures, one at Epsom and one at the Sesame Club and one at the Royal Colonial Institute – and Chapman and Hall have announced that wretched book and have written to him, but he won't open the letter because it may be about the book and he has none of it done yet.[2] Heigh-ho, why does he take on so much?

I suppose there is no idea when you get next leave. The weather here, from the house, looks wonderful – clear and fresh with the rose trees and ramblers budding little green shoots in the garden, but when I get little or no sleep for nights, I don't care whether I ever go out of doors again. I enclose the first golden crocus from the garden and the first blue scilla.

. . . Blessings and prayers and love and love and love to you – Mummy

Tuesday 25th January
[billets, Merville–Lestrem area[?]]

Dear Mummy

. . . I've been rather harassed, sending people to brigade, baths at unlikely hours, and tomorrow I have to inspect the company and waste time in fussing round it before the brigadier [General van Straubenzee] inspects it on Thursday. Too much inspection means short time for field training, which I want to practise. Probably my inside's upset and I'm viewing life with liverish eyes . . .

I was annoyed this afternoon. I had laid out, on a wee orchard promontory where two ditches joined (one very deep and wide) a little piece of almost impregnable entrenchment. I chose it because the earth was trodden brown and looked safe to dig in. Just as we dug the foundations, out came 'Madame', ruddy with strong features, and protests very nicely that the land is pasture and we'll spoil it forever by digging. So after a good deal of work we had to fill in and depart.

We practise the men, now and again, with gas helmets. How they hate it, puffing and blowing. I roar when they can't catch an order, and [they] turn round, stomach and snout out, and throw back their

---

2 In August 1915 the publishers Chapman & Hall, of which Garvin's one-time mentor W. L. Courtney was a director, suggested a book of his 'prophecies upon the political, military, and naval aspects of this Great War'. Garvin had reservations about the idea and the publication never materialised.

heads, all featureless and goggle-eyed, to stare and see, just like strange monsters.

Bye bye. Dearest love to you and Dad, Granny, Vi, Noonie, Gipsy and Bunny. Ged

Saturday 29th January
[billets, Merville–Lestrem area[?]]

Dear Mummy

I'm afraid I'm getting into a bad habit of writing to you last thing before going to bed. Whence no word last night. I felt too tired – not with work, because I really don't at all hard. Somehow I never feel able to settle down now. I'm always wanting to go round to Lumley or Hammill and chat. I can't feel any intimacy with my mess here. One of the subalterns is perpetually talking about a few not very marvellous experiences near Ypres, chanting again and again the wonderful feats accomplished in his neighbourhood. What's worse, he sniffs at everything he hasn't himself seen done, and assumes an airy superiority always.

One of the officers, Skelton, is keen and efficient and quite a nice fellow, but the third is vapid, though well-meaning. I can't talk to any of them about anything.

Lumley and Hammill dined with us last night. We played a new war-game, very like chess, with horse and footmen, cannon and aeroplanes. In the evening I went along the canal bank into the town and played on a piano in a shop. That was nice, a bit of Mozart and Beethoven (waltzes) and a delicious waltz of Offenbach's *La Grande Duchesse*.

Next week's programme towers like the adamant cliff before us and has rather damped our Saturday night. Even now I haven't thanked you for the nice letters I got today and the parcels, just what I wanted . . .

I'm getting very annoyed because every Sunday, instead of my morning rest, like everyone else, I have to get up at the same time as on a weekday to take Catholic church parade. Mass is at nine o'clock and battalion parade fifteen minutes earlier. Ordinary weekday parades are nine o'clock and close at hand, instead of several minutes' walk. What a grumble. I guess I'll feel alright in the morning . . . Bye bye. Dearest love . . . Ged

Monday 7th February
9 Greville Place, London NW

My dear old boy

This is a howling raving night with lashing rain and sends our thoughts naturally to sea and across it. I came home to find Mummy prepared for visitors and not having any, but she looks as pretty as you like in a new green Russian coat with fur edging, and the drawing room looked cosy . . .

We are going out to dine with Gordon Selfridge. Hoover is to be there, who is the head of food distribution in Belgium, and also a man named Kohlsaat, who is something important in the Chicago newspaper world. How the hyphenated baulk, yet some of them are friendly. We hate having so many social engagements, and when we find ourselves in the toils always wonder how we came to be so tied up . . .

Your books came and the letters. Mummy took charge of the letters. I arranged the books neatly in your little room, thinking about you a great deal. The one thing we are wondering about is whether there is a real chance of your getting leave or whether you may get stopped after all. There are all sorts of rumour about a great German attack on our lines in the west and about the tremendous concentration of guns that the enemy is making for the purpose . . . I wish infinitely that you could have got home this month.

The love of all our hearts to you and God bless you my son. Dad.

❖

Verdun

The city of Verdun in northern Lorraine stood at the centre of a large salient in the front line, epitomising French resistance to the German invaders. On 21 February German long-range artillery opened fire along

a twenty-kilometre front and up to forty shells a minute fell on parts of the city's defences. The next day six German divisions attacked, and when the stronghold of Fort Douaumont fell on 25 February it seemed that Verdun was lost. At that desperate hour the commander of the French Second Army, Philippe Pétain, took charge of the defence, and by skilled use of artillery he stemmed the tide. What had been meant as a German breakthrough became a battle of attrition that lasted until December, leaving around 143,000 Germans dead and 162,440 French. Verdun seriously weakened French commitment to the summer's planned Franco-British offensive on the Somme.

❖

Monday 7th February
[billets, Merville–Lestrem area[?]]

Dear Dad

The *Observer* came today, but nothing more personal. It always more nearly approaches a letter than any other substitute, even Mummy's parcels. We went for a route march today, planned spaciously, but cut short by a violent hailstorm which attacked us about eight miles out from home. Wherefore we wended speedily back. The sun came out and the wind dried us before we came in. This afternoon nothing happened. We didn't do much. Tomorrow we do more company training, which I like. I feel as if my own training were giving my fellows what they need. Educational responsibility, what? We go back to the trenches later this week, very likely. I'm afraid no leave before that, but from the trenches I fancy we may get leave. I hope so, though it is only three months . . .

The difficulty is that I have no one who can look after the company if I go. I'm always making mistakes, not serious as a rule; I expect that'll be worn off. But I don't think the others have much notion of what has to be done. A great difficulty for me is the comparative strangeness of the company. Even now I know very few of the men and haven't of course the old acquaintance I had with most men in B Company. That all takes time. Meanwhile I think all goes ahead well . . .

Bye bye. Dearest love to you and Mummy, Granny, Vi, Noonie, Gipsy and Bunny. Ged

Monday 7th February; 10.15 p.m.
9 Greville Place, London NW

Dearest and best beloved

I'm afraid my flesh is very weak, but the spirit so willing. I intend to write each morning and after the orders are given and the accounts attended to . . . the room is so cold and I'm tired that I put it off till evening – and that's fatal, because of meals and engagements and telephones and the etcs of life generally. I think Constantine Bay is what my soul longs for at the moment – so as to do as I like when I like. It shows, all this, that although I'm forty and fat, that the spring still has power to worry one somewhat . . .

I'm sorry you can't get over soon, but can't Dad get to some near point to you, for a rest? I wish he would. He misses you tremendously. I – well you know how much I long to see you, but both of us will soon perhaps. C. P. Scott has just arrived for a talk, which means midnight anyhow, I suppose. I think sometimes Heaven must be a place where one can sleep and rest and not worry and think.

Dearest beloved, I must say goodnight . . . Mammy.

Wednesday 9th February
[billets, Merville–Lestrem area[?]]

Dearest Mummy

I've had a regular day of rest, only troubled by a shower of notes from headquarters. More rain continued all last night, leaving a morning brilliant and warm, the sky blue as one always fancies a Greek sky, and here and there bunches of snowdrops nearly open and white buds on plum or damson trees. We are all enjoying the rest procured by inoculation, feeling languid, but fit.[3] The men who

3 The day before most of the battalion was inoculated with 'paratyphoid serum'. The men experienced constant aches and were rested for a couple of days.

hadn't been inoculated I sent off on a scheme by themselves, turning an Irish corporal for the morning into an amateur Napoleon . . .

Bye bye. Dearest love to you . . . Ged.

PS May I have another box (small) of Tiptree? Ration for jam is going off.

Monday 14th February
9 Greville Place [on 'Shootlands' notepaper]

Dear old boy

Here is obsolete notepaper to write to you on, but your mother is lying down: I don't want to disturb her and have nothing else, so use up this stuff. A few minutes ago you would have seen me on the floor evoking order out of chaos incredible: newspapers – English, American, French, German – the accumulation of weeks, until the Augean stable was more sightly than my study. I would rather have gone out and got some air, but it was impossible to tolerate that rubbish, so I fell upon it, and there is order after such a vigorous grappling as used to divert you of old . . .

[Friday] I went to the Royal Automobile Club to lunch with Andrew Fisher, late Prime Minister of Australia and now come here as High Commissioner for the Commonwealth. I had not seen him for five years . . . We had a capital talk about ANZAC, Australia and the difficulty of getting men of mark into the Government at home. 'Look here,' said Fisher, 'What are you doing, Garvin? When I was home last they told me you were one of the two or three most-coming men in England and here you are playing about with a newspaper. Why aren't you in Parliament long since, and where you should be?' I answered 'For two reasons, Mr Fisher. I have been so independent in action and judgement that the Mandarins, the wire pullers and the party machine have no reason to love me; second it's not worthwhile being an ordinary MP, and to be more, a man, at least men like me, must have money enough to devote entire time and resolution to parliamentary affairs.' He disputed this and thought I ought to enter the House of Commons anyhow. The hour is not yet. It may come, but of course, as I told him, I have more influence on affairs than any member of either

House of Parliament, outside the half-dozen leading ministers, and of course Northcliffe . . .

All the many many loves and constant blessings, oh bestest of sons. Dad

Thursday 17th February
[billets, Merville–Lestrem area[?]]

Dear Mummy

I'm writing you now about dusk in case a sudden call comes for the letters. We moved off at eight o'clock this morning and reached here about one or half past. Sky blue and a dry wind blowing, but rather cold. In spite of rain and flooded meadows I think the water level is sinking. I remember roads flooded in November, but now quite dry and ditches gone back within their banks. In spite of my month's riding, I found the march not at all trying. I'm permanently hardened to my pack and to the roads and came in fresh and even did a bit extra, going on with Skelton to see him into a post.

I'm getting that due-for-leave feeling, a kind of irresistible fatigue and want of a holiday. Curious how wearing a post of even minor responsibility becomes. I hope I get home soon. I may just possibly manage it, but, as before, don't be too – can I say hopeful? I've read another chapter of *Montrose* this afternoon.

Bye bye. Dearest love to you and Dad, Granny, Vi, Noonie, Gipsy and Bunny. Ged

Monday 21st February
9 Greville Place, London NW

Very dear son

If there's any chance of seeing you, as something in my bones insists, send a word as soon as ever you can, not only that we may be here for you, unlike last time, but that I may try to arrange work and engagements so as to have more time with you . . .

I don't know what to tell. Poor Mummy has a brute of a cough and if you come home we will take her about gaily for fresh air and entertainment. Your sisters seem full of spirits and Wiffles, whether from sheer reaction against his 'flu or because spring is in him as in birds and buds, invites us all eagerly to games . . .

No more to say today – but I'm having a long long talk with Jacky tomorrow. As much love to you as was ever freighted on paper. Bless you too. Dad.

Friday 25th February
[billets, Festubert–Givenchy front]

Dear Mummy

I'm afraid my letters have been very spasmodic lately. Partly I can blame the post, which goes at unearthly hours. I like to write at night or in the evening, but with frequent goings to the trenches and business there at night to tire one, I'm afraid I sometimes put off writing. We relieved again last night in a thick fog, all the trench black and long fringes of snow above the brim, marvellously white. Then a long march in single file along a snowy road, with dim trees here and there, or ruins seeming blind and gaunt in the fog. All the country is still white and crisp today, after a frost, and the sky dark . . .

We had some excitement these last two days. The Hun fired quite a few rifle-grenades. They are beastly things. You can hear a pop if you are listening, then sometimes high up you spot a little black thing twirling over. The next thing is to hide until it strikes the ground and goes off – tzing! – very loud. Fortunately the shooting was bad, but they're beastly things. We shut them up pretty well with artillery, though. Next, about tea-time, they dropped a mine on us from a trench-mortar. Very like a rifle-grenade in habits and visibility, but worse. The medium size – what we had – measures nine inches across the base and stands about fourteen, with forty pounds of high explosive in it, so you may imagine what it does. 'She' I ought to say – her name's 'Minnie', short for *Minenwerfer*. The first one did some harm, but no more came till about breakfast time next morning, when we had three, rapid. All went over and wrecked the unoffending ground. Beastly things they are when you aren't expecting them. But that wasn't very serious, merely tiresome, and as soon as we can fire up with the guns I expect we'll give the Hun a thin time just there. Nothing exciting happened otherwise.

Stuart is well, but getting on very badly with Winser. Lumley was for leave last night, but all leave was stopped at the last minute. I may get leave if I am lucky. Here I must knock off to inspect feet. Bye bye. Dearest love to you and Dad (I hope you're better), Granny and the girls. Ged

Sunday 27th February
9 Greville Place, London NW

Blessed person

Although this is do-nothing day, I'm going to write to you . . . Blaber says Mummy will come out all right; he was up again this morning. It has been a very severe 'flu, indeed almost choking at times . . .

There seems to be no earthly chance of your getting leave now that the fight for Verdun has become so thunderous and critical and the Boche are evidently determined to force, force the campaign, and, the situation being what it is, can scarcely do anything else. They would raise a fierce shout if they could get Verdun after all . . . What a thunderous game for everybody. I hear that all leave has been stopped; perhaps you are allowed to tell me. If you are not don't mind. If I thought there was no chance of your coming home I would like to get out there for a fortnight in the next month or two and think I could manage it . . .

You will be glad when the harsh weather is over, and then the sloppy weather – and I figure to myself what thaw in the trenches must be. If by chance there is any little thing I can do don't forget to ask. Of course here, as in France, people are all thinking and talking about Verdun . . . In all the war there has been no bigger, more dramatic fight on anything like the same area of ground. The Germans have gone so far in spite of their enormous losses [that] they are almost bound to try to get further, so it will be hammer and anvil in Vulcan's smithy . . . [*end of letter missing*]

Tuesday 29th February
[rest billets, behind Festubert–Givenchy front]

Dearest Mummy

We came back to our rest billet last night. I hope you don't worry at my letters being so irregular. One gets too tired in the trenches often to sit down and write letters . . . Of the war little news, except that we work hard, mainly filling sandbags. This trench warfare very much resembles the bondage in Egypt. I got so tired I could scarcely open your letters the other night – a freak of Nature, I suppose – and lo! just as I thought of sleep in my bunk I was enforced to depart in pitch dark on a long tramp to interview the colonel of a neighbouring regiment, replacing – as one handy, on the spot – another officer of ours who ought to have been doing the job but couldn't. I came back dead last night, but feel fitter than a double-bass this morning after sleep, breakfast in pyjamas and a sound leisurely wash . . .

I know you'll be disappointed if I don't tell you how we appreciated the Heinz things and sweets in your parcel. As for Tiptree: a pot of strawberry having been given to the colonel we have demolished the glorious blackberry, and the second strawberry pot, holding the cherry in reserve.

. . . Stuart keeps well, but is very tired, being short-handed in his company. Bye bye. Dearest love to you and Dad, Granny, Vi, Noonie, Gipsy and Bunny. I hope you're quite better. Ged

Wednesday 1st March
9 Greville Place, London NW

My very dearest

I have been too lazy to write all day and bed always leaves you so weary, more so I think after a diet of milk and water alone for five days – and likely to continue. I did manage a few business letters, that's all . . . My temp has gone down to just over a hundred, which is something. Dad went out to a lunch today looking very much the colour of the cigars he smokes and feeling rotten generally. Everyone is either in the throes of 'flu or neuralgia just now, so London is not cheerful . . .

We long for just a glimpse of you and hope to get that soon, but the fighting seems pretty bad . . . Goodnight best beloved, God guard you and guide you and bring you to your devoted Mummy.

Sunday 5th March
[rest billets, behind Festubert–Givenchy front]

Dearest One

I think I last wrote to you before going up to the trenches last time. Here's a short chronicle of events since that.

I personally took over as commander of the garrison, a little keep. You know both sides have everywhere along the trenches little keeps or strong points. Well, the Huns that afternoon had dropped eight-inch and five-inch howitzer shells all round this one. They didn't shoot too well, but managed to blow a crater in the post about fifteen feet deep and twenty across with no exaggeration. So all that night till just before daybreak we toiled to build fresh works. Then sleep till one next day. Again work at night with much reduced forces, the most part being needed for other work. The following afternoon our howitzers and other guns had a playful *strafe*. The Huns answered by firing more five-inchers too near us to be comfortable. You hear a howitzer bang in the distance, then the hum of the shell coming very leisurely. Of all the horrible feelings I know, none is worse than hearing that approach and wondering where the burst will come. Luckily they did no damage. We were relieved in the evening, very late, and came out in pitch dark, rain pouring, and an icy wind cutting like a knife. Then a long sleep between blankets. Did nothing yesterday except a chapter of Thucydides. Last night was dark, with stars bright in the pools and the trees towering darkly. Today blue and green, shining and windy.

Of military news, none. I don't yet abandon all hope of leave; tell Dad not to be too hasty about coming out . . .

Here's the orderly corporal. Bye bye. Dearest love . . . Ged.

Tuesday 7th March
9 Greville Place, London NW

Dearest of lads

No letter by first post, but just now – that is about 11.30 – Dr Blaber came up with one, having rescued it from the postman who had dropped it in the snow. What a jolly letter, now that I know you are, at the moment, out of the range of five- and eight-inch howitzers – but it must have been a warm corner in spite of the biting wind and cold. Here it has started snowing hard again and the poor little crocuses had only got their heads lifted from the last attack – and what the almond trees will look like at the end I've no idea, poor trees of the south to be treated in this frosty manner, just as their tiny blossoms were showing pink in our garden. I think, for once, I've shown great discrimination in my choice of date to be ill. I've escaped all the worst snow and now am in so much less pain that I can't believe it's me. No more poultices for the present as the mastoid ear has cleared up beautifully and the other nearly – only I'm horribly deaf, which is a nuisance.

. . . It's good to think there is a faint hope of leave for you, but I hope it is a day or two more than last time, so that your wardrobe can be attended to properly. I believe there is a new maid in the house, by name Ellen Cook, but I haven't seen her – but to have even another pair of hands is something . . .

Kitty has a sore throat with darts of pain to her ears, so that she is being dosed and kept at home. The snow was so thick this morning that although Jimmy valiantly set out for school, her two elders turned her back at the end of the street. I believe she and Kitty have been painting all morning in the small study. Now I must stop this gossip, which is all I have to do, and send you love and kisses, with my prayers and blessings ever, my dearest laddie – your most loving Mummy.

Wednesday 8th March
9 Greville Place, London NW

Little son

Mummy, I am infinitely relieved to say, is much better, sitting up and very cheerful, which makes a great difference to us here and will to you . . . There's no letter from you today, but you may imagine how we read and re-read the one written on Sunday after the hurly burly in your redoubt . . .

Winston made the great speech yesterday, and a most dramatic and startling episode it was when he advocated that Lord Fisher should be recalled. He made the big point too abruptly instead of leading the House up to it, but he spoke with admirable grip and vigour, and there will be large consequences sooner or later. The effect of his presence in vitalising the House was extraordinary. Before he rose the place looked conventional, unreal, inanimate, almost as though a gesture play were being performed; the moment he rose the House became a living, vivid scene, with a man of mind and force as the centre of it. Afterwards everyone felt that he ought not to go back to the trenches (everyone that is except his Fisher's enemies) when he might play so great a part in marshalling all the forces which believe in a stronger and more resourceful conduct of the war . . .[4]

Of course all the old hate and prejudice give tongue this morning in our precious press, half-rabid, half-ignorant as it is, but I have seen a good deal of Winston in the last few days and seek to sustain him. The position is difficult, but his duty is here. Jacky heard the speech and was delighted as a child. As he came out of the lobby with the Duchess of Hamilton, I met them both; he walked with the step of a young man and he knows well that but for me yesterday's scene in Parliament and the reconciliation never would have taken place . . .

More love to you dearest boy, than words can tell. God bless you.
Dad

Wednesday 8th March
9 Greville Place, London NW

Dearest and best beloved

Here it is, nearly eight o'clock, and I'm expecting dinner to be announced any moment, but I must write congratulations on really

---

4 Churchill voiced a general concern about a lack of driving power in the Admiralty, but his call for 'Jacky' Fisher's return amazed the Commons and turned 'one of the most serious and skilful speeches he had ever made into an object of derision' (Gilbert, p. 722). It also gave Balfour, the implied target of Churchill's criticism, grounds for a scathing reply, which he delivered the next day. The phrase 'his Fisher's enemies' alludes to those who opposed Churchill because of his support for Fisher.

having my 'Small Sonnie' as a full-fledged captain – gazetted this morning. For the very first time, I think, I've wanted *The Times* all day, and didn't know why. They brought it about half an hour ago, and there I saw 'S. Lan. R. Temp. Lt. R. G. Garvin to be temp. Capt. (Jan 15)'. There it is for you. I thought you were only acting for the time being and were now back as Lieut. – you wretch not to make it clear to a muddle-headed Mum. I can't tell you how pleased and proud I am and delighted that I was the first to find it, this day being about the only day Dad hasn't examined the *Gazette*.[5] Why I looked at it, I can't think. Vi says instinct – like Wiffles – I must have known. I'd like to give you something special for it – anyhow I'll instruct them to send you out a parcel tomorrow, now there is a third maid in the house.

Kathleen has come to do some sewing for the babies. I haven't seen the new girl, but John and Vi seem to resent the way she does her hair, but that I can't bother with at the moment. I can hear the kitchen cheering and clapping about you – they are pleased. No word this morning, but I hope you are all right, and hope too that you may get home on leave soon . . .

Now then, blessed thing, good night and God guard and bless you in all you do, and bring you safe back to a most loving family – with my special prayers and blessing and love. Mummy

Thursday 9th March
[billets, Festubert–Givenchy front]

Madonna mine

. . . I've no news except that last night was very clear and hideously cold. So is the morning. I saw a German aeroplane this morning with the black cross under its wings. It merely 'perped' and retired with

5 Christina enclosed the press cutting. In fact Ged had made the situation clear weeks earlier when he wrote that he had been replaced as company commander by Captain Ridley, who had returned after being wounded: 'He's an excellent fellow, and will make a splendid company commander. I'm half relieved at the removal of the responsibility. It affects one unconsciously. I'm awfully glad of my month's experience though.'

dignity. Last night wandering along our wire I was shot at, apparently from a line of willows close up. I don't know where the bullet went and we could discover no trace of the firer.

Our heavy howitzers have just been punching the German eye with considerable success. Last night I got the parcel with *Griffith Gaunt* which seems to promise well and *Great Expectations*. I advance slowly into *The Egoist*, enjoying it. Comedy is so refreshing out here . . .

Bye bye. Dearest love to you and Dad, Granny, Vi, Noonie, Gipsy and Bunny. Ged

Thursday 9th March
9 Greville Place, London NW

Dear Captain Courageous

Mummy found it first and you may imagine my pleasure that she discovered it and my delight in the step itself. I feel certain in my heart, without any question of personal pride in you, that you have deserved it by competence . . . The funny thing about yesterday was that I didn't know until the evening. For weeks I had faithfully run my eye through the *Gazette* in *The Times* day after day, but yesterday I was out early and away until late and had to get quickly through my morning papers. Then what was my surprise to hear Mummy call out and I found her sitting up in bed with glee accusing a hard-working editor of not having read *The Times*. It did her more good than doctor's stuff and had a serious effect on the kitchen where they clapped hands, and of course your sisters and Maima shone. Kitty and Jimmy didn't know until this morning, the little things – and as for me, how lumbering a way is this of saying I am awfully glad. I often wish to put a handshake into words but I can't . . .

You would have had a second letter last night but Winston rang me up and begged me to go round to see him and advise him whether he should resume his parliamentary career here. I said 'Yes': if he were strong enough to pass through the poison gas of mean imputation that assails every man against whom a cry is once raised. I stayed with him from 10.30 until long after midnight – his wife there too. I don't know what he will do, but here he could do infinitely more for the army and against the Germans. Today I saw him again at the Duchess of Hamilton's, Jacky ruthlessly booming 'stay' – Winston very legitimately torn. A strange episode . . .[6]

Little sleep for five nights owing to political excitements and must stop now. Son Captain I love thee exceeding and may God bless thee. Dad

Thursday 9th March
9 Greville Place, London NW

Dearest of sons

A real bright sunny morning, although no blue in the sky – just a heat sky – and nearly all traces of snow gone. Dad went out to see Winston at 10.30 last night and as he hadn't the key, Viva waited up for him. He came in just about one after a long talk with Winston and Mrs Winston. It seems Winston has been having a terrible rating in all the papers over his speech insisting on having Fisher back – after his speech in November, which was a scathing attack on Fisher. Balfour gave it to him hot and holy in the House, but Dad says Winston will have his own back – but about the conversation I know nothing and he will probably tell you. It is all awfully bad, I think, for ordinary people to have these recriminations in Parliament, and the hint that even the Navy isn't right – but I don't know . . .

Viola is still anxious to go to college and I am anxious she should have all she wants, in reason, and if to be afforded, but I imagine three of you at college at the same time with less income and heavier taxation will be a great drain – and yet she says for teaching or writing (if she can write) college is essential. She rather thinks Somerville. I wonder what you think of it all? . . .

Now, dear lad, I send you my dearest love and blessing . . . Mummy

---

6 Churchill 'returned to the trenches shaken by his Parliamentary humiliation of the previous week': Gilbert, p. 738.

March 11th Saturday
[trenches, Festubert–Givenchy front]

Dear Mummy

I love to get all these letters and was delighted to see your ear and cold are better. Do cuddle yourself up and keep warm and let Dad and Blaber have their way. I've no news. Our Huns are very quiet. We nearly all have steel helmets now. I don't know, but we hope to come out tonight. Nothing else. I'm reading *The Egoist* slowly. One needs plenty of leisure and reserve mental energy to read Meredith at his more reflective.

Asquith's speech to the congress of business men was amusing. Is it the habit of statesmen to answer the particular demand with Ciceronian generalisations?[7]

I know you'll all be pleased to hear that I'm becoming something of a marksman with the pistol. I've broken a lot of Perrier bottles. What a superb poise my revolver has.

Well, no more now. Bye bye. Dearest love to you and Dad, Granny (I hope her cold isn't affecting her too much), Vi, Noonie, Gipsy (give her a fairy book from me for her ear . . .) and Bunny. xxx Ged

Monday 13th March
[billets, Festubert–Givenchy front]

Dear Dad

I haven't much news. You haven't had a letter from me for some time. We came out of the trenches the night before last and yesterday morning, a day of devastating heat, marched back here to a straggling group of cottages and farms among stretches of flat open plough. Lumley and Ridley both seem heartily pleased I got my third star. Stuart too of course. Most others don't know yet. I am still second-

---

7 On Tuesday 7 March Asquith received a deputation from the Chambers of Commerce, who sought an undertaking that the government would defend imperial trade after the war. Having built a career on free trade it was unsurprising that Asquith 'declined for the present to make any pronouncement': *The Times*, 8 March 1916. Ged's use of 'Ciceronian' mocks Asquith's polished rhetoric.

in-command to Ridley. But for your letters I should still be vague. I've had no other formal word than Mummy's cutting . . .

The first indubitable breath of spring came today, a wafted fragrance of sunned grass, fresh and sweet. One shudders retrospectively at the past winter. I've been musing lately on the attitude of one's mind to the desolation and roughness of life out here: one only shrinks from the memory of it, the actual experience comes as a normal life at the moment. When one is actually in the rifle zone – or thereabouts – one passes into another existence, with trench conditions as the standard. What bosh! Bye bye. Dearest love to you . . . Ged. I hope the ears are better and Mummy [is] being sunned by warm days. Are the girls and Granny alright? And you – are you getting sound sleep again? Do try.

Monday 13th March
9 Greville Place, London NW

My dearest laddie

Your letter of Saturday came this morning, also one for Dad. It was so good to get them and I hope you left the trenches safely on Saturday night. This letter seems to have come quicker than most of them – only two days. The doctor hasn't been today, but I think the 'flu is clearing up, but slowly, and as I haven't had my afternoon's rest I'm feeling awfully tired. Staying in bed seems to make you as tired as being up and about . . .

I've had a pathetic letter from Melican, poor old man. You remember I told you, he seemed so done that last Monday he came – and Dad and I paid for a taxi to take him to Victoria. He hasn't been since and tonight he writes saying he is going into Bart's tomorrow for an operation; so I must write to him tonight and I think I'll send him £2.2.0 as an extra . . .

I didn't read Asquith's Ciceronian generalisations, but I do dread more and more the lawyer in the House of Commons – we've far too much of it. I'm dead sick of Asquith – pig and Nero, whichever you like to call him – only he can't fiddle, just swill.

God bless and guard you – prayers and blessings and love from Mammy.

14th March
[billets, Festubert–Givenchy front]

Dear Mummy

. . . The weather continues warm here, with a delicious mildness last night. With my book I picked out a new constellation 'Perseus and Andromeda' stretching from high to low at the back of 'Casiopeia'. Hammill, Lumley and Hoyle dined with us. We had an excellent dinner and a talk after, partly about social problems, partly as to why we should be fighting and the war be going on. Very pleasant. I dine with Lumley tonight.

By the way, will you have my new tunic altered – three stars and two stripes – and send it out; I fear the prospect of leave will be a mirage, though it may start again at any moment. And may I have another packet of 'Bromo' and some brandy, preferably in a worthless vessel? . . .

Verdun seems to be growing a worse bargain for the Huns every day. I wonder, will it be the last of their big land battles? We go on parade in a few minutes to be inspected by the colonel. My present billet is excellent, a nice little bedroom and a nice furnished messroom; the village also produces far from negligible beer.

Bye bye. Love to all. Ged.

Thursday 16th March
9 Greville Place, London NW

Very dear son

It was surprising and good to get a real letter this morning for myself after so long a time. Not that I at all needed it. What you say to your mother comes to me like a personal talk, so never send me one if it means her getting one less . . . The winter must have been a horrible experience. I knew it all the time and as for spring, I know what you feel but wonder what you see . . .

I'm all right, plenty of responsibility and thought in these difficult times at home, and one would give treasures to get a little more fresh air and some walking amongst hills . . . To tell the truth since the war began I forget for weeks together that there is any such person as myself, or how I am – which is one curious result of the war and not a bad one. I felt pretty sure you wouldn't get leave so soon. If you and Lumley and the rest have set out to find why you are at the war, the mess has tackled about the biggest theme for philosophy and investigation since Plato and Aristotle . . .

The third phase at Verdun was the most dangerous . . . but the defence is still magnificent and the Germans can get no more forward on the western side of the Meuse than they could on the eastern side. They haven't given up though, and I wonder what they will do before acknowledging defeat. Where is this expenditure of shells going to stop, geometrical progression through an infinite series of numbers? In September everyone said 'inconceivable', by comparison with June, and of course piled up alp on alp of ammunition. But again the amount used is utterly beyond all expectation, and 'inconceivable' is still the word – so that it is out of all true grasp, like astronomical distances . . .

This is a dull letter, but carries exceeding love and blessings from Dad.

Friday 17th March
9 Greville Place, London NW

My very dearest son

No letter this morning, so I have nothing to reply to. Your tunic came back today and I've paid (out of your a/c) 9/6 – for the extra stripe and two extra stars = fairly expensive. I'm thinking of letting you treat me to a theatre next week, 'cos the doctor thinks I might get up tomorrow if really fine – go to Helgesen's to see about a dress. The fashions have changed so much that I've nothing (although all my things are practically new) that is anything like the present fashion.

. . . I hope you get your tunic soon. I thought you had to have all the stars and stripes removed so that you looked like ordinary Tommies – isn't that so? Tell if all your parcels arrive safely, will you. I have no news, so this letter is really just to send my dearest love and thoughts to you, laddie dear. God bless and guard you in all you do – with hugs and kisses for you – ever your most loving Mummy.

Friday 17th March
[billets, Festubert–Givenchy front]

Dear Dad

The announcement was a mistake. Apparently I was captain while in command of the company, but not otherwise, owing to want of a vacancy. So the colonel told me tonight. I draw captain's pay for the month – that's all. I'm not worried as I didn't expect a third star anyway. Tell Mummy not to have the tunic altered; one band and two stars; but I'd like it out, please.

The jam is excellent. All the others got theirs. My feet are giving me torture, owing to the new boots still being hard, but as we are at rest it doesn't matter and will go off before we march again. I loved the letters today from all of you. Vi sounds very tired.

I went this afternoon to a demonstration of a system of bombing a trench, quite interesting. Yesterday I rode over to report on a post we shall hold in case of trouble. A little shelling at long range was going on, but nothing very nasty. Nothing else except that I'm nearly half way through *The Egoist*. I sleep in a room on the second floor here, with birds asleep on the branches outside the window, strange in the dark. The weather continues fine.

The town [Béthune] is straggly, with irregular tiled roofs, and a house, now and again, with two storeys and flat windows shuttered on the street . . . Of the Town Hall more later. It tells the hour from a clock of singularly sweet chime, reminiscent of Bruges.

Bye bye. Dearest love . . . Ged.

❖

Ged's pessimism about his prospects of leave proved to be misplaced and within a couple of days of writing to his father he was on his way home, probably arriving at 9 Greville Place on Tuesday 21 March. He returned to France on Friday 31st.

5

Training for the Somme

For the first three months of 1916 the 19th Division was engaged in trench warfare, but from mid-April it was taken out of the line to undergo training for the coming offensive on the Somme. It was led by the redoubtable Major-General Tom Bridges, who had assumed command on Christmas Day 1915. The 7th South Lancs left the Lys front on 12 April to begin its preparations in the Linghem area. The General Staff urged all ranks 'to endeavour to obtain the utmost instruction out of this short course of training', and placed great emphasis on the development of discipline and of esprit de corps.[1] *Platoons, battalions, brigades and divisions all underwent intensive training, and there could be little doubt that the summer would see a 'big push'.*

❖

Night of Friday 31st March 1916
9 Greville Place, London NW

My dearest boy

It is Friday and much to do, but a word must go to you before I turn in. Never have your mother and father and all of us loved you so much (where anything more seemed impossible) as in the last eleven days. They brightened us more than you can ever know. This morning on our return the house looked lost without you, and Wiffles, seeing the tail of his people come short, went to the front door after we came

---

1 Everard Wyrall, *The History of the 19th Division, 1914–1918*, London, 1932, p. 30.

in, searching for his soldier, and then went up and down the house for quite a while fussing into various rooms. Your respirator was nowhere to be seen, no trace of it, so we feel sure you must have it somewhere in your luggage . . .

Well I must stop and go to bed after I slip out and post this – good night our dear old son and God bless you. Mummy goes to Bess tomorrow and Vi with her for the weekend. Dad.

Saturday 1st April
Grand Hotel du Louvre et Terminus [Boulogne]

Dear Mummy

We leave here today at ten to one. By good luck we've had a grand night's rest to make up for yesterday morning. Of course we were held up; we came into harbour about two yesterday afternoon. Unless we had managed the extra day in London, though, we couldn't have done better. Last night's rest prepared one grandly for the trenches.

Of the journey not much to tell. Going across we had the sea calm and deep blue with wavelets breaking diamond crested. Naturally it's much better coming back to a future of summer and spring than meeting the beginning of winter as last time. Everywhere on the way to Folkestone we found the country fresh and green. London appears to have magnetised the bad weather . . .

Yesterday afternoon we saw a friend of Lumley's here, wandered about, went to the cinema to see Charlie Chaplin, who's quite funny, and dined out. There's no other news except I forgot my sponge; perhaps someone found it. If not will you have it sent, with a nail-cleaner and a box of Boots' tooth-soap? Here I am already starting to ask you to do things I could just as well have done myself.

By the way, I may as well warn you, anything I tell you isn't to go beyond yourself and Dad . . . If you do read out bits of the letters, keep them yourself and don't let anyone at all get hold of them, and just read what you think fit. Of course the girls are alright, but tell them not to chat. It really doesn't concern their friends to know that the trenches are muddy, or otherwise, or that we are working harder than usual, supposing we were, or anything else.

Bye bye. Dearest love . . . Ged

Sunday 2nd April
[trenches, Festubert–Givenchy front]

Dear Dad

Here I am back in the trenches. Not so bad after all. Even the trenches don't seem too bad in warm weather. Unless it changes we shall lead an idyllic life; the sun is warm today and everything dry. Very quiet everything too, not a sound except a very occasional cannon-shot or a rifle crack. Early this morning the birds sang deliciously, although the cold was a bit nippy!

Came back last night about eleven o'clock. How nasty after that jolly ten days at home. A really glorious time it was with the rest and the music and our jaunts, and of course being with you all. Pat Wiffles for me – is he wondering where I've gone to? Eccentricity of the worst kind it appears to him, I suppose.

Last night was very quiet. Leaving the base about one o'clock, we got to our station about seven, found our depot, dined with the padre, hugely hospitable, and rode off to come down here. Everybody seems very cheery. Winser greeted me this morning; he seems fit. I haven't seen Stuart yet. We're in the front trench . . .

Bye bye. Dearest love to you and Mummy, Granny, Vi, John, Gipsy and Bunny. Ged xxx

Monday 3rd April
9 Greville Place, London NW

My dear old boy

. . . I hope you got back to find the battalion all gay and lively, but I wonder what company you are to be attached to henceforth. All our thoughts are still mixed with you because we are not yet accustomed to your absence again, but all our talk is of Zepps and the weather . . . Of course nature is bursting forth – small leaves everywhere to brighten our eyes; yesterday the first yellow daffodil perfectly open in our garden . . . Wiffles is of course very importunate that I shall play with him, as if he knew that Monday was more an off day, but I hold up my finger and lecture him on the importance of learning to play by himself. He cocks his ear sagaciously but is probably no wiser than before.

Astonishing it is how foolishly pleased we are because one Zepp has been brought down, which shows that all our arrangements are improving (here's Wiffles again standing up, nosing and trying to stop my hand), though cases of women and children killed on successive nights makes one's heart stern with anger . . . Most killing and wounding have been caused by two bombs plumping on a Baptist chapel when it was pretty full: you may imagine what happened, but how much damage was caused last night we do not yet know . . .[2]

The love of loves to you dearest son. Dad

Wednesday 5th April
[billets, Festubert–Givenchy front]

Dear Mummy

I had no news at all yesterday, which was one reason for not writing. Came out of the trenches last night, back to rest billets a mile or so behind. Really this is very comfortable. Our mess has been done up with sacking on the walls and an open fire and a wood floor. I don't think we could be much cosier – except of course if we were all sent back home. By the way, you'd hardly credit how much fitter and fresher one feels living under civilised conditions. After all, I think a measure of civilised comfort has its advantages, though one accommodates oneself all right to this life. Really, though, it has occurred to me once or twice to wonder whether one's normal civilised existence is in any

2 Zeppelins raided Britain on three successive nights, Friday 31 March–Sunday 2 April, and according to *The Times* fifty-nine were killed on the Friday and Saturday, more than half of them in one incident when bombs fell on a Baptist chapel 'in a village of no military significance' in the north-east: *The Times*, 3 April 1916. In fact the chapel, in Cleethorpes, Lincolnshire, was being used as a temporary billet by the 3rd Battalion of the Manchester Regiment, thirty of whom died.

sense better than this? . . .

Stuart seems well but despondent about his leave. My respirator is undoubtedly somewhere at home. I have another, but could someone look for it again and send it . . .

Do take a genuine rest now while you can. Lie up mostly and just see some plays and pictures and a few nice people; restful ones for choice. If you meet Mrs Speed at No. 7 [Lansdowne Road] tell her I'm awfully sorry I couldn't come round to call. Also Mrs Heynemann – give her my special love. You know how tired I was. I really felt too slack to do a thing while I was home. I wish you had been able to share in the fun.

Bye bye. Dearest love to you and Dad, Granny, Vi, John, Gipsy and Bunny. Ged. Love to Mrs O'S. and the kiddies.

Sunday 9th April
9 Greville Place, London NW

Dearest laddie mine

I really have been specially bad about writing this time, but I have gone on again catching colds and being hoarse and sickish . . .

Mrs Cazalet sent me the most charming letters about you – and came up today to discuss with Dad if something could be done by a deputation of women of good social standing going to the Prime Minister, to see if a move-on couldn't be got, as they seem to think that women are contented to simply go on making bandages . . . She is a great creature.

I only found the respirator on Friday night (hung under a coat in the hall) and was furious. Did you get all the parcels (three) sent and do you want any more boots? Tell me please, at once. I have borrowed from you £3.15.0 for Mrs Saull, whose husband has not paid any rent for two months, and they were for putting her six small children out on the street, and you see with me being laid up she cannot spare the time to go out and see about rooms, but is going to tomorrow. I am sure you don't mind if she doesn't pay within a month . . .

This is all tonight, my heart's dearest one, with my blessings and prayers always. God guard you and bless you. Mummy.

Love to Stuart. Parting was much harder this time.

Monday 10th April
9 Greville Place, London NW

Dear old boy

There was nothing from you for three days or four, but this morning and since then there have come three letters – one as full and fresh as may be. The weather looked the brighter in consequence . . .

Of course I noticed at once and all through, how tired you were this time – though I said nothing – and how much you wanted just repose, just relaxing of mind and body, as the parched land takes rain. That was all natural and as it should be. On your account and our own, above all on your mother's, we were grateful to Winser for giving you those eleven days, that somehow grow more and more precious looked back upon. I'm very sorry Stuart does not get his leave, but it's a thing better left unjudged. A colonel's job is by no means easy and there's no worse curse to a battalion than a too-amiable colonel . . .[3]

Yesterday I went over to talk to Lady Randolph Churchill, who has had her house burgled and is in bed with a very bad foot. Said little Randolph, her grandson, a little joyous thing of four in a sailor suit: 'Granma's got to have her toe chopped off.' So she has, but it was a cheerful announcement. Mrs Winston came in from playing tennis, looking her best, which is very handsome indeed, and we talked of Winston. He is doing well as a soldier, but here he could do far more for the army and against the Germans. He must settle it himself. No man can advise another in certain matters where arises that most difficult of all things, a conflict of duties. Mrs Cazalet called to talk about how on earth we are to make the Asquith circle really realise that there's a war going on! . . . [*end of letter missing*]

---

3 In a short letter to his mother on 6 April, which his father would have seen, Ged had written: 'Stuart's leave is being withheld from him scandalously by [Colonel] Winser. Abominably petty.'

Wednesday 12th April [JLG's birthday]
[trenches, Festubert–Givenchy front]

Dear Dad

This is your real birthday letter – written on your birthday . . . I hope you're spending it in true celebration after the *Tribune* article.

The weather here has broken. We've had two days of the south-west, rather unpleasant in the trenches, where no house receives one after the shower. Still enjoyable enough. We go out tonight for our rest, back to the same little village . . .

I suppose you guessed where the violets came from. I'll get some cowslips this afternoon. We had a fine sunrise this morning, glowing in a broad band behind the ruins, with a jagged remnant of the church standing cold in front.

By the way, if you guess where I am, tell me what you think; just for my satisfaction. Bye bye. Dearest love to you and Mummy (I'll have to write her a proper letter), Granny, Vi, John, Gipsy and Bunny.
xxx Ged

Thursday 13th April
9 Greville Place, London NW

Dearest of sons

This has been such a blustery wet-by-turns and shivery day – April-like without her sun . . .

I couldn't write yesterday because the Saull family took up most of my time, the man having been allowed out of the infirmary by mistake and coming here, so that the wife was nearly distracted, and Dad had to interfere and we sent him off to another infirmary . . . By the way, Mrs Saull . . . repaid the debt to you, so I've put it back. She is very grateful . . .

You seem awful tired, old sonnie, but I expect that's 'like the old cab horse, who shouldn't take a rest'. You feel it more when you get back again and I expect you are kept terribly busy. You don't say what you want sent out in the way of clothes, and it was disgusting not going out more with you, but I think Dad preferred having you a lot and I know you loved being together. I'm sorry Stuart hasn't had his leave yet . . .

Isn't it funny, Dad has carried a letter of Lady Sackville's in his pocket for over a week, unopened – and when he opened it, it turns out to be an invitation for me and one daughter for four days last week to the peace of Knole. I don't know how he has answered it . . .

Did you know that Blaber has joined as Dr of the Middlesex and goes out in a fortnight. Isn't it sporting of him, and he is keen as mustard – so we shall have another doctor, I suppose, while he is gone . . .

With dearest love . . . Mummy

Saturday 15th April
[billets, Festubert–Givenchy front]

Dear Mummy

When I suddenly remembered I hadn't written yesterday, I resolved not to be baffled today. Herewith, as the military man says, the fruit of the resolution in question.

Nothing in this at all. I'm exactly in the same village where I was yesterday. We move tomorrow, back to another place about ten miles away I should think, though I wouldn't swear to it myself.

I'm still in charge of the company in Ridley's absence, a light task for the moment. Lumley breakfasted with me this morning. Stuart is a wee bit off; I see him every morning. His nerves want a rest badly I fancy. Naturally he's very disappointed about leave . . .

I sent home yesterday the Harrods tunic and my British Warm. Probably a bit more superfluous kit will go off by this afternoon's post. I found the bottle of brandy yesterday – many thanks. Don't send any more parcels for a week or so, though those already sent have been excellent.

Here I really must stop. Not a thing more to tell you, so bye bye. Dearest love . . . Ged.

Saturday 15th April
9 Greville Place, London NW

Dearest laddie

It's nearly bed time, but I thought perhaps that a word from home might be welcome . . . The weather was so bad this morning and the wind so cold that I didn't dare venture out, but stayed and domesticated; besides Saturday is always, as you know, a difficult day to leave the house. News none – except that I have got a fascinating green hat, rather Dolly Vardenish and not too youthful for your forty-year-old mother – and a new green frock, which the dressmaker, in mistake, made to come nine inches from the ground, so that I looked a very buxom and double-chinned Kitty. Back I went in a taxi with the dress on and now it's home and looks sedate enough to go with the Dolly Varden . . .

Dearest love, my own boy and my prayers and blessings ever. Mummy.

Palm Sunday, 16th April
[*en route* to Linghem area]

Dear Mummy

Forestalling the others I've secured my mail already. 'Rapture, rapture' – says Gilbert.[4] One letter from you and one from Dad. Bright and happy, both of them, as I judge. Evidently I counselled right when I bade you amuse yourself. Rollicking holidays the girls seem to be having; most seemly too. Except for their being just too late, I applaud heartily.

Today, rising at half past five to a morning bright and keen, with a Hun aeroplane hovering overhead, we marched back to a straggling hamlet of very neat farms among wide open fields. Zig-zag route because we missed the road and went a mile or two out of our way. Still, we had a bracing march, first along a great main way with traffic passing in both directions, wagons and infantry, and troops billeted by the road. A long avenue of trees, with blue circles of country – like so much French landscape – either side, and orchard or copse to round the distance, young, green with a white tower sometimes of blossom. The white cherry is out, excelling all others – unless it's the plums, as

4 From the duet between Dame Carruthers and Sergeant Meryll in Gilbert and Sullivan's *The Yeoman of the Guard*: 'Rapture, rapture / When love's Votary / Flushed with Capture / Seeks the Notary . . .'.

I fancy; purest white, only softer than snow. Easter has always seemed a white feast to me, to be thought of keen and sparkling – the light without the softness of summer . . .

Having spent the hour between, in attending commanding officer's orderly room, I take up the pencil again in a more sober frame of thought. You have all the news by now. Bye bye. Dearest love to you and Dad, Granny, Vi, John, Gipsy and Bunny. Ged

Maundy Thursday, 20th April
9 Greville Place, London NW

My dearest boy

A welcome little letter came to me this morning, enclosed in the one to Mummy, and I told Mummy that her cowslips came from the village right in the firing line, which makes them still more precious to her . . .

The [conscription] crisis is over. I saw Lloyd George for a few minutes at the Ministry of Munitions this evening. He looked brown, cheerful and more square-faced and determined than ever. He has fought a big fight, faced it single-handed at the start, and had won on the merits of the case backed by his own courage. 'It's all right,' he said, 'the army chiefs are satisfied.' Unless a last appeal for voluntaryism brings in, within the next few weeks, all the men wanted, general compulsion will come into play as a matter of course. There will be an end of that controversy, as there ought to have been within six months at furthest from the outbreak of war. The ordinary MP is almost as much in the dark as the ordinary citizen as regards the degree to which things are mishandled and blocked by inertia and mediocrity. There will be a secret session of the House of Commons next Tuesday and even the Labour members will be enlightened. This is all to the good and we shall now begin to get on, I really think, with the problem of shortening the war . . .

They are calling me to go and get dressed; it's my last minute. I envy you much reading Meredith. A Happy Easter to you my boy: God bless that festival to you and for you . . . Dad.

Saturday, 22nd April
training camp, Linghem

Dear Mummy

We've been run off our feet since we came here and with the post going at inconvenient times I haven't written you a proper letter for a long time. Yesterday we did platoon training, drill and skirmishing, with some jumping and scaling of the walls of a quarry by way of physical training. We were kept full up to tea-time. Then the colonel's orderly room lasts from six to seven. We're having a sing-song tonight, which ought to be fun. It's been raining in sheets all day.

Coming over here a great disaster befell. My valise was dropped in a pond, I think; at any rate the wagon went into a pond. My books, all cheap fortunately, are nearly ruined with all the bindings off. But they'll do for reading here. My wee Shakespeare and Milton suffered less than the others, except the 'comedies', which was soaked. My clothes are still drying, but I've borrowed a pair of pyjamas and have an ordinary bed in my billet.

I love all the letters . . . I'll try to write more regularly. Get the girls and the maids and Dad and Granny and yourself Easter things from me please and draw a cheque for them on my account.

Best love and Happy Easter to all of you . . . Ged

Easter Sunday, 23rd April
training camp, Linghem

Dear Dad

I was very glad to get your letter this afternoon. It was cheerful and sounded fit, as though you were feeling rested and Mummy getting better. I haven't much news. We went to Mass this morning and I went to Communion. We had a nice march of about twenty minutes across open fields, high and breezy. A blue day and warm. We had a cross-country run for the men this afternoon and a horse race for the officers, great fun. Last night we tried to get up a sing-song for the company but it wasn't very successful . . .

My cold has almost gone. I'm feeling much fitter. Please thank Granny for the moment – her parcel arrived this afternoon, very welcome. I'll write her a note.

Love to you and Mummy, Granny, Vi, John, Gipsy and Bunny. Ged xxx

❖

Easter 1916

It was one of Ged's duties as a Catholic officer, albeit not a practising one, to take his Catholic men to Mass, and in one of his letters to his father he made a casual reference to receiving general absolution on Easter Sunday, 23 April. He could not have anticipated the effect that this would have. J. L. Garvin had long wrestled with his own faith and had reached an uneasy equilibrium. Ged's letter shattered this, and swept along by his romantic imagination Garvin mistakenly thought that his son had undergone a religious conversion, and joined the church from which he felt himself divorced. Fearing that this would come between them he reached out to Ged with an anguished letter of self-explanation; as he later realised, his fears were groundless, and his reaction exaggerated.

That weekend saw the beginnings of the Easter Rising in Dublin, and for Garvin another strange revisitation of the memories of his youth. On Good Friday morning Sir Roger Casement, formerly a British diplomat, was arrested on the Kerry coast after landing from a German submarine; a shipment of arms that he had helped to secure from Berlin was scuttled. So began what Garvin called 'the melancholy opéra bouffe *of an Irish rebellion without any solidity or greatness'. He later revised this opinion, but his response to the unfolding drama was a mixture of revulsion and sympathy, reflecting his complex Anglo-Irish roots. Garvin had been a 'home-ruler' in his youth, and a supporter of Parnell, but he had long since left his 'Fenian past' behind, and he now moved in a different orbit.*

❖

Tuesday 25th April
9 Greville Place, London NW

Dearest son

Home again and to find a letter from you: we had not heard for some days. What a nuisance of an adventure to have your valise drowned in the pond: you did not say whether it was fished out or if you had any substitute for the drowned things? Do, like a dear lad, ask for what you want if there's anything you would like replaced – and n.b. – have you proper stores of light reading stuff? If not I'll get you what you want. What about sending you the French translation of Aristophanes? It is full of zest in that language. Also, what on earth do you do without your British Warm? . . .

This has been I would think, in a political sense, about the most exciting Easter Tuesday ever known . . . The morning and evening papers are almost worth preserving – the melancholy *opéra bouffe* of an Irish rebellion without any solidity or greatness to it – the sort of thing a feeble Government invites. There and more every day I understand Cromwell – seeing the Irish nature too, but so clearly that it was life and death for England that the western island should not become a hostile base between England and the ocean. Imagine it – a German auxiliary steamer escorted by a submarine tries to land arms but is sunk and Casement captured. He ought to be sentenced to death and then contemptuously refuted. In the meantime there had evidently been a plot carefully arranged in concert with Berlin, for the Sinn Féiners rose in Dublin at noon on Easter Monday, seized the post office and got most of the city in their hands. The authorities must have been owls, for there was no backbone to the thing, and it was over as soon as soldiers appeared.

. . . Wiffles gave me the nicest romping welcome today I have had for a long time. Untold love to you and all my blessings. Dad.

Wednesday 26th April
training camp, Linghem

Dear Mummy

The posts caught me again yesterday, and your letter didn't go . . . We are still in the same wee village working pretty hard. The weather has been lovely, warm and bright. I've had no time for any odd reading though . . .

Ridley has come back to the company this morning, so I shall be his second-in-command. I hardly feel myself fit to command a company at present, for want of experience. It requires an older man, like Hammill or Lumley. Ridley is nearly twenty-nine, if not more. The company goes to the baths this afternoon, and in the evening we all do night operations. I saw a jay in the wood this morning. The frogs croak amazingly here, just like many knife-grinders. The violets are opening wide in the banks of the lanes, and anemones smell deliciously. Bye bye. Dearest love . . . Ged xxx

PS Will you send me two sets of summer underclothing, the silk sort, from my chest of drawers please?

Wednesday 26th April
9 Greville Place, London NW

My dearest son

Your letter came this morning and I was profoundly moved to know that you had made your first Communion in Flanders on Easter Sunday, and Shakespeare's [birth]day, and I daresay in sound of the guns. Somehow it touched me to the heart, with I know not what mingling of emotions that I shall never forget. It has been always difficult for me to speak about religion, and a thousand times when near you I have longed for an utterance that would not come. I could teach you little but the three words that are my faith – 'God-Truth-Prayer' – but how numberless have been my prayers for you all your life you never can know. Undogmatic as I am, you know that I have always remained deeply religious in my solitary way. Your letter was a surprise in a way that I could never describe and awakened a life's memories . . .

The surprise was utter. I had no idea that you were preparing, and to feel that I had not known this, of so profound concern to me, made me feel a stranger in the world. For an instant I had a passionate wish that I could have remained orthodox; with what rendings and tearings I ceased to be, you cannot guess . . . Let us go to Mass together sometimes: we can at least do that, for to be parted from you altogether, when you are of the Church that I have so infinitely loved, would be more than I could bear . . . It is many and many a long year since my heart was so full: silence about my religion had so long become a second nature that I suppose it insensibly became a frost. I have not been able to think about anything else all day and won't try to write much about anything else . . .

I am going to Lady Randolph's to dine with Winston: he spoke in the secret session last night, though of course I don't know what he said and under the new Draconian regulations one must not enquire! Of course everybody who counts will know, and the order prohibiting any newspaper from 'speculating' as to what goes on in the Cabinet or in secret session will have to be modified. Even the faithful radical journals are rebelling. There's nothing new to say about the Irish business. The sparks of the rising seem to be going out here and there, but it is clear that the plot was widely spread and carefully concerted with the Germans. Probably communication passed by way of America. Well, that is about all, except that it has been a day of sudden summer, heavy with heat, and Wiffles, seeing me trying to modulate in the garden, where the cherry blossom is full on two little trees, made valiant attempts to induce me to gambol. He had my old sponge, as they have got me a new one, and worried it with joyous ferocity. But as I said I can really think or feel nothing today except this wish that I could have been at your side on Easter Sunday morning and this strange throng of memories from long long ago. The pilgrim soul had not known how far it had wandered. Love not to be told: may God bless you. Dad

Thursday 27th April
training camp, Linghem

[Dear Dad]

. . . The night affair was a farce last night. We marched up with great scraping of feet to the point of assembly, formed up, lay down and waited some time; then we prepared to advance. Everyone lost himself and everybody else, our company collided with two others. Eventually we deployed. Then an order came down wrong. We formed up and marched back to the starting point, whence we were retrieved after more waiting; so we came back, deployed again, continued the advance, and in the end arrived home about midnight. This morning the usual work. The heat is terrific. I forgot to tell you that the company marched over to the baths yesterday. We all had a bath, which was good, though the march was long and hot . . .

Well, here comes parade. Bye bye. Dearest love to you and Mummy, both Grannies, Aunt Maggie, Vi, John (thank her for her letter), Gipsy and Bunny. Ged xxx

Thursday 27th April
9 Greville Place, London NW

Dearest old son

I hope my letter yesterday didn't upset you: today I have relapsed into the usual stoicism in the subject, but feel much better for having talked to you at length. We could have had such a heart to heart talk [long] ago, and not on paper, but I always meant to postpone it until you were of an age to settle for yourself: then the war came and you grew a man unawares, while one was absorbed with all that the war brought . . .

Winston and I had a very jolly dinner together last night. In spite of official injunctions little birds carry secrets and I hear from several sources that Winston recovered his parliamentary position completely on Wednesday night by a splendid speech on the army. He must return permanently and as soon as he can manage it to parliamentary life. The only other persons there were his wife and his mother. We stayed very late together. The Government have received slap on slap this week. The miserable Irish business is spreading, but will be got firmly in hand in a day or two . . . It is all crass, maddening and stupid and German money must have had a good deal to do with it . . .

Good will come out of all these muddles, but the credit of the 'wait-and-see' ministry has received a mortal blow. I think we should have a new Government of five or seven persons . . .

This has been a strange sweltering day, more like August than April. The town has been prostrate. Going up to your room last night what was my amazement to see Wiffles on the pillow if you please. He looked so abashed and appealing I let him stay all night. The love of my heart to you, many many blessings. Dad

Saturday 29th April
training camp, Linghem

Dear Dad

Thank you ever so much for your letters tonight. I'm just sending you a short note because of what you said about Communion. I didn't prepare for it. I took Communion last Sunday because the Padre gave me general absolution on account of Easter. I've received Communion twice before, the first time in November, just before going into the trenches. I'll have a talk with padre tomorrow if I can get hold of him, or else early next week. He's very sensible. Bye bye. Dearest love . . . Ged.

Mayday, Monday 1st May
9 Greville Place, London NW

Dearest son

Tonight comes your short word to Mummy . . . and it's clear you are having any amount of hard work – we hope enjoying it, weather permitting. For a full week we have had as wonderful a short summer as ever I remember. The thunder has begun to rumble as I write this, so I suppose the break we have quite been expecting is about to come . . .

We can of course think and talk of little but the Irish trouble. The Government at first minimised everything as usual and it was not until the *Daily Mail* was allowed to come out last Saturday morning with two pages of excellent messages that we could realise the fierceness and desperation of the outbreak. Imagine from Queen's Hall to the Thames held by rebels fortified in the Piccadilly Hotel, the Trocadero, part of Whitehall and so on, and imagine Regent Street reduced for the most part to ruin by fires and shell, and you can conceive part of what has happened to Dublin. It makes one mad to think that, but for a purblind, inert, fumbling administration, this would never have happened.

Redmond has behaved admirably and I am profoundly sorry for the decent Nationalists of whom there are very many, though they have not had fundamental decision enough to face unflinchingly the madness which they knew to be abroad in the land. Good will come out of it all. The atmosphere of Ireland has been full of falsehood and constraint, and all this thunder and lightning will have cleared the air. Lunatics as the rebels were in the mischief and futility of their rising, the thing was thoroughly well planned, and the Sinn Féiners showed any amount of skill and courage in action, though mixed with the exceptionally repulsive ruffianism and rascality of the Dublin slums . . .

Of course I meant to have finished, long since, preparing my speech for the Ladies' Imperial Club on Wednesday; and of course I have been interrupted even today and there's not a word framed so I must do it tomorrow. It will be a rather important gathering, with Lady Edmund Talbot, wife of the Unionist chief whip, in the chair, and the theme 'The War and the British Empire' is big and momentous enough to demand some arranging of mind.

Well, this is about all I have to tell. All the love to you that is communicable by this paper and God bless you little boy. Dad

Tuesday 2nd May
9 Greville Place, London NW

Best son

Just a scrap tonight for I am still bothered by this wretched speech for tomorrow. I could not get at it until today and have found it not easy to shape and compress . . . I fear I wrote you a stupid letter after coming back from Buckhurst, but I was infinitely touched, not knowing you had been to Communion before, and Easter carrying the dear associations it does. Then my thoughts being always and ever with you, not to know such a thing made me feel isolated, or rather as if you were on one side of a gate and I on the other and outside. Any course of yours I never questioned for a moment, if we differed it would only mean a deeper harmony really; but I wondered whether perhaps I had failed you in my chief duty, whether in my care for you I had been wise for you, whether I ought not to have said more to you long ago about the obstinate questions. But now I understand the whole thing better and am certain you are right, especially with your Catholic men to lead and your example to set . . . Poor padre. Do not trouble him on my account; Forgive me if in my wish to keep very close to your mind I disturbed you without meaning it . . .

Infinite love and God bless you. Dad

Wednesday 3rd May
9 Greville Place, London NW

Dear old son

There is nothing from you today. The military posts are still erratic. Sometimes what you write comes in twenty-four hours, while letters you have written earlier come a day or two days after. That seems – as Lord Dundreary used to say in the generation I can just remember, but you can't – 'One of the things no fellah can understand'; but I suppose the simple secret is that the railway routes necessarily vary.

This has been a dull, close, heavy day, but at least another speech is off my chest, and the story thereof is amusing. I could not get my preparation finished, even by working in a dressing gown this morning. So I scratched up some skeleton notes. They were scribbled out about twenty past three. The meeting at the Ladies' Imperial Club, Dover Street, was due to start at half past three! Away with Mummy in a taxi, Grandma Wilson and John following in another. Mad driving. Not very late. At once to business. Lady Edmund Talbot a nice chairwoman, with one of those firm faces not always taking at first which often make one realise suddenly how strong and kind they are. But the meeting! I can only call it a 'Frump-Zoo' of most elderly though undoubtedly well-meaning females. About three men of funny types. And a most awkward room. And the heat. And the soporific moral atmosphere of any afternoon meeting. Then it was cloudy outside and the room was dark. To my horror I could not read a word of my notes when I tried, but was continuous.

Mummy and John swear it was good, and as much as my precious audience could understand of my plea for Imperial unity and organisation seemed to impress them. But what a headache after. Viva didn't come because she had one too. To tea at Fullers, or rather to ice-cream soda for me, and then John and I, in the interests of the latter craving air, walked up Portland Place and through Regent's Park to Hanover Gate. By the lake in the park there was a coolness at last. I always think on such occasions now how I would feel carrying a military pack and feel much lowered in my own esteem . . .

As I anticipated the Bill for General Compulsion was brought in today. Three of the Dublin leaders were shot this morning under martial law – a melancholy end for infatuated fanatics who have caused many deaths and endless mischief, but one wonders whether logical insanity, as distinguished from the illogical insanity recognised as madness, has ever received the deep psychological study it deserves . . .[5]

All the loves and blessings. Dad

Thursday 4th May
training camp, Linghem

Dear Dad

Just a line. We move from here in a day or two. Tomorrow we have a divisional scheme. Today was easy, after a practice mobilising in the morning, when the weighing of officer's kit was ridiculously comic. No one had less than fifty pounds, and most seventy or upwards. We're allowed thirty-five.

I didn't tell you about the little shopman in A— on Sunday, prosperous and content, who overflowed with enthusiasm when we noticed his beautiful Roquefort. He would have us taste a bit on a biscuit, and ran for butter because it much improved the flavour. We've been having a lot of fruit. All the apple trees are pink, and the lilac nearly full. Bye-bye. Dearest love to you and Mummy, Granny (both), Vi, John, Gipsy and Bunny. I mustn't forget Aunt Maggie. Ged. I'm having cold baths.

---

5 The three leaders of the Easter Rising who were shot at Kilmainham Gaol that day were Patrick Pearse, Thomas Clarke and Thomas MacDonagh. In all, fifteen were executed in Dublin between 3 and 12 May.

❖

On Saturday 6 May the 7th South Lancs moved from Linghem to the Somme valley, and in the last fortnight of the month the battalion was involved in digging new trenches along the front line north-east of Albert, opposite the German-held villages of la-Boisselle and Ovillers-la-Boisselle.

❖

May 8th Monday
[billets, Somme area]

Dear Mummy

I think I told you that owing to the move I was going on to the station as a general help to the entrainment officer. Lively enough too. I had to be up and dressed by five o'clock yesterday morning. Loading mules is rather fun, though, because they have a way of flying around suddenly and tangling everything up. Looking after horses is fairly easy. Everything is going well. Really there's very little for me to do. Seeing animals into trucks and looking hugely official in a great helmet about sums up my job. Captain Spender-Clay introduced himself yesterday. He's in charge of the whole affair. I like him very much. He seems thoroughly competent . . .

Nothing else, except that in view of an afternoon off (I come on at midnight) I indulged in a Chartreuse after lunch today. The lunch was plain. After the war I must bring you to this town . . .

Here I went to dine – sardines, veal, ragout, cake, coffee – *Voilà*. Nothing else to tell. Bye-bye. Dearest love to you and Dad, Granny, Vi, John, Gipsy and Bunny. Ged

Tuesday 9th May
9 Greville Place, London NW

Dearest and best beloved

No letter this ninth day of May – or if there is one, it is in the post still. The posts are so scarce and so bad . . . and the last collection goes out at 8.30 at night, so if Dad's and my letters are a bit late you mustn't mind. Your parcels did go – but tell me why all the woollies are coming back. Don't you know the old saying 'Dinna cast a cloot till May gangs oot'? And I think you should not do, round your waist anyhow . . .

Dad, at last, has had his secretary up to do some letters at the house and so relieve the pressure. Otherwise he looks well, sleeps well in my room, eats well, but he takes no exercise. Viola at this moment working hard in the dining room. John also working hard (for matric.) at my writing table. Jimmy and Kitty asleep. If you do get a moment to write and scold Jimmy I wish you would. She will not do music and Miss Snowden is furious with her, and Vi and John say she is awful altogether and leads Kitty a terrible life, Kit being a dear. We got two of Mrs Saull's children off to Barnado's this morning, she, poor thing, being very upset at the parting – also horribly tired.

We've had quite a frivolous table tonight – over the Daylight Saving Bill and what it entails. We shall see how it works. With dearest love – blessings – prayers always, dearest lad. Mummy.

Wednesday 10th May
9 Greville Place, London NW

Dear old boy

Nothing from you today again, so there is the usual absurd sense of vacancy at the end. My letters must have been a day delayed in reaching you lately for I didn't know (and as an editor, professing to preside over news sheets, my ignorance was shameful) that posts have been reduced to three a day, and if I don't pop into the pillar box before seven the letter doesn't go that evening. So this is written earlier. There's still little to tell. Mummy is still a bit nervy and is at tea with Bess. I wish she would go to the O'Sullivan house again for a few weeks. Vi is with her majestic Miss Brumy for Martin Harvey's tercentenary performance of *Hamlet*, and the other three are grinding in various rooms – young Jimmy practising mutinously at the piano under penalty that if she doesn't mend she shall be packed off to boarding school!

Happily she doesn't know how hard it would be to pay for boarding school. Our finances are indeed far better than most people's of our class, yet the makers have again put up the price of paper so as to clap £165 a week on to the expenses of the *Observer* and sweep away all profit. When the last rise in price came, I revived the business side of my mind, usually dormant, saved £200 a week one fine morning, and more than kept up the profit. By more practical ingenuities I hope to make a good balance again, but doubt whether, after the next rise in the price of paper – and I don't doubt there will be another rise a few months hence – our share in the *Observer* profits will be worth much until after the war. But by comparison with most people – not munition makers! – we are doing very well . . .

Winston is back for good. His battalion is one of those disbanded, owing to want of drafts I suppose, so he is free in any case to come home. He made a little speech on the Irish question last night and was excellent in tone and temper. Quite as I foresaw, execution by driblets is going to give rise to angry and deplorable debates. I had tea with Winston in the House of Commons this afternoon – he is in good form physically and mentally, that capacious cranium of his full of strong ideas. He asked about you with his unfailing cordial memory. Well, if I am to catch your post I must close . . .

All my love and blessings on you. Dad

Thursday 11th May
[billets near Pecquigny, west of Amiens]

Dear Mummy

We had a little scheme this morning and dined out on the downs, but nothing much happened. Later we had a race home, a good two miles. I didn't come in very soon, but was fitter than I used to be after running a good part of the way . . .

These French people amaze me: in our billet is a tiny back garden with a fowl-run taking up a good piece; in the rest are small patches of potatoes, lettuce, onions, currants, beetroot, peas or sweet peas, a few rose bushes and flowers on the edges, and oh yes, strawberries. Isn't that extraordinary? Just enough for the old man and the old woman.

Bye-bye. Dearest love to you and Dad . . . Ged.

Thursday 11th May
9 Greville Place, London NW

Dear old boy

. . . I can't quite make out what kind of job you are at now. It seems as though you were a sort of deputy horse-master and mule-master and also a sort of assistant station master, which seems a comic combination that you would not have believed of yourself had anyone prophesised it to you before the war . . .

Last night I wrote part of my *Tribune* article and finished it this morning before getting out of bed, which was exceptional economy of time for me. I wrote on the Irish question and the earnest attempts to get Carson and Redmond to work out some solution together. It would be a blessed sequel and I do not despair of seeing it realised, though we are still threatened with that terrible emotional egoism, if I may call it so, which makes the Irish Nationalists think that to shoot a dozen Sinn Féiners is an agonising tragedy, while the deaths of two hundred officers and men were, by comparison, a commonplace. It is so hard to convince those whose feelings are so strong that other people have feelings as humane and powerful. But we must make the least, not the most, of such points, and remember that history has not been calculated to give the Celt in Ireland a balanced psychology . . .

I must finish like a flying man coming down or I shall never catch your post . . . Much much love and these with the blessings unfailing.
Dad

Thursday 11th May
9 Greville Place, London NW

Dearest and best

. . . I'm glad you've met Spender-Clay. You know he is Waldorf's brother-in-law and quite a charming person, very capable, but somewhat silent. Still I hope you are kept – wherever you are – doing work which keeps you safe for a bit and is interesting.

Here life goes on as usual, only that economics must go on more than usual, which, in a way makes me pleased. I have bought <u>some</u> clothes, as I don't think ever again I shall see any.

By the way, have you taken to smoking – reason why? – this morning's letter had quite a big bit burnt in its side. Chartreuse is good, but seldom, dear lad. Why don't you ask Dad to come over to you for a change. He is more than fed up here and very nervy, even though I took him to *Caroline* this afternoon – a delightful thing, which, if published in a book form I'll send you. It's so amusing . . .

Now good night, blessed thing. God bless and keep you safe for your own Mummy.

Friday 12th May
[billets near Pecquigny, west of Amiens]

Dear Mummy

I've no news at all. We went up to an old Roman camp this morning, a fine mound across a scarped spur with a wide view of the river. We practised siting trenches with Ridley, who is really very good. This afternoon we bathed in the river and after tea there was an hour's drill for officers.

I saw three swallow-tailed butterflies; they're common on these chalk downs, big yellow and black ones with swallow tails, very beautiful and rare in England. That's all. We had a gramophone tonight, borrowed, that played *Carmen* and the *Casse-noisette* for us and *Who is Sylvia?* The weather is sultry . . .

Bye-bye. Dearest love to you and Dad, Granny, Vi, John, Gipsy and Bunny. Ged . . .

Monday 15th May a.m.
[billets near Pecquigny, west of Amiens]

Dear Mummy

This is really yesterday's letter, written before breakfast today . . . Don't worry about my warm clothing, the climate is warmer here than at home. I haven't felt the want of it at all. It's raining heavily here today. The country looks beautiful, with all the trees and high green wheat. Yesterday we had a gymkhana . . . Great fun it was, I did nothing else except take a hand in the tug. Coming home I tried to ride a bare-backed mule but fell off. Stuart did the same and hurt himself rather badly. The doctor thinks he has bruised a rib and will have to lie up for a week. He was going on leave tomorrow morning. Bad luck wasn't it?

Bye-bye. Dearest love to you and Dad, Granny, Vi, John, Gipsy and Bunny. Ged.

Monday 15th May p.m.
[billets near Pecquigny, west of Amiens]

Dear Mummy

The post was again favourable today, and brought me two letters, one from each of you. The burn on the notepaper was made by a cigarette end by Smith. I'm not smoking. You needn't worry . . .

The night is beautiful (I'm writing this in bed, as the electric light in the mess goes off at ten o'clock) with a bright moon and the grove rustling in long cadences. I think I heard a nightingale, but it was only a snatch. I read a bit of the *Merchant of Venice*. This afternoon, the rain having given way to a dry wind, we had a paper-chase. I and Wilsher were hares. We had a four-mile run about, across fields and up a high hill (the Roman camp, with scarped sides about fifty feet high) and through swamp. Great fun and I feel very fit . . .

Stuart went to hospital today. I just missed him. I think he'll be well in a week, I hope he'll get his leave then at once.

Bye-bye. Dearest love to you and Dad, Granny, Vi, John, Gipsy and Bunny. Ged.

Tuesday 16th May
The *Observer* office [on *Pall Mall Gazette* notepaper]

Dearest old boy

Searching for notepaper I find these ancient relics of a bygone age in my drawer and use them with a feeling like chipping out fossils. We go to the new office in a fortnight as we expect, and shall then be done with all connected with the old *PMG*. I'm writing with a quill pen too, which is a very rare thing. Your letter to me came this morning and somehow I gather that the whole battalion is a happy family. I'm particularly glad that Stuart is having a better time: tell him so from me. Of course I mustn't try to guess exactly where you are, but knowing the geography of those parts as I do, I can't help guessing you are on higher ground . . . So I think of Artois and the Somme valley . . .

. . . I see among the wounded in *The Times* this morning is a Second-Lieutenant J. Garvin of the Welsh Regiment. The 'phone was going all morning, many anxious enquirers wondering whether the casualty was our son. We had funny feelings . . . Accordingly I took your Mummy out impromptu to Pagani's and gave her lunch on a peace basis, and afterwards, when we went down Great Portland Street, she saw in the window a brass door-stopper in the shape of a fox-head, so of course had to have it; and in the shop she saw the poems of Dante Gabriel Rossetti bound in calf and complete in one volume, like most of your other poets, so we bought it for you . . .

All my love: God bless you. Dad.

Wednesday 17th May
9 Greville Place, London NW

My Dear old boy

Nothing from you today, which is perhaps as wholesome as occasionally missing one's lunch – one has such an appetite for dinner. I see there has been a scrap somewhere near Arras and we ripped across into a trench, but I can't tell how near or how far you are from that particular scene. Note how I said 'we' then like the organ blower who said of the Bach fugue: 'Didn't we do that fine sir?' – if a citizen so far away from the front is even a organ blower . . .

Last night we had dinner – very indifferent at most points – at the Pall Mall Restaurant and then went to *Follow the Crowd*; not as good as either *Joyland* or *Bric-a-Brac* – indeed not a patch on the latter, but very hustling, tuneful uproarious stuff, rather on the lower plane of the vulgarities . . . The costumes were of course gorgeous in audacity and it is odd to notice how the Russian ballet has influenced theatrical dancing and dressing. I wish it could do as much to make dialogues, plots and the words of songs less brainless. We had the good luck to get a taxi and finished by reaching home nearly at midnight – a wonderful night, with the full moonlight working magic even amongst the trees in Leicester Square – but the big day's amusement did us good . . .

Heaven bless you, dear boy. Dad

Sunday 21st May

[billets, close to front north-west of Albert]

Dear Mummy

I'm writing this by candle-light just before going off on a working party; nothing in it.

The letter I wrote this morning was delayed on account of some indiscretion. I always rely on your never telling a soul anything I let you know. I haven't warned you before; but don't let anyone see my letters except Dad and the family for at least a fortnight . . .

Anyhow, we've done two days' hard marching and we're now bivouacking. We have shelters and our valises, so I had a very comfortable night last night; and hope to have a good sleep tomorrow. My shift is from midnight to dawn. I can't tell you what the job is.

The night before last we bivouacked in the gardens of an empty chateau, with big old trees. The candles are red and white on the chestnuts and the red hawthorn curtained with bloom. The nights are clear and starry; the day scorches one to the bone, and unluckily water is very scarce just here. I begin to realise how troops may suffer from want of water – not of course that we are enduring more than a temporary inconvenience. I've taken on a new servant, a very nice boy, rather shy, who'll make a good one I fancy, after a bit . . .

How good that you're having some fun together. If you can't take a holiday, that'll help you both to keep well and cheerful. You should get a proper change of air though. Do try both of you. Give my love to the girls . . . Ged.

Tuesday 23rd May

[billets, close to front north-west of Albert]

Dear Dad

I wrote a letter for the afternoon post, but couldn't send it; and I've since lost it. There wasn't anything in it, nor is there in this. Last night I went out for my digging earlier and got back in time to sleep from one of the morning till nine. The day has been sultry, with rain threatening. Yesterday a slight shower alarmed us for our bivouacs and caused some inconvenience. Today we're cut back into the bank, and got some stuff from the engineers, so I write this in a very cosy little shelter.

The men have been singing merrily down below, while waiting for their turn to work. I go off tonight at half past eleven. It's curious how these fellows veer from the most languid sentimentalism to the vilest filth. Nothing between.

We have a queer fellow in the mess – I'm not mentioning names. He's knocked about the world a good deal, has been a boxer, and an oil-well superintendent in India, and been elsewhere. He talks very big and blusters mightily when he loses his temper, which frequently happens – especially with me – owing to his entire want of the vaguest sense of humour. We all ragged him a lot at first. He really has a lot of experience and common sense all the same . . .

All letters from you are more welcome even than water, a primitive statement which you will appreciate when I tell you that water, both for drinking and washing, is exceedingly scarce. It's only an inconvenience, but it serves to give one an idea of how people may suffer from thirst. As a matter of fact the heat wave has passed over for the time being. Just think! We had to put ourselves on a ration of Perrier, one bottle each for the day. Perrier and mineral waters are greatly sought after out here; so are oranges just now . . .

Bye-bye. Dearest love to you and Mummy, Granny, Vi, John, Gipsy and Bunny. Ged . . .

Thursday 25th May
9 Greville Place, London NW

My dearest laddie

No letter again this morning, but I hope that means you are quite well, though working hard. I also hope you are not suffering from want of water in this appalling heat. Here we are in mid-summer weather, which I always detest. The heat coming suddenly always prostrates me, or nearly does. Last night a beautiful night of stars and clear sky, so that the many searchlights looked like numerous aeroplanes crossing each other in the sky.

I suppose Stuart will not get his leave after all and if he does he will have to get a permit to get to Ireland. Gerty had to get one coming over because of the disturbance. Expect you'll see that Asquith is sending Lloyd George to try to settle the whole question. Poor man – to try to settle the Irish question. I rather agree with Tim Healy on one thing – although he has been absolutely without control and as thoroughly stupid as he can be in the House – but this is the story: [Max] Aitken asked him when all this trouble had started? Tim: 'When Strongbow came to Ireland.' 'And when will it end?' Tim: 'When the world ends.' I believe him there. What a time to live in and how awful it all is . . .

Dearest dearest lad – God bless you, guard you and guide you – my blessings and prayers and my love ever and ever. Mummy.

Friday 26th May
[billets, close to front north-west of Albert]

Dear Mummy

I had nothing to write about last night and have little enough now. Yesterday afternoon I went . . . to look at the trenches close to us. I can't tell you what they were like, but we got to a place only about fifty yards from the Germans. There are several places of the kind along the front, where the French or our own people have pushed back the enemy on to points where he has contrived to hang on, and both sides have dug in. They're generally very unhealthy, with bombs and mines, but yesterday was a quiet day – not a shot or a bomb anywhere near.

Going and returning we had a meal in a neighbouring hostel, where the remnant of a cellar still provides a change from camp rations. Don't be alarmed – indulgence was limited to a light lunch with a bottle of Sauterne, and tea with lemon squash and Perrier.

Last night I took out a working party, but a steady rainstorm and murky night drove us in before long. I've been doing the same this morning, meditating between whiles on ways of fortifying villages, a very interesting subject on which I shall doubtless be able to give you several hints when I come home again. That Vimy affair was a nasty slap. We must give the Boche something back[6] . . .

Bye-bye. Dearest love to you both, Granny, Vi, John, Gipsy and Bunny. Ged.

Friday 26th May
9 Greville Place, London NW

My very dearest boy

Nothing from you this morning, but a field card addressed to me came last night like a handshake. I feel somehow that you and your comrades are going through a stiff time, perhaps the stiffest you've had. I may be wrong, but you are so much on my mind that I practically dwell with you . . .

There was no chance to write to you yesterday, so I am writing on a Friday morning this week as last. Here's my diary. I came down in a dressing gown and got through my *Tribune* article – asking the Americans to leave us Allies to handle our war in our own way if [the] US stand out. This done against time, yet carefully in the way that makes my job peculiar. I jumped into a hot bath and had a cheerful chaffing lunch with Mummy . . . In the afternoon I went down to the House of Commons and had tea on the terrace with Winston – a blue sky with high white clouds and a splendid light on the Thames. Winston, of course, full of ideas, not ill-content with the advance he has already made in the delicate process of regaining the ear of the House. Equally, of course, he asked about you. His speech on the army, and handling to better advantage the huge numbers of men we now have, was crammed full of excellent suggestions. The morning papers give no proper idea of it. It must be read in *Hansard* in full . . . Then came Philip Kerr, the editor of the *Round Table*, for a long talk about Ireland and everything. When he was gone there was just time

6 On 21 May the Germans attacked at the north end of Vimy Ridge and, according to General Headquarters, 'succeeded in penetrating our front-line trenches on a front of about 1,500 yards': *The Times*, 23 May 1916, p. 8.

to dress and none for your letter, so I sped to Lady Sarah Wilson's for dinner – Lord French there, he on her right hand, I on her left, and several Peers and millionaires and a number of beautiful women, rather brilliant, rather boring too, for nobody had anything to say that wasn't banal – not because some were not clever, but because the affinities were not brought together in the way that makes a dinner party go. Home before midnight and now it's Friday morning. So back to work!

All love and blessings to you, my boy. Dad.

Sunday 28th May
[billets, close to front north-west of Albert]

Dear Mummy

I'm afraid my letters will be irregular for a day or two because I am detailed from the battalion. After it went back on Saturday morning a party of officers was left to have a look round the trenches. Luckily we have a very decent billet – I can't say where – in an abandoned house of some pretensions with a fine garden round. Broken windows of course, and bare rooms, but shelter and an excellent mess, white panelled and carpeted. Except that we got no letters during our stay – four days or so – nothing more could be desired.

Really there's no news to speak of. Trenches are a forbidden topic and as our day has consisted of a morning stroll round them followed by an afternoon sleep in the sun, what can one talk about?

The nights are dark, and lovely in the garden to smell honeysuckle and look up to the stars through gaps in the branches, like the damsel in *Prince Otto*. We had a vigorous argument after dinner on various points suggested by the war, alliances and finance, and the possible course of the first weeks. Rightly or wrongly, Prince Louis has the credit of having the fleet ready and on the spot in the first instance.[7]

---

7 Prince Louis of Battenberg (1854–1921), first sea lord 1912–1914, took the important decision not to demobilise the fleet after its manoeuvres, 25–7 July 1914, thus ensuring that it was fully mobilised before the declaration of war on 4 August. Notwithstanding this, the Austrian-born prince was compelled to resign his post on 29 October because of his 'German origins'. In 1917, at the

I'm finishing *Guy Mannering* and enjoying every word of it. And there the bulletin must end.

Dearest love to you and Dad, Granny, Vi, John, Gipsy and Bunny. Ged.

PS Will you send me two more pairs of light wool socks and may I send my dirty clothes home for washing?

Tuesday 30th May
9 Greville Place, London NW

Dear old boy . . .

I'm writing this on my back again in the garden chair – there's something demoralising about this daylight saving. It's a quarter past nine by legal time, yet the birds are still singing, the swallows darting with keen notes and the sparrows too talkative to sleep, while out here I can see to write perfectly well. Wiffles approves all this, but fails to understand why it doesn't mean more games. Mummy is so active and gay . . . that she has done and posted her letter to you, stealing a march on me, so you will get this by a later post.

I was delayed by an odd reason. I went to Pagani's for lunch to meet Mr Dmowski, one of the chief Polish leaders and a member of the Duma. We had an extraordinary talk, of course in English, his command of it being astonishing since he lived here years ago. We ranged Heaven and Earth. I wanted to talk in detail about Poland and what is to be done, but Dmowski insisted on the importance of the fact that the Poles were Catholic, with the Roman tradition, but Russians [were] Orthodox, with the Byzantine. So of course that opened all history and we had to discuss religion, race, Charles Darwin, the Vatican and the latter-day Papacy, all the peoples of South-Eastern Europe, whether Danzig should be Polish again someday, and the absurdity of [the] popular error, shared by intelligent people, that there is any useful analogy between the Polish question and the Irish question – you can imagine, and our host Mr Usher listened amazed . . .

---

request of George V, he changed his name to Louis Alexander Mountbatten, 1st Marquis of Milford Haven.

[Dmowski's] claims for Poland [are] so large, his anti-Russian feeling so profound, though subordinated for the present to his anti-German feeling, that one felt the enormous difficulty of bringing about any reasonable solution. They are a splendid race, but there is the old difficulty that went to ruin them – the want of strong geographical boundaries and clear ethnographical limits. It was nearly five in the afternoon before I could get away, but I wasn't sorry. How hard the world is to put straight. He told a good story from a Polish comic paper in Warsaw: 'There was a day and the Russians went away in the evening. There was another day and the Germans came in the morning. Next night I had a beautiful dream. I dreamed we were alone' . . .

All manner of love to thee and the blessings too. Dad.

Thursday 1st June
9 Greville Place, London NW

Dearest of sons

Before anyone arrives on this Thursday June 1st I will try to get a word to you. It is a grey bleak day, with wind and dust and showery clouds and grey sky – not at all a good June day, more like late September or early October.

7.30 p.m. – just at that point Mrs Halsey arrived and stayed for two hours. Also Madam Marchesi, who is anxious to know if you wear your St Gerard's medal pinned inside your pocket as I put it. She claims for it that nothing can hurt you while you have it. So, in case she may be right (and he is your patron saint), please do wear it where I pinned it, laddie mine. She was the same nice, kind-hearted, exuberant person, so full of vitality that she does one good, always. She always makes one wish one knew French really well – she speaks it so wonderfully.

Our new cook has arrived and the between maid gone and I have written to four others hoping to get one . . . Now no more – and what a bad, tame thing at that, but the intention is good, and anyhow it brings you devoted love and prayers from Mummy. May God guard you always, dear lad. Mummy.

Friday 2nd June
9 Greville Place, London NW

Dearest of sons

Today the skies are blue and cloudy as June skies should be, but there is a nip in the air which is far from summery. No letter from you this morning, but we are not worrying as you told us that posts would be uncertain for some days. Dad was allowed to sleep in this morning, so is not very pleased. He had told Vi to call him and she overslept herself. The new cook is Kate, who knew you at the O'Sullivans – and I hope she gets into the odd and erratic hotel-like ways of this house, which is difficult for any maid. To have to be up till 11.00 or 12.00 and up at 6.30 they can't stand for long . . .

Mrs Lumley told me that there was a rumour that all letters from the front were to be stopped for a month, but I haven't heard it and nor has Dad, so I expect it can't be true. If it is it will be a nuisance and worrying.

I expect to hear all your experiences later – and all you have been doing. I'm so sorry I forgot about your new lamp for the torch and have now ordered it. Let me know if it comes all right. Dearest son, God bless and guard you. My tenderest love and blessings for you. Mummy.

Saturday 3rd June
[billets, Somme area]

Dear Dad

It was jolly to read your long letter yesterday, sitting on a bank during a halt . . . I'm as busy as can be. I barely found a moment yesterday and I've been up doing papers for nearly an hour this morning. I'm writing to you before breakfast with a plate of porridge smoking at my elbow. I daresay after a day or two I shall get a grip of the state of affairs and find more leisure. The country is delightful, waving cornfields still green, and bright threads of colour, cornflower and poppy.

The garden here is full of flowers, pinks and roses and columbine. Our landlady makes us excellent salad and custards and last night she made us meat turnovers, little ones. Yesterday we cleaned kit and marched out in the morning to a place where we did an attack after dinner, very comic and operatic. We got back about six.

I hear nothing of Stuart. A card a week ago said that he was at a hospital on the coast. No other news. I'll try to send a proper letter when I can.

Bye-bye. Dearest love to you and Mummy, Granny, Vi, John, Gipsy and Bunny. Ged.

Tuesday 6th June
9 Greville Place, London NW

My very dearest old thing

How decent of you to write me a little letter this morning, full too of the sweet o'the year in your countryside there, at a time when you are pressed early and late . . . It is execrable of me to make so bad a return as not to have written for four whole days, which has hardly happened since you went out, but [you] would guess there was a reason and perhaps the real reason. The truth is that the biggest naval fight since Trafalgar in importance . . . has for all sorts of causes thrown us into a sullen sort of pother, and filled up your father's measure with such business that to send you the usual long Monday's letter was impossible yesterday . . . We must, at all costs, keep up the Trafalgar ideal as a standard, otherwise we shall [fall] back into a dangerous casuistical complacency, but for any other people except us, and against any other foe but the Germans (who came out of it all most ably, though their subsequent boasting and lying are a disgrace to them), the battle of Jutland . . . would count as a very respectable victory. With a little more cold fighting-brain in moments, added to our fighting pluck, nay ferocity in attack, it would have been either a more signal success, achieved with much less loss, or for the enemy *Der Tag* indeed, and *Der Letzte Tag* . . .

Verdict? Not quite up to Nelsonic standard. The Germans handled their business with great judgement both in engaging, manoeuvring and breaking off . . . Altogether they have done by no means badly in their first considerable grapple with the greatest navy in the world, and have proved quite the tough and brainy antagonists we expected

. . . We have gained invaluable experience – though at a bitter price – in the trial run. Our sea power is absolutely intact. Next time, if they give us a next time, I feel we shall smash them . . .

My dear boy, what a gigantic age our lot is cast in. Three more months should see the worst of it all, though very far from the end of it. I never felt more certain, somehow, that we are going to beat the enemy with a real beating, unless weak politicians amongst the Allies are lured into a bad peace. I don't think it will be so, though there is something about the naval battle which has had an invaluable effect in making our people set their teeth . . .

Mummy is resting and keeps very bright. Dear old Viva was first in English at Somerville and top on the list of vacancies. The rest are all right . . . Ever so much love and many blessings. Dad.

Thursday 8th June
[billet in Flesselles]

Dear Mummy

. . . Yesterday we made a little move, only about a two-hour march. We're still well out of danger so you needn't worry. We're in a fair-sized village, very poor and dirty, on the edge of a kind of tableland, a flat ridge, very much indented. The country round is all upland, undulating in low hills and valleys, with villages bunched up on hill-tops in the middle of little woods. No hedges, only wide fields, corn mainly with occasional patches of yellow mustard or a peculiar kind of clover with a deep crimson flower, almost too dazzling to look at in a mass. The poppies and cornflowers glow scattered or in groups with a lot of colour that one can't miss . . .

I dined with Lumley the other night. We had a very jolly dinner. The adjutant was there and we had a bit of a talk about history and kindred things. Today we did a scheme, which was rather comic, as usual. When is a field-day not comic? It rained a bit, but not to speak of. We all came back rather chilly, but a glass of Benedictine after a cold lunch warmed us up again.

I'm at present in a little iron bed (with very clean sheets and a comfortable mattress fortunately) in a bare loft with a swallow's nest on the rafters: like the *Odyssey* isn't it? . . .[8]

Bye-bye. Dearest love to you and Dad, Granny, Vi, John, Gipsy and Bunny . . . Ged

Tuesday 13th June
9 Greville Place, London NW

Dear old boy

This morning brought a note from your loft, where the swallow builds, and you remind me of a thing or two. When we had our last weekend at Wargrave we had all our meals in a sort of square loggia that Edward has. Two swallows nested over the door going into the house and one jolly little bird usually perched on top of the open door, while the other above peered down out of the nest. Lovesome creatures and one gets fonder and fonder of them. As for the country about you, I feel I have seen the very place and probably I have . . .

Mummy is a little better today and Gerty is an immense comfort to her as helpful and kind as may be. Vi and John and I were amused last night at the Ambassadors. *Pell-Mell* is a bright racketing brainless piece of folly . . . Home in the rain a long way before we got a taxi – a terrible dripping cold night. I asked the veteran driver whether he ever remembered a worse June? 'Yus,' he said, with authority, 'it was worse than this in 1882.' Why, an antiquary of weather nemesis! I see we are attacking at Ypres: the Canadians are very sore to have been exposed so long in that terrible hollow (they suffered casualties ten days ago) and they are furious at having lost a little ground[9] . . . With deepest love and blessings on thee – Dad.

---

8 In book twenty-two of the *Odyssey* Athena appears at Odysseus' side during his confrontation with Penelope's suitors: wishing to see him demonstrate his prowess she does not intervene, but instead flies up to one of the rafters in the cloister roof and sits there in the form of a swallow.

9 On 2 June the Germans attacked in force at Ypres and gained significant ground along a sector south of Hooge held principally by the Canadians. The Canadians counter-attacked the next day, and again on 13 June, when they retook the greater part of what they had lost.

6

The Somme Offensive

Thursday 15th June
19th Division Headquarters, St Gratien

Dear Dad

Yet another transmigration; where and what am I this time, you ask? If you please, I'm attached to divisional headquarters for instruction, under Captain Spender-Clay – who's on leave just at present.[1] I haven't much to do, just a certain amount of writing. When I get a chance I'll write a proper letter; please excuse this being so short. I loved getting your letter yesterday.

Last night we brought in Daylight Saving. Things go on as usual, but I was very sleepy this morning. Bye-bye. Dearest love to all. Ged.

Friday 16th June
9 Greville Place, London NW

My dearest lad

I have been scandalously delayed and prevented for two whole days and cannot put much into this to make up. Mummy is not very well again, rather over-wrought by various things, so Mrs O'Sullivan, who is the guardian angel of this family in your absence, descended on her yesterday, kind and enveloping – and Mummy is going to Lansdowne

---

1 Ged had been recommended for attachment to divisional headquarters by his commanding officer, Colonel Winser, 'as he was so capable and hard working': the *Observer*, 30 July 1916. St Gratien was about six miles north-east of Amiens.

Road tomorrow . . .

Gerty has been very kind and helpful. She says Gerry has got the Military Cross after that very bad scrap at Vimy, and I see that Winser is mentioned in despatches this morning amongst the other names that fill about twelve columns or more of *The Times*. People are being allowed to talk very openly, even in public lectures, about the imminence of the big push, but then the Paris press heralds it also. I don't suppose it makes much difference and probably helps a little to embarrass the Germans, as long as they don't know on what features we mean to make the real punch. You may imagine with what interest I follow things . . .

The Germans are clearly preparing a tip-top effort against Verdun. How I hope we hold it – that is, they hold it. Dearest love to you and all my blessings. Dad.

Saturday 17th June
19th Division Headquarters, St Gratien

Dear Mummy

I'm writing this to you from the office . . . They give me very little to do, just putting one or two things on maps, and writing a note about once a day. I answer the telephone when it rings, but I can't see what use I am otherwise, and anyway, my answering the telephone is about as much use as announcing a visitor, because there are no wrong numbers and nobody who rings up is anyone I can speak to.

I'm quartered in an attic of a chateau, with beautifully clean linen on a little bed, and a superb view through a high cleft in the trees across a valley to a sunny ridge . . . The trees almost without exception are very tall and well-grown – and of every kind, ash, acacia, copper beech and fir and others I don't know.

The chateau was finished, so the Countess told me yesterday – she speaks English very well with a noticeable accent – in the year of the Revolution and appears to me about as full of bad taste as it could be. The hall glories in looking-glass doors and Corinthian pillars of wood painted to look like marble. All the panels are the same; though the actual design of the room isn't at all unattractive: frigid of course, not like the English country house, but with a certain stiff pomposity, rather suggestive of the bad actor playing the Roman Emperor . . .

I share my room with another officer attached for instruction, Fletcher by name, from the North Lancs, a very frank, decent fellow with whom I get on very well. And that, I think, is all. I'm afraid I can't write again at this length for a day or two. Don't worry if I only send a field card or can't manage to get anything off at all . . .

Bye-bye. Dearest love to you and Dad, Granny, Vi, John, Gipsy and Bunny. Ged.

Sunday 18th June
19th Division Headquarters, St Gratien

Dear Dad

. . . I've done very little all day, except copy a few things on to a map in the afternoon. That's the worst of having no definite job. Nor have I anything to talk about, except that we have a very good little gramophone in the mess with some nice records, among them a little Schubert piece, some Grieg and one or two other things good to hear again . . .

There I broke off to draw rainbow lines on a map. This part is written in my bedroom. I feel so fresh that I'm going to read a bit of *Napoleon* before I go to sleep. What's more, after forgetting for two nights the wherewithal to light my candle, I've managed to make a light by striking my third and last match on the window pane. I looked out from the front door just now – a lovely night, cool and fresh, and what a delicious vista of the black tree-tops and twinkling stars . . .

Did you see that Winser was mentioned in despatches? We've been doing rather well lately. Bye-bye. Dearest love to you and Mummy, Granny, Vi, John, Gipsy and Bunny. Ged.

PS Can Mummy send me (urgently) two new khaki ties and a pair of 'Lotus' boots (Harrods). My Hook Knowles were being dried too close to the fire by Madame.

Tuesday 20th June
9 Greville Place, London NW

Dear old son

This is written in pencil in the garden . . . because there is nowhere else to go. Today, in my absence at the office, [Mummy, Mrs Saull and Hilda] laid violent hands on my Augean stable, and when I came home they were at work stacking and scattering my mountainous litter and I had to come out here. It is very good of them and my den will look beautiful, no doubt, at the end of this clearing up, but once my papers are put all in order I shall not be able to find anything when I want it . . .

We wonder what on earth you are doing exactly. There is so much open talk both in Paris and London about the British push that everyone assumes big things are toward, and of course they must be. The advertisement is so general that I don't suppose much harm is done, if any, and it may serve the good purpose of keeping the German line taut everywhere and preventing them having at Verdun the freer hand they would like just at this moment . . .

Fountains of love to you, my boy and God bless you always. Dad.

Friday 23rd June
19th Division Headquarters, St Gratien

Dear Mummy

I'm awfully sorry to hear about your not having been so well. Do please take a rest and look after yourself. Couldn't you and Vi have a rest by yourselves? You both need it . . .

We had an amusing time this morning. The Army Commander announced his intention of coming to decorate various people with their medals on a parade this morning. The message came yesterday afternoon. Vast excitement: the major of this office sent in a car to the nearest big town for ribbon – one special ribbon nowhere to be had. The office spent an evening of wires, telephoning and excitement, ending in a despatch rider dashing off to fetch ribbon at midnight from a neighbouring division. Then this morning no flagstaff or Union

Jack to be had for a saluting base. A motor-cyclist went off for a flag and I went down to get his flag-pole from a harassed ordnance officer. I brought it back in a car, about twenty minutes before the ceremony. Just as it was being put up, the Army Commander wired that he couldn't come. The general took his place though and everything went alright.

The weather, after a glorious warm yesterday, full of the smell of new-dried hay, broke this afternoon in a thunderstorm, deluging the country for half an hour. I'm still doing maps in little bits at a time. I feel all the sensations of the monk scrivening and illuminating at the monastery desk . . .

Bye-bye. Dearest love to you and Dad, Granny, Vi, John, Gipsy and Bunny. Ged

Friday 23rd June
9 Greville Place, London NW

Dearest of Sons

I was so glad Dad got a letter this morning. He always especially appreciates it, even although it may be only a line. You seem to be having almost a peaceful time out there in spite of all the fighting going on. Yes, I did notice about Winser, or rather Gerty told me of it.

Dad got his *Tribune* article done last night in spite of all, but didn't get to bed till one o'clock and of course I had practically no sleep because I must be up in the morning.

Thank goodness the papers are all out of the house today. I expect it will cost about £2.0.0 to have them removed to the office and we had two very beery-looking individuals up and downstairs for some hours getting them into a van to take them to the new office in Tudor Street. I sent Mrs Saull to see they were put in the proper place and I truly believe Dad will sell them at the finish. In any case I am sure he will never read two tons of papers from the beginning of the war till now . . .

Too sad to tell you, Dad has just had a letter from Mrs Melican saying that Sergt Melican died last week after going to hospital twice and being X-rayed and nothing found. Then he went to Ireland and when he came back he was examined again and was found to be tubercular; then pneumonia set in and we shall never see him again. Poor John is so upset and so are we all, and as always wonder why we didn't do more sooner . . .

I wish I hadn't to tell you such sad news. Dearest dearest son, good night and God bless you and guard you and my tenderest love and blessings to you. Mummy.

Friday 23rd June
9 Greville Place, London NW

My dearest son

. . . We cannot quite make out what you are doing, but anything connected with map-making or other such games in war must be a kind of a sort of responsible employment. You will hardly relish so much desk work, but it as needful as any other . . .

This evening Mrs O'S. and Harry Butters came round after dinner. He is suffering rather badly in nerves from shell-shock, but the few days' leave will do him good. He is a very fine, honest fellow. When they went the postman, just as I was at this, brought sad news – a black-edged card from Melican's wife. It shocked us, as it would you. Poor Melican is dead. He died on Monday afternoon. He had been ailing strangely a long while . . . His wife seems heartbroken as well she may be, for it casts a gloom over us. I liked him from the first and he knew how much you were attached to him and was devoted to you in return . . . Well, it might have happened even in peace, but seems sadder somehow in war. There's nothing else to say tonight, except that Viva seems much better and we have happily succeeded in keeping her at home for the rest of the week. Deepest love of my heart to you, my son and God bless you always. Dad.

❖

Saturday 24 June – The Opening of the Somme Offensive

On Saturday 24 June the Fourth Army began an intense bombardment of the German lines between the Somme and the Ancre in preparation for the much anticipated offensive. The shelling was meant to last for six days, but bad weather on Monday 26th and Tuesday 27th meant that the attack was postponed for twenty-four hours, and the bombardment therefore lasted a full week: zero hour became 07.30 a.m. on Saturday 1 July. The British deployed more guns on the Somme than the Germans had amassed at Verdun – over 1,400 – but these were spread along a front line that was twice as long, and although they fired more than 1.5 million shells their effect was dissipated. The bombardment was meant to destroy German barbed-wire, dug-outs and gun batteries, but it achieved none of these objectives: too few guns were given too much to do and the infantry paid the price.[2]

❖

Sunday 25th June
19th Division Headquarters, St Gratien

Dear Mummy

Today's post brought the unexpected joy of five letters. Two of them the 23rd and others older from both of you. I had a fine time reading them all at lunch. A parcel came too with nuts and putties. Thank you very much for all . . .

Can one do anything for Mrs Melican? If you can, draw on my account as much as you like. I'm sure it would please her to have Masses said for him. Could you fix that up and let me supply the money. I don't know what the exact arrangement is. I'm very sorry to hear of the sergeant's being dead . . .

I went into the town [Amiens?] yesterday, in the afternoon, got a pair of boots, puttees and a fearsome stick with a steel spike, very well balanced and absolute death to any marauding nettle by the roadside . . .

If this is to go I must stop here. I did some work this morning but had a pleasant hour in the afternoon lying in the hay under the sun, chatting with Fletcher about cathedrals and other matters of travel.

---

2 See Gary Sheffield, *The Somme*, London, 2003, p.40; Strachan, *The First World War, A New Illustrated History*, p. 188.

Bye-bye. Dearest love to all of you, you and Dad, Granny, Vi, John, Gipsy and Bunny. Ged.

Monday 26th June
9 Greville Place, London NW

My very dearest son

Only a field card from you this morning and both our own communiqués and the German's reveal that the big thing or its unmistakeable preliminaries has begun on our front. You may imagine how we long to hear, though we know the more we wish for news the more you mustn't send us any. Discretion, though far from perfect, has been better kept on our side this time and that in every way is wise. However the general conditions are too clear for the Boches to be astonished everywhere, but I pray they may get somehow somewhere even more than they expect. You will be hardly able to send a line for some little time, but don't bother about us until it is easy to do so. You know that our whole thoughts, hearts and souls are ever and always with our dear soldier.

When I think of what is going on since our guns opened, home things seem so small, so trivial, one hardly likes to write them, but let us keep up the chronicle however little there may be in it. Your Mummy is so lively and competent about the house, I don't know when I saw her so much like her old self as she is just now. The house looks ever so much better since she cleared out the mass of journalistic rubbish and, rather than let it accumulate again in the same way, will take a couple of rooms near here and use them as working and storing places so as to prevent the newspapers of all nations from piling themselves up into mountains here. Talking of them, the German newspapers show a remarkable change. They are quite chastened by comparison with their tone of even a few weeks ago, and they know well now that they have got themselves into a desperate business. There is no need to get to the Rhine to finish with them; if we could even get to Lille on one wing and Metz on the other, they would concede the terms of a pretty thorough settlement . . .

Winston Churchill is asking Harry Butters to dine tonight which will vastly please that excellent American citizen in khaki. He returns to his guns on Wednesday morning. June is very capricious – if we have one splendid interval, as yesterday, it sulks again like today, which is gusty and clouded. Wiffles, for some reason, was exceptionally gay yesterday, perhaps because we were all in the garden for tea . . . I really think he was trying to amuse. The love of our hearts with this and God bless you. Dad.

Tuesday 27th June
19th Division Headquarters, St Gratien

Dear Mummy

Just after putting last night's letter in the box, I went for a walk; my colonel in the office here told me to go out and get some exercise, so I went off with Anson, the adjutant of the North Lancs. We had a jolly brisk round, through a delightful valley full of oat and barley and bright yellow mustard fields, and corn paling to ripeness with poppies thick among the stalks. This is a rolling country of narrow valleys and smooth wood-crowned hills, mostly with a chateau or spire and two or three farmhouses on top. We were driven in by the approach of rain which absolutely deluged the place a while after, coming down like a sword. Today I did a little more mapping and had a short bike ride. No other news. Bye-bye. Dearest love to you and Dad, Granny, Vi, John, Gipsy and Bunny. Ged . . .

Thursday 29th June
19th Division Headquarters, St Gratien

Dear Mummy

. . . Yesterday began with fine steady rain which soaked everything till about noon, when the weather began to clear. Today a dry wind has set things right and the sky this evening held out hopes of fine weather for a while to come. Life continues normal. Yesterday I hadn't much to do. Today I was kept busy – in a leisurely way – till tea-time in making copies of a map. I didn't make many, but quite enjoyed the work. It was a traced map, and I got quite cunning at the end in putting on all lines of one colour and then another like a printer. Truly I gain cunning in many arts . . .

Dad asked about war-books. Will you ask him for me to hold them up for a while; I'll write for them later on . . . I played rounders tonight for a while in the garden, which made me very hot and, I daresay, fit. I really think that's all I have to put in. Not very exciting is it? You must wait awhile for that.

Bye-bye. Dearest love to you and Dad, Granny, Vi, John, Gipsy and Bunny.

Ged xxxxx

❖

Saturday 1 July – The First Day of the Somme

On Friday 30 June the 7th South Lancs were in temporary billets at Hénencourt Wood, about four miles due west of Albert, and Ged visited his comrades to wish them luck. The next morning, at divisional headquarters, he awoke to a 'shattering bombardment'. The shelling of the German lines intensified ten minutes before zero hour, 07.30 a.m., and there was then a brief lull while the gunners shifted their range to find new objectives behind the German front lines. As the barrage lifted the infantry attacked. They advanced into the annihilating fire of German machine guns that had reappeared within minutes of the barrage ending. The first day of the Somme had been planned as a hammer blow, but it delivered only modest territorial gains for massive human losses: total British casualties were 57,470, of whom 19,240 were dead. In the early hours of Sunday 2 July Ged spoke to returning officers from the 8th Division, which had fought unsuccessfully for control of the Ovillers spur north of the Albert–Bapaume road: the division was, Ged noted, 'evidently badly cut up and demoralised'. The reality of the first day was kept from the British public, and the press took at face value the optimistic reports coming through official channels: the Observer *of Sunday 2nd heralded 'Britain's Day – The Big Push at Last – A Great Beginning'.*

❖

Sunday 2nd July
9 Greville Place, London NW

Dearest of sons

I was too busy, with a hundred and one things, to write yesterday (no letter from you). Kate has left and now we have Grant for a few weeks, but still we are without the chance of a cook.

Dad had the usual Saturday rush and as the news of our push and taking over sixteen miles of the German trenches came in too late, it knocked his article sky high, so that he had to revise greatly[3] . . . When we got downstairs this morning, it was to hear that Grant had been knocked up by a policeman at three o'clock in the morning – with the latch key. The front door had been left wide open and the key in the lock. Dad had had piles of maps and papers and forgot to tell anyone that he hadn't shut the door. So Grant wandered through the house to see that no burglar was hidden. Today we've breakfasted late and lunched later and now it is nearly four and Dad has just gone out to sit in the garden in a long chair.

Love to you and constant thoughts and prayers for you. May God guard and guide and bless you always, dear lad – Mummy.

Monday 3rd July
9 Greville Place, London NW

Our son

. . . Of course we can hardly think of anything but the beginning of the big, slow push, and as we have heard nothing from you since Friday you may conceive how we wait. I felt certain that even your mapping was part of the infinite detail which seems to have been well done this time. I have not cared to speculate much in writing

3 Early reports from the Somme stated that the British had 'broken into the German forward system of defences on a front of sixteen miles': *The Times*, 3 July 1916. This was misleading: the British made no appreciable advance along two-thirds of their twenty-mile front. In the week following 1 July *The Times* speculated on the number of Germans taken prisoner, but not the number of Allied soldiers killed or wounded.

to you recently; just because of being by way of hearing a good deal, I have sometimes to use in writing to you more reticence than another father would need, and that for your sake, not mine. But of course we knew long since the big effort was coming . . . Somehow 1 July had been assumed as the opening date amongst the initiated, and when our bombardment opened a week before, with Verdun near the last extremity, had things remained unchanged, imagine our tension. So many things might intervene. Who could answer for the weather of this perverse morose season; and who could answer for the Hun and what he might get to know and what he might do, being a tough, crafty beast, bound to try every shift and tax every fibre now.

On Thursday night took place one of our Other Club dinners . . . Winston only came in after ten o'clock. We did not talk in very much detail about prospects, though we were full of nothing else, but it was assumed that our affairs had been baulked a bit owing to the weather. It was a nuisance for me having to begin on Saturday morning without being sure of being able to give any hint of the main thing in my article . . .

Then about three o'clock the news boys come shouting through the streets and there in the stop-press corner . . . was the short telegram from headquarters that our advance in concert with the French had begun that morning over a front of twenty miles and was going well! It sent an extraordinary thrill through the town and newspapers disappeared in the streets, I believe like leaves before locusts. There was no shouting, no froth, no expectation of great spectacular things, but a sound feeling somehow that we were on the right lines at last. With all that, there was a proud and thankful feeling, I can call it nothing else, that we were doing something strong at last to help the French . . . But what a devil of a pinch for me. I finished the article on the lines planned before the news came, wrote a leading article on the Irish question, then rushed down to the office, transformed my stuff . . . repeated the process for the later editions . . . and at last when my article was complete for the London edition, no one would have guessed, I think, how hard it had been. I have been in many tight places, but never in a worse one. But here I go bragging in these infinitesimal personalities, when all one is really thinking about is the historic stroke and the price – less, no doubt, than the cost of the old Neuve Chapelle and Loos methods, but certain to be heavy all the same.

Of course a most stubborn prolonged business has been entered upon and if the Boche doesn't bring up his guns well at some points we shall be surprised, but we – I mean the more thoughtful sort – are more than well content. Military brains were in the plan as well as valour . . . Not that it would be at all wise to drive back the Boche too soon, even if we could do it. Better to reduce and diminish him considerably more or less where he stands. We long and long to hear from you. I will say no more of that . . .

The weather still dull, though it is July. Heart's love to you and soul's blessings. Dad.

❖

Monday 3 July – The 7th South Lancs at la-Boisselle

At zero hour on Saturday 1 July the 7th South Lancs had been kept in reserve north-west of Albert waiting to support a cavalry breakthrough that never materialised. The battalion first saw action on the Somme on Monday 3 July, when it was placed under the orders of the 57th Brigade for a hazardous night attack on the strongly fortified hamlet of la-Boisselle. The communication trenches around the 57th Brigade headquarters were full of dead men, and the commanding officer of the 7th Battalion, Colonel Winser, was forced to walk on corpses as he travelled backwards and forwards from his unit. 'It was', he later recalled, 'a beastly and never-to-be-forgotten experience.'[4] *The attack on la-Boisselle began at 9.30 p.m. and it was not until 3 p.m. the next day, Tuesday 4th, that the village was cleared of the enemy after 'bitter fighting against stubbornly held positions'. Some of the German dug-outs*

4 Captain H. Whalley-Kelly, *'Ich Dien': The Prince of Wales's Volunteers (South Lancashire) 1914–1934*, Aldershot, 1935, p. 180.

were forty feet deep, and the British losses were heavy: all four company commanders of the 57th Brigade were either killed or wounded, and it was in these circumstances that Colonel Winser assumed overall command and pressed home the attack. He was later awarded the DSO for his leadership at la-Boisselle.

❖

Tuesday 4th July
9 Greville Place, London NW

My dearest son

Mummy is out and dinner a little delayed and I have been out till now and have come into the garden to write this – so forgive pencil. Just after I came in the postman – a doddering old grey chap we have now for a postman – brought a field card for me. It makes me think you have been in the trenches or in the push, but I quite thought it might be so. The field card is dated Thursday. Of course our thoughts have been with you every moment of the time since and we long and long for more news. It is a big business and we have paid a very big price, I imagine, but for my part I always thought that inevitable when it came to the pinch – on that chalk ground where the German dug-outs are so deep, and no matter how heavy the shelling has been so many machine guns must jump up out of their caves as soon as we begin to charge.

Still, it is in no common or vulgar sense a great and glorious adventure . . . Considering everything, though some people expected more gains and smaller losses, I think we have opened admirably and that, for the first time on land, the balance of war is being turned definitely against the Germans. But of course the Huns will fight with great energy on all sides before they go down. They can do nothing else and there is credit in measuring with them. We are full of affection and pride in the army, and what it has done these four days makes the nation itself feel greater somehow. Yet we are all very quiet; and very determined. I hear it has been very difficult to keep our men from charging too far once they get loose . . .

There's not much gossip. Mummy seems so bright and happy

and active that it would do you good to see her. She has not been so entirely her dear self for three years at least. What a nuisance money is, and how I wish, often, to have had a lot of it so that I could give those I cared for every single thing they wanted and never let them be bothered by a care. Of course with four daughters in the family I have got to think about it! . . . God bless you most beloved one. Dad

PS Since your field card Mummy has a jolly letter from you written the same Thursday night. You were playing with colours and contours, very necessary things, but were certainly not in the trenches then. What a nuisance that one can't telephone to one's offspring, or aeroplane over for a talk. Yet you will be full of things, having been so close to the pulse of battle. How I wish you kept a diary . . . Dad.

Wednesday 5th July
9 Greville Place, London NW

Dearest laddie

No letter today, but a card dated Sunday so I know you were all right up till then – and a letter from Stuart who wrote as though he were busy. The one item, apart from his health welfare, he told me – of interest – that you were where you are for good, but it still leaves me burning with curiosity to know the whys and wherefores and what really your particular job is – and why you are moved from your company . . .

This morning I went and spent more money. I'm so jubilant at having no bills that I'm getting my wardrobe put right, for a year anyhow . . . Still no cook in the offing, although I've got my name in four offices and I've written to about twelve.

Dearest son, good night and God bless and guard you – dearest and tenderest love from Mummy.

Friday 7th July
9 Greville Place, London NW

Dear old boy

Such a rush yesterday, I couldn't write to you at all, so break the rule to write to you now, interrupting Friday's labours such as they are. . . .

Nothing from you this morning, so our enquiring minds are still left to speculate. I suppose it will be some time yet before you are allowed to write a full letter. Yesterday I met Courtney of the *Fortnightly Review*. His son has been in the thick of it, a flyer: Courtney looks so many years older since his boy went out. He asked me whether I ever made any inward communication to you, such as he had to his lad. I said not – that you and I could never express our inmost, but we knew what was in each other's heart, and trusting each other's depth of soul there was, in some sort, a perpetual silent conversation between us, and we had become content with it somehow. Did I interpret aright? James Knott, the Newcastle ship owner, has lost his third son in this push and has no boy left now. He has turned into a very old man suddenly and goes about talking to himself.[5] Many more things one hears. The Ulster Division has been frightfully cut up, that is clear. Heaven help us, but it is the price of honour and less, by far yet, than France and all the other nations have paid. The New Armies have made the military name of Britain greater, more splendid by far than it has ever been.

Yet they are only beginning. The Boches I think will never scoff again. And that there has been real staff brains behind our attack this time and a careful preparation of our business is what completes our immeasurable, speechless pride in you all, of that great army. Terrible as the casualties must have been in many sectors, I hear that a very high percentage of the wounds are slight. The job is bound to be a slow one for a bit, though it may very well go faster a few months hence, but it is wonderful to think that the tide has turned for good, so far as human judgement can estimate and that we Allies are on the right road at last . . .

A thunderstorm has passed and it is a most radiant evening – all leaves glistening. God bless you. Hearts love. Dad.

---

5 In fact Knott's eldest son survived the war: see Biographical Notes.

Saturday 8th July
19th Division Headquarters, St Gratien

Dear Dad

After missing the post two evenings, I'm in danger of doing the same tonight, so I must hurry with this. I've had a full evening for once.

I must tell you one thing which will bring grief to all of you. Stuart has been killed. Some men were running away in an attack on one of these places – not ours thank God – and he was shot through the head trying to rally them. It makes it more bitter to think of his life going that way, but he could not have died more bravely; he was close to the enemy at the time, in one of the worst battles since the affair began and one of the strongest points. I haven't yet found out the exact spot, but I'll get to know it. His people will like to know. I'll write to them as soon as I can.

I can't write much, for want of time. You won't have been worrying – or I hope not – knowing I'm doing office work at divisional headquarters. Your letters and Mummy's always brighten the morning. She was immensely pleased you settled up all her household bills. I'm as glad as can be that you all seem so fit and happy now.

Bye-bye. Dearest love to you and Mummy, Granny, Vi, John, Gipsy and Bunny. Ged.

Sunday 9th July
19th Division Headquarters, St Gratien

Dear Mummy

Today has been very quiet; I've no news. We're very tired, even back here. Not that I've any reason for being tired, because only on the first and second nights of the scrap I sat up late, or rather most of the night. I told you I met Solano the other day. The battalion is coming a little way back tonight for a short rest. I saw them the other night and they appeared rather fit and cheery.

In my fairly frequent leisure intervals I go on reading the *First Seven Divisions*, a rather flabby book lacking in quality. I wish I had a definite job; I'm messing about here too much. The major does everything himself, so I'm reduced to helping in odd ways.

Nothing else. Bye-bye. Dearest love to you and Dad, Granny, Vi, John, Gipsy and Bunny. Ged.

❖

Monday 10 July – The 7th South Lancs Rested

After its harrowing work at la-Boisselle on 3–4 July the 7th South Lancs endured several more days at the front under heavy shell fire. On Monday 10th the battalion was taken out of the line and sent to Hénencourt Wood to repair and refit. Colonel Winser was obliged to make good his losses: on 12 July he recommended Lieutenant R. G. Garvin for promotion to captain, and the next day requested his return from divisional headquarters, which had moved to Millencourt. Ged rejoined his battalion at Hénencourt Wood on Thursday 13 July, with the effective rank of captain.

❖

Wednesday 12th July
9 Greville Place, London NW

My dearest son

I had hardly finished writing to you last night when your letter came to tell us of the death of poor Stuart. We were cut to the heart and a shadow lies still on us all. Heaven help us in these grim times. We have known so many tragedies in our own circle or near it that we ought to be steeled, and yet nothing made us so sorrowful as Stuart being killed. He seemed to come into our little circle so intimately and to be part of our home life ever since he became your chum. I don't know how to write to his father and mother, what is there to say except alas, alas! Words seem so utterly empty and vain where the truth is so quiet and desolating. It's the poor little finely-strung mother that one grieves for and I will try to frame something that at least may be so simple as not to jar. What will help them most is that mourning is the common portion in Belfast today, owing to the way in which the Ulster Division has been cut up, and they are full of stern pride that their stock has been proven and found true unto death. We long to hear more details when you can give them. It was a gallant death. God grant that his brothers may come through safely. That all is over with Stuart, even as I write this, it seems impossible to believe.

As for our worrying over you, it is true we did, for of course we could not tell whether you were taken for permanent work at headquarters nor what emergency would arise. Of course parents at home go through a thousand deaths, as Courtney said to me the other day, saying aloud what I have said aloud to no one, but it is true and it is also unavoidable. It has been an infinite mercy for your mother that you are where you have been. Edward Goulding has written me regulated letters of reproach for not using my influence to try and get you on the Staff, which was dictated on his part by love of us all, but excruciating for me, whose love of you as you know is speechless, but I knew you would not wish me to move in that way, though I longed for it to come to you by your fitness for Staff duties, which from top to bottom are the most vital, the most indispensable business of all, and cannot be done with too much intelligence and care. That has not always been remembered and the army has suffered accordingly. So I never spoke a word nor lifted a finger, but when we knew you were attached to headquarters on your merits, inexpressible was our relief. That has done more than anything to make Mummy a different woman from what she had been for many a long month. You know, being your parents, we are not less brave and true than any other parents, nor would we be less so if the worst came, which God forbid; yet we thank God as long as you are at your present duties . . .[6]

Today I had a long talk with a very distinguished Frenchman, who has acted as liaison officer for over a year and knows and loves our army; thinks our infantry unsurpassed in the world; but he says that even yet our Staff work in certain respects can learn

6 Katharine Garvin later wrote: 'Week after week in the *Observer* my father thundered for parents to let their sons go. It was honour with him that his own should not be sheltered.': *J. L. Garvin: A Memoir*, London, 1948, p. 85.

from the experiences of last week. A number of French officers, I imagine, have been specifically attached to us since the push began, so you in your turn are at present part of the brain of the thing; but if you are summoned to rejoin your battalion you will be equal to all that honour and the glory our country demands, and your parents will not be unworthy of you. Heaven bless and keep you in all circumstances.

We have just learned this moment that Lumley arrived home on Saturday, wounded in the cheek and is getting on very well. We know no more yet, but Mummy will of course pay a call in the next day or two. I rejoice that your battalion showed itself to be solid stuff. I wonder in what corner of hell it was.

. . . Your letters are the best things that happen to us. As for the war, all the more thoughtful and informed amongst us are well satisfied: the generality of course are enormously pleased, but they cannot know what a stupendous job we are at, nor can grasp the theory of the grinding method. Berlin is shaken and more sombre than before the push, but of course the brutes will be tough for a long time yet. But they know we are on the right lines and cannot be stopped however slow the process . . . Infinite love to you, our best son and may God ever bless and guard you. Dad.

Wednesday 12th July
9 Greville Place, London NW

Dearest of sons

I have had two days such a rush that I have not had time to send you a line. Yesterday home dressmaker, lunch to Gerty and her cousin, then theatrical garden-party till 7 p.m., then dinner with Bess at 7.45, home at 11.30. Got your tragic little note about Stuart – poor, poor lad, and worse for poor mother. I must write to her tomorrow. On Monday we got back late from Aitken's, where we had a most enjoyable time. Peaceful and restful, while you poor dears were going through such times. It is awful, the whole of it . . .

Of course you feel restless, knowing what's going on. I suppose I'm selfish and pray God all the time he keeps you there and safe for a bit.

Wear Marchesi's medal please dear, all the time, for my superstition's sake.

Dearest love and blessings and prayers for you, dearest of dear sons. May God guide you and guard you in all you do and may he bless you always.

Mummy.

We were all terribly grieved about Stuart. Now we hear Lumley is home, wounded, but not much, I believe. I'll ring up tomorrow again.

Thursday 13th July
[Hénencourt Wood]

Dear Dad

I've come back to the battalion. The colonel came round this morning to the office, and when he saw me he said he wanted me back, and I was quite ready to go, so here I am. I hear they put me in yesterday for a proper captaincy, which sounds very nice. Of course I learned a fair amount with the division, but I hadn't much to do, and felt very fit and cheerful tonight with the battalion. We're camping in a field, relaxing war-worn limbs for a few days. The division did admirably in the fighting, winning commendation from the Army Commander even. Headquarters moved today. We've been in a dilapidated cottage in a poky little village, but we shifted about a mile today to a vacant chateau, which I'll tell you about tomorrow. Will you thank Mummy for the letter, and by the way, the old address now again.

Bye-bye. Dearest love to you and Mummy, Vi, John, Gipsy and Bunny. Ged.

Thursday 13th July
9 Greville Place, London NW

Dear old boy

You must have had plenty of work last week and pretty trying in its way we think, though this is a pure guess on our part. I am such a sensitive register now for all your vibrations that [I] take slighter waves than you suppose – probably things imperceptible to yourself: so, though you didn't say a word about it, [I knew] that you had passed through some depressing hours. Even when the day goes well, how must you feel if we here keep thinking of lost comrades with sighs. I hope we at home here don't make the impression on you of living a life of exaggerated jollity. That's not so, but we must all try to be cheerful there and here, now and then, otherwise it would be much worse . . . If only we could have half an hour together . . .

Mummy had a talk with Lumley today over the 'phone. He is in hospital in Berkeley Square. He told us about poor Harvey, but did not know about Stuart and was very much cut up. What a thinning. Lumley isn't allowed to be out late at night, so we are going to get him and his wife to lunch at Princes' on Tuesday. He evidently wants to meet as much as we do ourselves. There's nothing much to tell about here. We went to the Colvins' last night and of course it was dull, but yet they were dears and we were glad to have been. One doesn't want to go out to dine in order to talk about the war, not at least at such a time, and one can't always bring oneself to talk with real zest about anything else, not even about books and the theatre . . .

I see we still have very heavy fighting in the Trones Wood, but keep a strong footing there, and I am glad we are striking to the Mametz Wood and Contalmaison. I hope you can read this. I am trying to use a new fountain pen . . . Hearts love. God bless you, best son. Dad.

Thursday 13th July
9 Greville Place, London NW

Dearest of sons – my boy

I got your letter dated Monday 10th this morning and I'm glad you're getting the letters fairly regularly. We are busy here and fairly cheerful – as cheerful as one can be, though we know [what] is going on over there and we are so tired at night that we sleep and are up early . . .

I've sent your tunic back and the only pair of breeches I can find. Please dear, did you ever get those cakes from Withers – I want to know because I've paid. Also did you get the boots and ties I sent out. That I want to know, so please do try and remember to tell me when you get things.

I haven't yet written to Mrs McClinton, but will though it is a difficult letter to write . . .

Did Dad tell you there was a bare chance of our getting over in September through the French Government, and he wants me to take up French at once – but I want to get the household settled first.

Dear Lad, good night, and God bless you and guard you in all you do. My blessings and prayers for you constantly, dear heart. Mummy

Is there nothing you want sent out?

❖

Friday 14 July – The Battle of Bazentin Ridge

At dawn on Friday 14 July, the day after Ged rejoined his battalion, Rawlinson's Fourth Army launched a highly successful attack on the Bazentin Ridge. The battle lasted until 17 July, but the greatest gains were made on the first day. As on 1 July massive artillery fire-power was deployed, but on this occasion it was concentrated on a narrow front and proved decisive. The British took the ridge, the villages of Bazentin-le-Petit and Bazentin-le-Grand, and their adjacent woods, and were poised to take High Wood roughly a mile to the north-east. The attack demonstrated the offensive potential of the 'New Armies', but it also exposed the limitations of the corps command, which stopped divisional commanders from advancing on High Wood, a key strategic point, when it was only lightly defended. The enemy rapidly reinforced High Wood, which, together with Delville Wood one mile to the south-east, became a bloody drain on the British infantry for the next two months, withstanding repeated attacks. Rawlinson ordered the first of these for the night of 22–23 July, aimed at the German defences between Guillemont and Pozières. The key objective was to be the 'switch line' trench that ran through the northern tip of High Wood across open land to the north of Bazentin-le-Petit. 56th Brigade had not partaken in the battle for Bazentin Ridge, but it was to be closely involved in the attack on the switch line.

❖

Sunday 16th July
[Hénencourt Wood]

Dear Mummy

I hope you didn't worry when no letter came yesterday. Foolishly I spent the afternoon with papers and only found out the post had gone when I asked when letters were to go in. Today's letter won't have much to compensate, owing to the want of news. Yesterday we had to keep ourselves ready to move, but nothing came of it. I've got the company again and I'm allowed to wear the badges of captaincy pending formal promotion. I'm getting straight again with various papers and arrangements . . . I'm lightening my kit. All the old letters from both of you are coming home – will you put them in my bureau . . .

I can't tell you any more about Stuart. We haven't heard any more, as to who buried him, and whether his personal effects have been sent home. I saw him and we shook hands the night before the push began.

Please don't fret about me. I'm quite secure here behind the chateau.

. . . Do have a proper holiday. Bye-bye. Dearest love to you and Dad, Granny, Vi, John, Gipsy and Bunny. Ged.

Monday 17th July
[Hénencourt Wood]

Dear Mummy

This letter can claim no virtues except that it will reassure you as to my whereabouts. I'm still where I was, but with no atom of news for you. The rain is fairly persistent and heavy. Everybody is well, in spite of the weather. The men are all having baths this afternoon.

I feel very drowsy, which I hope isn't the fault of the excellent Corneille. I've nothing else at all to tell you; but can you send me some Tiptree, or some of Beach's Farm, which I'm told is as good, and a folding knife, fork and spoon. Please don't send many sweets, because I don't eat them much now.

The post goes in a few minutes. Bye-bye. Dearest love to you and Dad, Granny, Vi, John, Gipsy and Bunny. Ged.

Monday 17th July
9 Greville Place, London NW

My dearest old son

It's great news entirely as they say in the Distressful Isle, that you are back with the battalion and in prospect, too, of being a pukka captain. That will be a proud day somehow when you are a captain. The odd thing is that I thought this would happen. You know what a psychic sort of person I am and it was in my bones that your attachment to divisional HQ would not be permanent. Then when the battalion got knocked about a bit, you were certain to be wanted. It is an honourable thing for you that the colonel should want you and I feel you are happier with the old mess and among the rank and file to whom you have so long been a sort of little father. I don't suppose you will be very long out of the show. I told you we are lunching the Lumleys at Princes' tomorrow. They will be very interested and Lumley, I'm sure, will look forward more cheerfully to rejoining when he knows you are there . . .

I hope you are keeping some sort of diary, if only the very briefest and sketchiest jottings – a few lines a day. On that basis we should at least be able to ask you a few questions. Otherwise you will never tell, and will dislike to be interrogated, and we shall never know anything of our son's experience in the Great War. You must have been not so very far from the bombardments last Thursday night and up to first dawn on Friday. When the gun-work gets to a certain magnitude I don't know how on earth people compare one bombardment with another, but some think that the one you heard was the biggest shoot ever known in relation to the area it played on . . .

News of my own have I none – or none to speak of. Your Mummy is very bright and looks exceedingly pretty and when she comes in – she is out just now – she will be more than brave about your going back to the battalion, much as she liked your being at DHQ . . . Then, as the state of my wardrobe makes even old Grant wag a hopeless head, Mummy got [me] down to the tailors at last – an achievement worthy to rank almost with the Big Push – and let me in for several suits at once, so that I should no longer be the shabbiest man in London. And tonight I am taking Mummy . . . and Aunt Maggie to a comedy called *Hobson's Choice*. No more now. All the love of my heart to the best of sons and God bless and guard him. Dad.

Tuesday 18th July
9 Greville Place, London NW

Dearest and best beloved

I've been so rushed since I last wrote to you that, in spite of all my attempts, I haven't succeeded in getting you a letter written . . . Sunday we intended to rest – and the O'S.s arrived for tea and talk. Bess had been seeing John Redmond in the morning and was interesting, but we were tired. Then yesterday morning your Friday's letter arrived, telling of the chateau and in the afternoon the Thursday letter saying you were back with the battalion. I'm sorry for my own sake and glad for yours, but I wish so many of your special intimates had been spared to be with you . . .

I'm awfully pleased about Colonel Winser putting you up for a captaincy, but I'd rather you were safe – but I know the good God will take care of you. Do always wear St Gerard's medal; Lumley wears one to please his wife. I did like him so much and she is a dear . . .

No more tonight dear, dear lad. God's blessing on you always and my prayers and thoughts for ever for you. Mummy.

❖

Wednesday 19 July – The 7th South Lancs Rejoin the Battle

At 7.00 p.m. on the evening of Wednesday 19 July the 7th South Lancs, with Ged in command of D Company, left Hénencourt for trenches near Mametz Wood, where they were to relieve the 4th King's Liverpool Regiment, in readiness for the night attack of 22–23 July. The ten-mile night march was, according to Colonel Winser, 'hellish': the roads leading to the front were congested and the guides who met them at Fricourt could not find the way. As dawn broke on Thursday 20th the battalion found itself in the valley north of Caterpillar Wood, a few hundred yards from Mametz Wood. The valley offered the only suitable ground for forward gun batteries and it was packed with field artillery, which attracted heavy German shelling.[7] *Colonel Winser therefore moved his battalion to a ravine on the eastern edge of Mametz Wood, where they dug in at once. They were shelled by German 5.9-inch guns all of that day and the next, and suffered casualties. The battalion received no orders or information until the evening of Friday 21 July, when two companies were instructed to relieve the 10th Worcesters in a sector of trench north of Bazentin-le-Petit. Colonel Winser chose A Company, under Captain C. M. Hewlett, and D Company, under Captain R. G. Garvin, and they moved off in the early hours of Saturday 22nd. Zero hour for the attack was 12.30 a.m. on Sunday 23rd.*

❖

Wednesday 19th July
9 Greville Place, London NW

Dearest of sons

I have come out into the garden after dinner to write to you and hope you don't mind my scribbling on these oddments. Although it is half past nine the swallows, recking naught of daylight saving, are twittering with the long keen note that always reminds me of Orvieto and Cliveden – I suppose because at both places they swept just past one's windows. There they go again like mad, and every other bird abed . . . How jolly for you to be authorised to sport the signs of captaincy pending your being gazetted. I suppose one mustn't change the way we address you yet, until the warrant of your new rank is

---

7 Gerard Gliddon, *When the Barrage Lifts: A Topographical History of the Battle of the Somme, 1916*, Stroud, 1994, p. 91.

signed, sealed and delivered. We shall be excessively proud when you have full headship of a company. We note that you are sending a lot of little things home and they shall be stored in your room . . .

There's nothing to tell except the usual trifles – how priceless a dog Wiffles is, how he assumes dramatic ferocity when we tell him to scuffle with the kitten, which has the queerest large round paddy feet, like pen-wipers; how Jimmy grows subtle at wheedling; what a very sweet, gentle little kid Kitty is. How John goes in for vigour now, as a budding Bob Sawyer, and how Viva grinds with incredible perseverance and yet remains humorous. All things you hear for the thousandth time . . . I can of course think of little else but you and your battalion, and feel as though I knew the trench-map by heart . . .

Your operations (Haig's I mean!) seem to have been stopped by rain and mist and the Germans, by hefty attacks, have got back a bit of Delville Wood and Longueval – not for long . . .

Well, well, since I can't see to write this, you will hardly be able to read it. We wear you in our inmost hearts, Mummy and I and pray God to bless our boy. Dad.

Wednesday 19th July
9 Greville Place, London NW

Dearest of Beloved Sons

It was a joy to get your Sunday's letter by first post this morning and to learn that you were safe and sound, till that day anyhow. Hilda called out from the front door step when she was collecting from the postman 'Letter from Master Ged' – which meant a happy breakfast for us all.

As I have already sent out your tunic and the only pair of breeches I could find – the tunic minus the star and stripe – I am sending out two stars and the stripe taken off it, which I should think anyone could sew on for you.

I'm awfully pleased and proud you have got your captaincy and I'm sure you have done enough to deserve it. What is your company? D or C or B? Also did you get those boots and ties and the cakes from Withers.

I'm so glad you saw Stuart before the push and shook hands with him – and surely they will send his personal effects home . . .

Mrs Melican is coming to see me tomorrow. What a dull letter and stodgy – but I'm so tired it takes me all my time to get up in the morning and I'm almost too tired to get undressed for bed.

Good night beloved and God bless you and keep you. My prayers and blessings and love always. Mummy.

Thursday 20th July
[Ravine near Mametz Wood]

Dearest Ones

This is just a short note for you. We go into action in a day or two and I'm leaving this in case I don't come back. It brings you both, and to the girls and Granny, my very deepest love. Try not to grieve too much for me.

I hope my death will have been worthy of your trust and I couldn't die for a better cause.

Please give one of my books or something else of mine to Chidson and each of the O'Sullivans. Everything else and of course any money belongs to you to handle as you will.

Bye-bye. Heart's love and kisses.

xxx Ged.

Thursday 20th July
9 Greville Place, London NW

Dearest

It's nearly post time, so I must hurry to catch it. Reason – none, only that I was so lazy and dawdled the morning away, after I'd seen to orders and seen the new maid. The afternoon was taken up by visitors – the first Mrs Melican who came by appointment – and I've promised to get Dad to write and try to get her a post in the kitchen to wash up, for which she would get £1.0.0 a week. She brought a gift for you and only that the sergeant loved you so much, she wouldn't part with it. I opened it when she'd gone and I found his gold watch and chain, which I must return with a nice letter. Also £10, which pays the only debt the sergeant left behind him. I'm not quite sure of her, but we must do our best at any rate . . .

I've ordered the knife, fork and spoon and I've sent an order to Tiptree. Beach's isn't so good really – and I'll note about the sweets.

Do, dear lad, tell me any – the least thing – I can get or send. I wasn't sure you wanted things just now with the push and you in hot weather – but I've noted the sweets.

Dearest one, good night and God bless you. My love and prayers and blessings always for you. Mummy

Friday 21st July
9 Greville Place, London NW

My dearest old son

As it's Friday I can only send you a few hasty lines in pencil. My head was so crammed with business affairs yesterday that for once I forgot your letter, but felt something was wrong and wakened up about one in the morning, exclaiming very sleepily but very loud: 'Good heavens, I haven't written to Ged': Mummy was startled and then amused. She continues serene and active and wonderfully her best dear self as she has not been for years. She feels under God that you will surely come back to her and will be guarded through the war: that is why she is bright to a degree that will do you good to think of . . .

Your returned letters came in a batch today. What a funny little lump they make: one would have thought there would be a pile of stuff big enough to relieve the paper famine. They shall all be preserved for you like the others and what a sifting you will have and what huge archives you will have accumulated at your age. Of course there's no fresh letter from you and we didn't expect it. But we hope, all the same, to get word tomorrow . . .

It has really been a most extraordinary day; a sort of leaden, solid, still, oppressive heat . . . How sick one's infirm nature – but especially one's infirm eyes – gets over these endless masses of print and manuscript which are my portion. I feel sometimes wild to be a young man again out in the war. I see we have very heavy fighting, which was to be expected, but, like the French, are doing excellently. The Russians are slow-sure, like *That's Him* in your favourite Kipling.[8] It's a great squeeze all round on the Boche. Love past words and God bless you. Dad.

❖

J. L. Garvin wrote one more letter to his son, on 24 July, but neither this, nor that of the 21st, nor Christina Garvin's of the 20th, reached Ged. They were returned to 9 Greville Place unopened, the envelope of 21 July stamped 'Undelivered for reason stated. Return to sender': written on the front was 'Killed in Action'. This would have been a brutal way for Ged's parents to have learnt the news, but it was mercifully broken to his father by a friend, Waldorf Astor, on Tuesday 25th. Astor had learned through private channels: official confirmation came two days later. So far as can be ascertained Ged died shortly after 12.30 a.m. on 23 July, caught by machine-gun fire while leading his company against the strongly fortified German positions north of Bazentin-le-Petit. His body was never found.

8 In the *Just So Stories* (1902) there is the tale '*The beginning of the Armadilloes*', in which the young painted Jaguar recalls his mother's advice on how to tell the hedgehog and tortoise apart so that he can employ the correct technique to eat them: 'Can't curl, but can swim – / Slow-Solid, that's him! / Curls up, but can't swim – / Stickly-Prickly, that's him!'

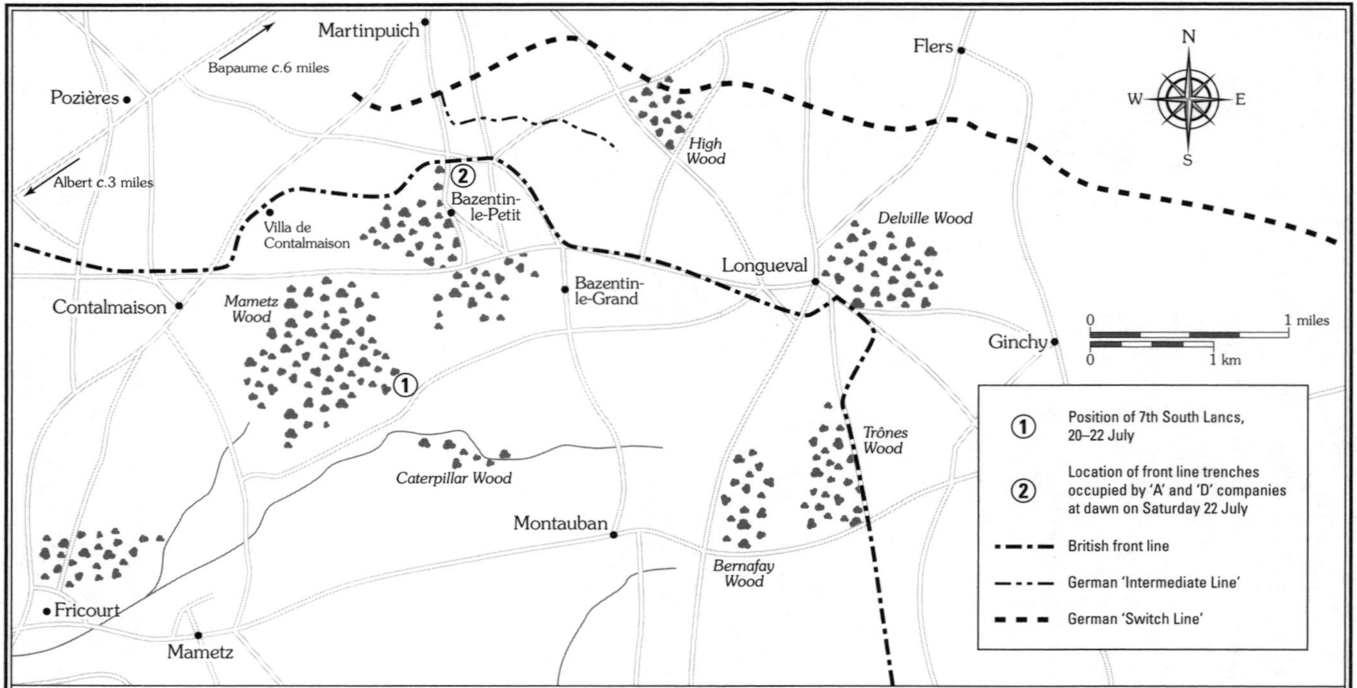

British and German Front Lines from Pozières to Guillemont, Prior to the Night Attack on the German 'Switch Line', 22–23 July 1916

EPILOGUE

I. The Battle for the 'Switch Line', 22–23 July[1]

After leaving the rest of the 7th South Lancs in the early hours of Saturday 22 July, Captains C. M. Hewlett and R. G. Garvin guided A and D Companies, respectively, towards trenches on the road line directly north of Bazentin-le-Petit, in readiness for the attack on the German 'switch line', now less than twenty-four hours away. After Hewlett was wounded during heavy shelling *en route* Ged took command of both companies, and at dawn he reported to brigade headquarters that the 7th South Lancs had relieved the 10th Worcesters, as instructed. He was also obliged to note, however, that the forward trench from which they were to advance that night, just north of their present position, 'had not been dug yet'. Neither this fact, nor headquarters' proposed solution, described in the following communiqué, could have been reassuring:

22.7.16   SECRET

1. The line of trench . . . has not been dug, and it is necessary to create a position from which 7 S.LAN.R. can advance tonight.

2. 88th Bde. R.F.A. are to create a series of shell holes along this line by fire from their How[itzer]: Batty. commencing at 2 p.m.

3. 7 N.LAN.R. will warn their advanced company at present holding the line . . . to keep down during the

1 Unattributed quotations are from the war diary of the 56th Brigade: see Bibliography.

shelling. 7 S.LAN.R. will warn their 2 companies now holding the line . . . to note the position of these shell holes, as they will be occupied by 7 S.Lan.R. as soon as it is dark, and will as far as possible join up these shell holes so as to form a continuous line.

J. N. Gilbey
Captain.
Brigade Major.
56th Infantry Brigade.

Copies to O/C 7 S.LAN.R.; 7 N.LAN.R; 88 Bde R.F.A.

Ged must have wondered how he was to identify the shell holes in question, still less make them into a 'continuous line'. His position was enfiladed by machine-gun fire from a position near High Wood, which prevented accurate observation. The 10th Worcesters had sent four platoons to capture the machine gun but had failed. There was also the difficulty posed by the terrain itself. According to the history of the 19th Division: 'The state of the ground in the neighbourhood of Mametz Wood and Bazentin was almost indescribable. Everything was pulverised and smashed beyond recognition. The whole area was a mass of shell craters, and it was difficult, if not impossible, to recognise any landmarks'.[2] This confused landscape favoured the defenders, who did not have to move across it and had chosen their positions well. Ged spoke to an officer who had patrolled the previous day towards the ridge line some 250 yards in front. He had only travelled a short distance when he was spotted by two Germans in a 'trench or keep' and was subsequently fired upon 'from several directions'. Ged reported to headquarters: 'The officer is of opinion that a German trench or possibly string of advanced posts, is just above the first crest.' This proved correct: it later became clear that the enemy had dug a defensive line, known as the 'intermediate trench', to protect the 'switch line'.

Headquarters were initially reluctant to believe in the existence of the intermediate trench, which meant that the enemy was dug in much

2 Whalley-Kelly, p. 183.

closer than previously thought, but the new information nevertheless forced a late change of plan: the 56th Brigade would now have two distinct objectives, which would be realised in two distinct phases.[3] At 10.30 p.m. on 22 July the divisional artillery would begin a general bombardment of the German defences. Before zero hour, 12.30 a.m. on the 23rd, A and D Companies would move into the 'shell-hole line', leaving B and C companies to take their place in the vacated road-line trench. At five minutes before zero hour the artillery would bring 'intense fire' to bear on the intermediate trench, and two platoons from each of A and D Companies would move to within 150 yards of it. At three minutes to zero, when only 'percussion shrapnel' would be used, 'they should creep up to within 75 yards of the objective.' Once the first line was taken the same method would be repeated for the second line – the 'switch line' – exactly one hour later.

The congestion of the battlefield, the difficulties in communication, and the strength of the German defences conspired to make a mockery of this plan. Bad weather during the day had prevented the Royal Flying Corps from spotting targets for the artillery, and that night the British guns were literally left shooting in the dark. Half an hour into the bombardment, at 11.00 p.m., Major P. C. Vellacott of the 7th South Lancs reported that: 'Enemy shelling is heavy and have suffered a few casualties . . . Our shells are occasionally bursting very near our front line.' Vellacott was in the road-line trench, but neither the signalling officer and his men, nor Colonel Winser and the rest of the battalion, had yet arrived. The communication trenches were so congested that Winser eventually took his men across open ground, and was not long delayed, but the 57th Brigade, on Vellacott's right, were so slow in assembling that their attack did not begin until 2.00 a.m., by which time the 56th Brigade were on the point of abandoning theirs.

According to Vellacott, A and D Companies moved out to the 'shell-hole line' before midnight, but there was confusion on his right, where a company of the 10th Worcesters was waiting to be relieved by the 8th Glosters. Vellacott reported: 'Have got into communication with 10th

3 For headquarters' reluctance see Wyrall, p. 54.

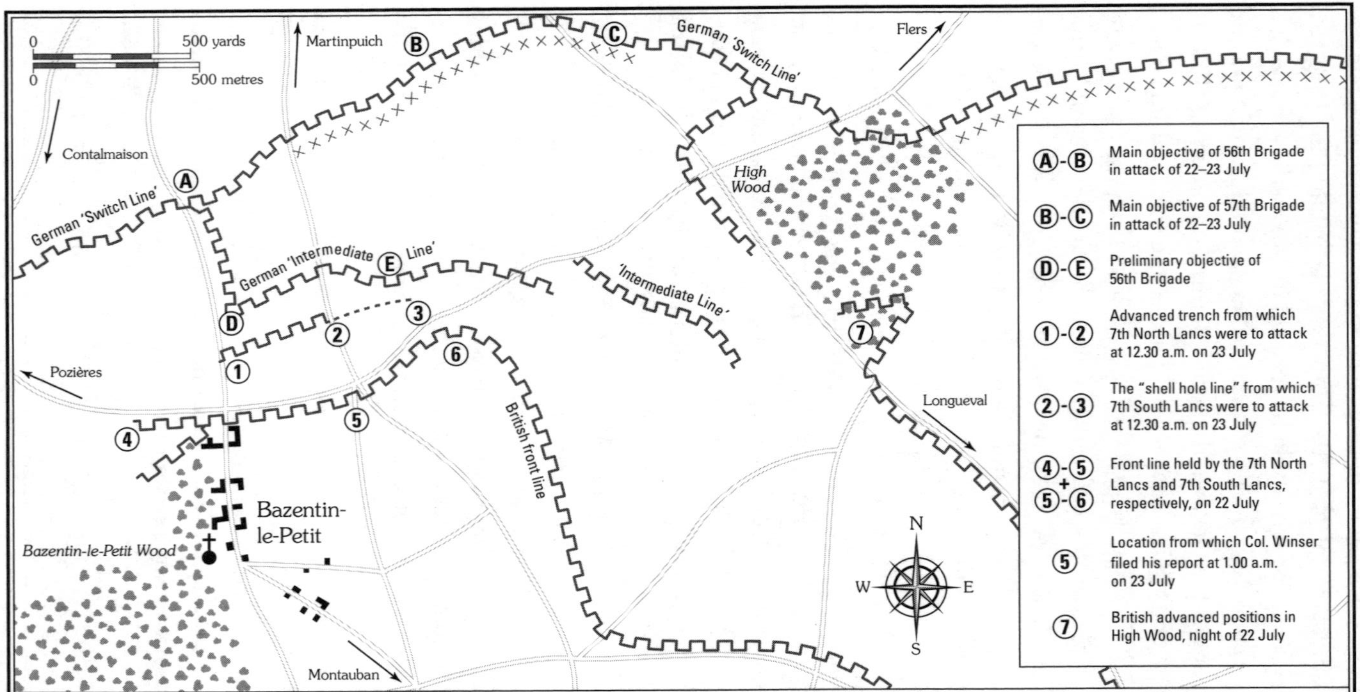

0
500 yards
0
500 metres
Martinpuich
Contalmaison
Pozières
Montauban
Flers
Longueval
German 'Switch Line'
German 'Switch Line'
German 'Intermediate Line'
'Intermediate Line'
British front line
High Wood
Bazentin-le-Petit
Bazentin-le-Petit Wood
N
S
E
W
A
B
C
D
E
1
2
3
4
5
6
7
A-B Main objective of 56th Brigade in attack of 22–23 July
B-C Main objective of 57th Brigade in attack of 22–23 July
D-E Preliminary objective of 56th Brigade
1-2 Advanced trench from which 7th North Lancs were to attack at 12.30 a.m. on 23 July
2-3 The "shell hole line" from which 7th South Lancs were to attack at 12.30 a.m. on 23 July
4-5 + 5-6 Front line held by the 7th North Lancs and 7th South Lancs, respectively, on 22 July
5 Location from which Col. Winser filed his report at 1.00 a.m. on 23 July
7 British advanced positions in High Wood, night of 22 July

THE BRITISH AND GERMAN FRONT LINES BETWEEN BAZENTIN-LE-PETIT AND HIGH WOOD, 22 JULY 1916

Worcester Regt who state that they are NOT going TO ATTACK but are waiting to be relieved by 8th Glosters. If they are not relieved they are not going to move from present position, in which case our right flank will be unprotected.' In the event the unfortunate Worcesters joined the advance, alongside the Glosters, but it was too late to cover the 7th South Lancs. At 1.00 a.m. Colonel Winser reported that his first two companies had been forced to withdraw after their initial advance, but that they had gone forward again, reinforced by a third company: 'We are having many casualties from M.G. fire from right flank and front. All the officers except one in the two leading coys are reported hit which has disorganised the companies considerably'. At 1.55 a.m. he filed another report:

23.7.16 56th Inf Bde

At 1.15 A.M. an officer of 7. N.LAN.R. reported to me that they had not advanced from their forward trench as he had read no orders. I ordered him to attack at once. From the amount of hostile M.G.fire and the number of our casualties I gather that our attack is not meeting with any great success. From reports received the majority of my officers are out of action. Enemy rifle and M.G.fire is very severe indeed and apparently is unaffected by our artillery fire. Owing to darkness and confusion cannot ascertain the exact situation. Wounded officer has just reported that he got close to 1st objective but that his men were mown down by enemy M.G. Are you arranging telephone communication with me please . . . I have no information from the right or left at present.

P. Winser
Lt Col
1.55 A.M. 7. S.Lan.R

Half an hour later he requested 'bearers and stretchers from field ambulance as soon as possible. There are a great quantity of wounded in the open who must be collected and brought in before daylight.' At 2.50 a.m. he reported that his right-hand company was 'unable to advance owing to enfilade M.G. fire – that they are digging in', and that the Glosters and Warwicks were 'quite unable to advance . . . Please send me instructions'. At 4.10 a.m. Captain G. W. Anson of the 7th North Lancs reported to Winser: 'Am enfiladed by machine gun fire which appears to come from High Wood. Afraid our casualties are very heavy.' Around this time Winser ordered a withdrawal, and the following evening, 24 July, the 7th South Lancs moved back to Mametz Wood. On 31 July, after twelve days continuously in the trenches, the battalion was relieved.[4]

According to the *Official History*, the preliminary artillery bombardment of 22 July 'undoubtedly put the enemy on his guard, but, there being no moon, the British infantry, advancing in the darkness, was expected to offer few targets to such German machine guns as might contrive to come into action'.[5] Such reckless optimism made no allowance for the illuminating effect of flares, the close proximity of the enemy, or blind firing from the German machine gunners – who knew the ground intimately and could be relied upon to 'contrive to come into action'. That they had not been disabled by the British artillery was obvious as soon as the first attacks were launched – yet the attacks continued, without any prospect of success. There had been a general failure along the whole front that night: 'The quality of the troops was not at fault. What was wrong was that the night attack of 22–23 July was poorly coordinated.'[6] Six divisions were involved, yet there were four different zero hours.

It is hard to be certain when Ged fell. It seems likely that he was killed by machine-gun fire close to the German intermediate trench between zero hour and 1.00 a.m., when Colonel Winser reported that his leading companies had been forced to retreat. Casualties from shelling had been heavy, and Ged had taken command of

---

4 The 7th South Lancs later moved north to Flanders but returned to the Somme area in October, and on the last day of the offensive, 18 November, undertook inconclusive and hazardous operations on the western outskirts of Grandcourt. The onset of winter finally closed the battle down.

5 Sir J. E. Edmonds, *History of the Great War Based on Official Documents: Military Operations France and Belgium, 1916*, London, 1932, p. 136.

6 Sheffield, p. 93.

what remained of A and D Companies. One of his comrades later recalled: 'Although his orders came at the last minute and there were a thousand things to distract him, he concentrated all his energy on working out his plan of attack.'[7] He was urging his men to spread out and hold a line when he was hit, and he was able to pass on the command before he died. The British did not advance across the same ground for a considerable time and his body was never recovered. In the hours before the attack he had discussed with a brother officer the absurdity of their position: 'Gerard said, very shrewdly, "Isn't it extraordinary that these gunners should spend the whole of a pleasant summer afternoon shooting at one another in this way?" – and then he added "and enjoy it too . . . Unless you are very near the front line it is amazingly easy to forget all about the human element."' They fell to wondering whether this human element 'came back to Army Commanders . . . whether, for example, it ever kept them awake at night'.[8] According to another officer in the 7th South Lancs: 'When orders came through for our last move into the firing line, after we had finished our packing and the rest of us were pacing about restlessly, he took out a pocket edition of la Bruyère's *Caractères* and continued to read until we moved off.' It was a significant gesture, a statement of who and what he was, and an affirmation that these things would not be obliterated by 'the crash and thunder of the Somme'.[9]

II. In Memoriam

One of the many letters of condolence that J. L. Garvin received on the death of his son was from Ged's commanding officer, Colonel Winser, who wrote: 'Personally his loss has affected me more than did that of any of the other fellows I have seen for the last time. I

7 The *Observer*, 30 July 1916.

8 Second-Lieutenant Douglas Sharp, quoted in David Ayerst, *Garvin of the Observer*, London, 1985, p. 157.

9 The *Observer*, 30 July 1916; the phrase is Churchill's: *Great Contemporaries*, (paperback edition), London, 1990, p. 84.

thought he would live and become a great man. It has been willed otherwise. I cannot write more. Of the original lot who joined at Tidworth Pennings, Vellacott and I alone remain with the battalion.'[10] In the summer of 1917 Garvin visited the Somme with his old friend Sir Edward Goulding, and almost on the anniversary of Ged's death he stood in Mametz Wood and quoted Wordsworth, whose poetry father and son had both loved: 'Not for a moment could I now behold / A smiling sea, and be what I have been: / The feeling of my loss will ne'er be old; / This, which I know, I speak with mind serene.'[11] A few days later he wrote home to Christina:

> On Thursday I went to the place where our little boy went under and thanked God you were not with me to see the dreariness of that desolation. One could not be sure of the exact spot within a hundred yards; the ground is so altered by gunfire. Thousands upon thousands of dead lie around. I will say no more, but I shall have much to tell you.[12]

On his return to England Garvin included a short note on this experience in his weekly article for the *Observer*:

> Here are poppies, deep cornflower, wild mustard, thyme and the rest . . . The spirit of earth is weaving patterns of bright wonders and robing our dead as kings. In this wilderness, half dreadful and half gay, whether we find one spot we search for, or find it not – but it must be hard by – they who rest here, rest well. They were above all that was ever dreamed of, uttermost courage, honour, truth to something above self: 'This way have men come out of brutishness / To spell the letters of the sky and read / A reflex upon earth else meaningless.'[13]

---

10 Ayerst, pp. 157–8.

11 William Wordsworth, *The Poetical Works*: VI. 'Elegiac Stanzas, suggested by a picture of Peele Castle, in a storm, painted by Sir George Beaumont' (1805).

12 JLG to CG, 25 July 1917.

13 George Meredith, 'Hymn to Colour', from the anthology *Lyra Celtica* (1896) edited by Elizabeth Sharp, quoted in Garvin's article in the *Observer*, 22 July 1917.

The poet was Meredith, whose works had helped sustain Ged during the winter of 1915–16.

Close to the time when J. L. Garvin was at Mametz Wood, Christina was visited at 9 Greville Place by two of the officers who had been with Ged in the attack on the switch line. There was little that they could offer by way of consolation. Katharine Garvin remembered her mother crying through all the rejoicing on Armistice Day, and lamenting: 'It is too late for me.'[14] She died soon after, on Christmas Eve 1918, from heart failure, which complicated an attack of the Spanish 'flu that was so lethal at that time. In the space of three years J. L. Garvin had lost his son, his mother and his wife: it was a bleak New Year in 1919, but with typical industry he began the long process of trying to make sense out of Ged's death. In March, less than four months after the armistice, he published the massive *The Economic Foundations of Peace* – a personal statement on the post-war settlement and 'a plea that his son's death should not have been in vain'.[15] Garvin sought nothing less than a new world order, and feared that another war would result from the unjust peace emanating from Paris. The first edition of the work sold out in one day. It was dedicated to Christina and to Ged, 'To The Memory of Mother And Son'. Garvin beat the same drum in his weekly articles in the *Observer*, the most notable appearing on 11 May 1919 when he likened the peace terms to the scattering across Europe of the dragon's teeth of Greek mythology: 'They will spring up as armed men unless the mischief is eradicated by other and better labours.' He concluded:

> We fought and worked, let us repeat it, not for the mere domination of the victors nor for the selfish security of a few, but for the redemption even of the enemy and for the reconciliation of mankind. That alone is worthy of the pure hearts of our young dead who fought without hate. That alone is the truth, and it will prevail.[16]

Ged was commemorated on the First World War memorial erected

---

14 Garvin, p. 88.
15 Ayerst, p. 175.
16 The *Observer*, 11 May 1919.

by Westminster School. In an irony that justified his father's fears about the post-war peace settlement this memorial was destroyed by German bombing in May 1941; Ged's name was recorded on the replacement. It is also inscribed on the war memorial at Christ Church, Oxford: although he never matriculated at the university he was admitted to the college, which did not forget him. And on the Thiepval Memorial to the Missing of the Somme there is inscribed the name of: 'Garvin, G.'. He was twenty years of age.

Chronology

A concise chronology intended primarily to give a framework to the events described in this volume. More detailed chronologies may be found in many of the reference works covering the First World War (see Bibliography).

1914

June	28	Assassination of Archduke Franz Ferdinand, heir apparent to the Austro-Hungarian throne, in Sarajevo; Austria-Hungary holds Serbia responsible
July	6	Germany communicates support for Austria-Hungary
	23	Austria delivers an ultimatum to Serbia; Serbia appeals to Russia for support
	25	Serbian army mobilises against Austria-Hungary
	28	Austria-Hungary declares war on Serbia and bombs Belgrade; the Tsar orders partial Russian mobilisation
	30	Russia proceeds to general mobilisation
August	1	Germany declares war on Russia; France begins mobilisation
	3	Germany declares war on France; the British Cabinet authorises mobilisation
	4	German army invades Belgium; Britain (and Empire) declare war on Germany
	5	Austria-Hungary declares war on Russia
	6	Kitchener appointed Secretary of State for War
	7	Kitchener appeals for 'the first hundred thousand' volunteers for the new armies
	15	Russia invades East Prussia
	23	British Expeditionary Force (BEF) engages German army at Mons, Belgium

	26	Battle of Tannenberg, East Prussia (to 30 August): German victory over Russians
	29	Kitchener's First New Army ('K1') created from first six volunteer divisions
September	2	French government leaves Paris
	6	First battle of the Marne (to 10 September): Germans retreat and entrench
	12	First battle of the Aisne, followed by the 'race to the sea' (to late October)
October	1	First battle of Arras (to 4 October)
	10	Fall of Antwerp
	15	First battle of Ypres, Flanders (to 16 November)
	29	Turkey joins the war on the side of the Central Powers
November	29	German offensive at Ypres (to 13 December)
December	10	French offensive in Champagne (to 17 March 1915)
	16	German navy bombards Scarborough and other east coast towns
	25	British and German troops share unofficial Christmas truce on Western Front

1915

January	19–20	First Zeppelin raid on Britain, over East Anglia: four killed and sixteen injured
	28	War council approves naval attack on Dardanelles
February	4	Germany announces submarine campaign in British waters (begins 18 February)
	19	Anglo-French naval bombardment of Turkish defences at Dardanelles
March	10	BEF attacks at Neuve Chapelle (to 13 March)
	11	Britain bans all 'neutral' parties from trade with Germany
	18	Naval attempt to force Dardanelles Straits fails, leading to plans for invasion
April	22	Second battle of Ypres (to 24 May); first use of gas by Germans, near Ypres

	25	First Gallipoli landings, at Cape Helles and Anzac Cove
	26	Treaty of London, by which Italy joins the Entente
	28	Allied attack on Krithia, Gallipoli
May	7	Sinking of the *Lusitania* off Ireland
	9	Aubers Ridge offensive: British attack impeded by shortage of shells
	14	*The Times*' military correspondent alleges shortage of shells on Western Front
	15	Fisher resigns as first sea lord
	17	Asquith visited by Bonar Law: he agrees to form a coalition
	18	Turkish offensive at Anzac Cove (to 24 May)
	23	Italy declares war on Austria-Hungary
	31	First Zeppelin raid on London
June	4	Allies attack on all fronts in Gallipoli
August	6	Allied landings at Suvla Bay in Gallipoli (to 10 August)
September	25	Allied offensives begin in Champagne and Artois-Loos (to 4 November)
October	12	Execution of nurse Edith Cavell by the Germans
	14	Decision taken to replace Hamilton by Monro as commander-in-chief, Gallipoli
December	7	Anglo-Indian forces besieged in Kut, Mesopotamia
	18–20	Evacuation of Suvla Bay and Anzac Cove, Gallipoli
	19	Haig replaces French as commander-in-chief on the Western Front

1916

January	8–9	Evacuation of Cape Helles, Gallipoli
	27	Military Service Act introduces conscription of single men aged eighteen to forty-one
February	21	Start of German offensive at Verdun (to 18 December)
	25	Germans take Fort Douaumont, Verdun
April	24	Easter Rising in Dublin (to 1 May)
	30	Fall of Kut
May	3–12	Execution of the leaders of the Easter Rising in Dublin

	25	Second Military Service Act extends conscription to married men
	31	Battle of Jutland, North Sea (to 2 June)
June	5	Lord Kitchener drowns in sinking of HMS *Hampshire*
	24	Beginning of bombardment of German positions on the Somme
July	1	Start of Allied Somme offensive along a twenty-five-mile front (continues to 18 November)
	4	Lloyd George becomes Secretary of State for War
	14	Battle of Bazentin Ridge on Somme (to 17 July)
August	29	Hindenburg appointed chief of German General Staff in place of Falkenhayn
September	15	Allies take Flers, Martinpuich, Courcelette and High Wood on the Somme; tanks used for first time, at Flers-Courcelette
	23	Germans begin construction of the Hindenburg Line
	26	British capture Thiepval
October	1	Beginning of the battle of Ancre Heights and Transloy Ridge
	24	French re-take Fort Douaumont, Verdun
November	13	Battle of the Ancre: British take Beaumont Hamel
	18	Winter ends Somme offensive: casualties in region of 419,000 for the British, and 204,000 for the French; estimates of German losses vary greatly
December	5	Asquith resigns
	6	Lloyd George becomes premier and forms a coalition government
	18	President Wilson's 'peace note' issued

1917

January	22	Wilson's 'peace without victory' speech to Congress
February	1	Renewed German campaign of unrestricted submarine warfare
	3	USA breaks off diplomatic relations with Germany
	24	British retake Kut

March	8	Beginning of the 'February Revolution' in Russia
	15	Tsar Nicolas II abdicates; beginning of 'Operation Alberich' – the German tactical withdrawal to Hindenburg Line
April	6	America declares war on Germany
	9	Battle of Arras, in support of the Nivelle offensive (to 17 May)
	29	Mutinies in French army (to early June) follow failure of Nivelle offensive
May	15	Pétain replaces Nivelle as the French commander-in-chief
	26	First American troops arrive in France
July	31	Beginning of the third battle of Ypres (Passchendaele) (to 6 November)
November	5	'October Revolution' in Russia
	15	Clemenceau becomes premier in France
	20	British tanks attack in force at Cambrai (to 7 December)
December	9	British take Jerusalem, Palestine
	16	Armistice on the Eastern Front

1918

January	8	Wilson's programme for peace, or 'Fourteen Points', announced
March	3	Treaty of Brest–Litovsk between Germany and Bolshevik Russia
April	9	Beginning of the German Lys offensive
	12	Haig's 'backs to the wall' order of the day
	14	Foch appointed Allied commander-in-chief on Western Front
May	27	Third battle of the Aisne: Germans reach the Marne (to 5 July)
June	3	German offensive on the Aisne halted at Château-Thierry and Belleau Wood
July	20	Beginning of the German retreat on the Marne

August	8	Allied counter-offensive in Amiens (to 15 August) triggers German collapse: Ludendorff's 'black day of the German army'
September	29	Allies cross the St Quentin canal on the Hindenburg Line
October	4	Germany and Austria-Hungary seek an armistice with American government
	5	Main Hindenburg Line positions taken by Allied armies
	30	Turkish government signs armistice of surrender with Allies; German High Seas Fleet mutinies
November	2	Allied Sambre offensive on Western Front (to 11 November)
	3	Austria-Hungary signs armistice with Allies
	5	Allied Supreme War Council accepts the terms of German armistice
	8	Foch receives German armistice delegates
	9	Kaiser flees to Holland, and abdicates; republic proclaimed in Berlin
	11	German delegation signs armistice of surrender; armistice on all fronts
December	14	Wilson arrives in Paris; Lloyd George coalition wins general election

1919

January	18	Peace conference opens in Paris
June	21	German High Seas Fleet scuttled at Scapa Flow
	28	Treaty of Versailles signed by Germany and the Allies

Biographical Notes

Of necessity the career details given below cover only those individuals who are mentioned in the text. They are also concise: the information is mostly restricted to the period pre-1918, and marriages are only noted where the spouse also appears in the text. The principal sources of reference were *Who Was Who* and the *Oxford Dictionary of National Biography* (*ODNB*). Surnames, Christian names, nicknames and initials are cross-referenced in the Index: e.g. 'AJB' will point to 'Balfour, Arthur James', and 'Gipsy' to 'Garvin, Katharine'.

Aitken, William Maxwell ('Max') (1879–1964), cr. Baron Beaverbrook, 1916; Canadian businessman, newspaper owner, politician; owner of *Daily Express*, *Sunday Express*, *Evening Standard*; Unionist MP; minister of information, 1918.

Amery, Leopold Stennett ('Leo') (1873–1955), politician and writer; tariff reformer and imperialist; on *The Times* editorial staff, 1899–1909; Unionist MP; served in Flanders and Near East, 1914–16.

Astor, Waldorf (1879–1952), 2nd Viscount; owner of the *Observer* from 1915; enjoyed good relations with Garvin until late 1930s when latter's unwavering support of Churchill caused breach; in February 1942 Astor declined to renew Garvin's contract.

Astor, William Waldorf (1848–1919), Baron, 1916; Viscount, 1917; born in New York; moved to England 1891 after inheriting fortune; British subject, 1899; purchased *Pall Mall Gazette*, 1893, and the *Observer*, 1911 – on condition its editor, J. L. Garvin, relinquish his one-fifth share and become editor of *Pall Mall Gazette*; in 1915 he gave both titles to his son, Waldorf.

Asquith, Herbert Henry (1852–1928), cr. Earl of Oxford and Asquith, 1925; Liberal statesman; home secretary, 1892–5; chancellor of the exchequer, 1905–8; prime minister 1908–16; secretary for war, March–August 1914; resigned as premier 5 December 1916; succeeded by David Lloyd George; lost his eldest son, Raymond, on the Somme.

Balfour, Arthur James ('AJB') (1848–1930), cr. Earl, 1922; nephew of Conservative statesman, Lord Salisbury, under whom he served as foreign secretary, and whom he succeeded as premier; Unionist leader in Commons, 1891–1911; prime minister, 1902–5; first lord of the admiralty, 1915–16; foreign secretary, 1916–19.

Bonar Law, Andrew (1858–1923), Canadian-born statesman and politician; succeeded Balfour as Unionist leader, 1911; colonial secretary, 1915–16; chancellor of the exchequer, 1916–18; prime minister 1922–3; lost two sons in the war.

Bottomley, Horatio (1860–1933), newspaper proprietor, politician and convicted swindler; produced the patriotic paper *John Bull*; violently anti-German; a highly effective public orator who made many recruiting speeches.

Bridges, (Major-General) Sir (George) Tom (Molesworth) (1871–1939), KCMG, 1919; GOC of the 19th (Western) Division from December 1915 until September 1917, when severely wounded; head of the British War Mission in United States, 1918. The nephew of the poet laureate, Robert Bridges, and a hero of the retreat from Mons.

Butters, Henry Augustus ('Harry') (1892–1916), California-born son of a San Francisco industrialist; educated in England; became friendly with the O'Sullivan family; an Anglophile, he volunteered in 1915, and was commissioned in the Royal Field Artillery; saw action at Loos; although shell-shocked in June 1916 he returned to his unit and was killed on 31 August. Winston Churchill wrote an appreciation of his life that was published in the *Observer*, alongside another by J. L. Garvin.

Carson, Sir Edward (1854–1935), knighted, 1900; Baron, 1921; Dublin-born lawyer, leader of the Ulster Unionists; implacable opponent of home rule; attorney-general, 1915; first lord of the admiralty, 1917; member of war cabinet without portfolio, 1917–18.

Casement, Sir Roger (1864–1916), born in Dublin; entered British consular service; exposed human rights violations in Africa and South America; knighted, 1911; joined Irish volunteers, 1913; tried to raise Irish brigade from prisoners of war in Berlin; captured on Kerry coast, 21 April 1916; tried for treason and hanged, 3 August 1916.

Cazalet, Maud Lucia *née* Heron-Maxwell, wife of William Marshall Cazalet of Fairlawne, Tonbridge, Kent, and the mother of the Conservative MPs Victor Cazalet and Thelma Cazalet-Keir.

Cecil, Lord (Edgar Algernon) Robert Gascoyne- (1864–1958), third son of the Marquess of Salisbury; Viscount Chelwood, 1923; lawyer, politician and diplomat; under-secretary of state for foreign affairs, 1915–19; an architect of the League of Nations and Nobel Peace Prize winner, 1937.

Chamberlain, (Joseph) Austen (1863–1937), statesman and Unionist politician, the son of Joseph, and half-brother of Neville; secretary of state for India, 1915–17; member of war cabinet, 1918.

Chidson, (Lowthian) Hume (1896–1946), Ged's school friend; joined Westminster School as a non-resident King's Scholar, 1910; admitted to Trinity College, Cambridge, with scholarship, 1914; second-lieutenant, 4th Battalion East Surrey Regiment, 15 August 1914; in France until October 1915, and Macedonia from November; attached to machine gun corps; promoted major, 1918; took BA at Cambridge after war; barrister, 1926.

Churchill, Jeanette *née* Jerome ('Jennie'), Lady Randolph (1854–1921), society hostess and writer, the mother of Winston Churchill.

Churchill, Sir Winston Leonard Spencer (1874–1965), eldest son of Lord Randolph Churchill and Jennie (*née* Jerome) of New York; first entered Parliament as a Unionist in 1900, but broke with his party over tariff reform, and sat as a Liberal from 1906 (though later rejoining the Conservatives); first lord of the admiralty, 1911–15; chancellor of the duchy of Lancaster, 1915; battalion commander, 6th Royal Scots Fusiliers, France, 1915–16; minister of munitions, 1917–19. He married Clementine Ogilvy *née* Hozier (1885–1977), the second of the four children of Sir Henry and Lady Blanche Hozier; much admired for her classical beauty she married Churchill after a brief courtship, September 1908.

Colefax, Sir Arthur (1866–1936), patent lawyer and briefly (1910) Unionist MP; head of scientific department, ministry of munitions, 1914–18. He married, in 1901, Sybil *née* Halsey (1874–1950), daughter of William Halsey, of the Indian civil service; the Colefaxes were society figures and friends of J. L. Garvin.

Colvin, Sir Sidney (1845–1927), knighted, 1911; Slade professor of fine art at Cambridge; keeper of prints and drawings at British Museum, 1884–1912; in 1903 married his long-term companion, Frances Sitwell (1839–1924), after the death of her husband.

Courtney, William Leonard (1850–1928), philosophy tutor at New College, Oxford; left Oxford for journalism, becoming editor of *Daily Telegraph* and *Fortnightly Review*; in 1895 he accepted an article for the *Review* from the young and unknown J. L. Garvin, beginning a long association that was important to both men.

Cowans, (General) Sir John (1862–1921), knighted, 1913; quartermaster-general, and a member of the army council; at War Office, 1912–19.

Croft, Henry Page (1881–1947), 1st Baron Croft, 1940; entered Parliament as Unionist, 1910; joined Hertfordshire Regiment, 1914; temporary brigadier-general, February 1916.

Darling, Charles John (1849–1936), 1st Baron Darling; high court judge, 1897–1923; author of (*inter alia*) *On the Oxford Circuit and Other Verses* (1924): 'a professional oddity' given to 'inveterate facetiousness' (*ODNB*).

Davis, Sir Edmund Gabriel (1861–1939), knighted, 1927; Melbourne-born, Paris-educated mining financier and art collector; gave major collection of modern British artists to Luxembourg gallery in Paris, 1915. Married, in 1889, his cousin Mary Zilla Hartford.

Dillon, John (1851–1927), Irish Nationalist leader; land reform agitator; opponent of Parnell; first entered Parliament 1880; supported third Home Rule bill; succeeded Redmond as leader of the Irish Parliamentary Party, 1918.

Dmowski, Roman (1864–1939), Polish politician and statesman, and principal leader of nationalist movement; saw Triple Entente as best guarantee of Polish independence.

Fasken, (Major-General) Charles (1855–1928), veteran of Afghan War, 1878–80; commander of Ferozepore Brigade, India, 1906–11; retired January 1914; recalled to train 19th Division, 1914–15; divisional commander from September 1914 to June 1916.

Fisher, Andrew (1862–1928), Ayrshire coal miner and union official; emigrated to Queensland, 1885; became leading trade unionist and politician; three times prime minister of Australia; high commissioner for Australia in London, 1916–21.

Fisher, (Admiral) John Arbuthnot ('Jacky') (1841–1920), OM, 1905; cr. Baron, 1909; innovatory, effective and ruthless first sea lord, 1904–10; recalled to Admiralty by Churchill, October 1914; precipitately resigned, 15 May 1915, over Churchill's Dardanelles' policy; laid before prime minister memorandum setting out terms on which he would return to Admiralty and win the war; never returned.

French, Sir John Denston (1852–1925), Viscount, 1916; Earl of Ypres, 1921; field marshal, 1913; commander-in-chief, BEF, August 1914–December 1915; of home forces, 1915–18.

Garvin, Catherine *née* Fahy ('Maima') (d. November 1916), mother of Michael and James Louis Garvin; widowed when her sons were age five and two, respectively; lived with JLG throughout his married life, and was a severe trial to her daughter-in-law, Christina.

Garvin, Christina Ellen *née* Wilson ('Tina') (1876–1918), daughter of Robert Wilson, superintendent of police in Newcastle upon Tyne; married J. L. Garvin in 1894 and they had five children, of which the first-born was Roland Gerard, 'Ged'; four daughters followed (see below); Christina suffered from chronic ill-health and died of heart failure on Christmas Eve 1918.

Garvin, James Louis (1868–1947), born in Birkenhead, 12 April 1868, the second of the two sons of Michael Garvin (1832–1870), labourer, and his wife Catherine Fahy (d. 1916); married, 1894, Christina *née* Wilson – one son and four daughters (see below); after her death in 1918 he married, 1921, Viola Taylor Woods; in 1920s purchased a house in Beaconsfield, 'Gregories', and withdrew from London political and social scene; editor of the *Observer*, 1908–1942; left the *Observer* February 1942 over his support for Winston Churchill; continued in journalism; declined public honour from Lloyd George, but accepted Companion of Honour from Churchill, 1941; died 23 January 1947.

Garvin, Katharine ('Kitty' or 'Gipsy') (1904–70), the Garvins' fourth child; she followed her elder sister Viola to Somerville College, Oxford, and pursued an academic career in English literature; wrote a memoir of her father, published 1948.

Garvin, Michael (1865–1914), J. L. Garvin's elder brother; schoolmaster; worked in Hull and Newcastle; emigrated to South Africa; died in Cape Town, 31 December 1914.

Garvin, Roland Gerard ('Ged') (1895–1916), the Garvins' first child, born 12 October 1895; homeboarder, Westminster School, 1908–1914; admitted to Christ Church, Oxford, 1914; joined 7th Battalion, South Lancashire Regiment, 28 August 1914; commissioned second-lieutenant, 19 September; lieutenant, 3 August 1915; temporary captain, 12 July 1916; killed in action, Bazentin-le-Petit, 23 July 1916.

Garvin, Una Christina ('Noonie' or 'John') (1900–65), the Garvins' third child; married Dr John Ledingham; studied medicine, London School of Medicine for Women (later the Royal Free Hospital School); physician at the Royal Free Hospital, 1931–65.

Garvin, Ursula ('Bunny' or 'Jimmy') (1907–2007), youngest of the Garvin children; studied at Sorbonne; became a linguist; librarian at British Library in Florence; married, in 1936, Leo Slaghek, Italian engineer; lived in Milan during Second World War.

Garvin, Viola ('Vi' or 'Viva') (1898–1959), the Garvins' second child and eldest daughter; she read English at Somerville College, Oxford, and was literary editor of the *Observer*, 1926–42; thereafter a freelance writer.

Goulding, Edward Alfred (1862–1936), Baron Wargrave, 1922; politician and financier; later chairman of Rolls Royce Ltd; dedicated tariff reformer, and influential member of Unionist Party; one of J. L. Garvin's greatest friends.

Greenwood, Hamar (1870–1948), Viscount, 1937; Canadian-born lawyer and politician; lieutenant-colonel commanding 10th (Service) Battalion, South Wales Borderers; served European War, 1914–16.

Gwynne, H. A. (1865–1950), journalist with wide experience of foreign affairs; editor of the *Morning Post*, 1911–37.

Haig, Douglas (1861–1928), cr. 1st Earl Haig, 1919; became field marshal at end of December 1916 (noted in *The Times*, 1 January 1917); commander, First Army, 1914–15; commander-in-chief, BEF, 1915–19.

Haldane, Richard Burdon (1856–1928), 1st Viscount Haldane, 1911; Liberal statesman; reforming secretary of state for war, 1905–12; lord chancellor, 1912–15; once a close friend of H. H. Asquith, he was a casualty of the May 1915 political crisis.

Hamilton, Nina Mary Douglas- *née* Poore (1878–1951), Duchess of Hamilton; married, in 1901, Alfred Douglas-Hamilton (1862–1940), 13th Duke; she was the long-term companion of Admiral 'Jacky' Fisher, and his literary executor.

Hamilton, (General) Sir Ian Standish (1853–1947), KCB, 1900; Chief of Staff to Kitchener in Boer War; commander, Mediterranean Expeditionary Force, 1915; commander-in-chief at Gallipoli; replaced in October by General Sir Charles Monro (1860–1929), who oversaw the successful evacuation of the peninsula.

Hankey, Maurice Pascale (1877–1963), cr. Baron, 1939; secretary to committee of imperial defence, 1912–38, and to war cabinet, 1916–19; highly valued for his judgement; in the opinion of Balfour: 'Without Hankey we should not have won the war.'

Harvey, Sir John Martin (1863–1944), actor and theatre manager, who started under Irving at the Lyceum; first played *Hamlet* in 1904.

Healy, Timothy Michael (1855–1931), Irish Nationalist, first entered Parliament 1880; land reformer, but later anti-Parnellite; sympathised with Sinn Féin, and was the first governor-general of the Irish Free State.

Hoover, Herbert (1874–1964), thirty-first president of the United States of America, 1929–33; in October 1914 Hoover established a neutral organisation to obtain and distribute food in Belgium, which the British and German governments allowed.

Jellicoe, (Admiral) Sir John (1859–1935), in command of the Grand Fleet, 1914; criticised for excessive caution at the battle of Jutland, 1916, but, according to Churchill, 'The only man on either side who could lose the war in an afternoon.'

Jones, Sir Roderick (1872–1962), KBE, 1919; with Reuters Agency and, from 1915, principal proprietor; in charge of cable and wireless propaganda, 1916–18.

Kerr, Philip (1882–1940), 11th Marquess of Lothian; politician and diplomat; founder and editor of the *Round Table*, 1910–16; secretary to prime minister, 1916–21.

Kitchener, Horatio Herbert ('K of K' or simply 'K') (1850–1916), 1st Baron Kitchener of Khartoum, 1898; 1st Earl Kitchener, 1914; as sirdar of the Egyptian army, 1892, retook the Sudan, 1896–8; Lord Roberts's Chief of Staff in South African war, 1899–1902; commander-in-chief, Indian army, 1902–9; secretary for war, 1914–16; drowned when HMS *Hampshire* torpedoed, 5 June 1916.

Knott, Sir James (1855–1934), cr. Baronet, 1917; rose from office boy to ship owner, and founded the Prince Line; Unionist MP; lost two of his three sons in war: the youngest Henry, died of wounds, September 1914; James died on the Somme, 1916; the eldest, Thomas, had been thought dead at Gallipoli but survived the war.

Kohlsaat, Herman H. (1853–1924), millionaire publisher, and editor of the *Chicago Times-Herald* and the *Chicago Record-Herald*; a friend of Taft, Roosevelt, etc.

Lloyd George, David (1863–1945), Viscount, 1945; Liberal statesman; president of board of trade, 1905–8; chancellor of the exchequer, 1908–15; minister of munitions, 1915–16; secretary for war, 1916; prime minister, 1916–1922; in popular parlance 'the man who won the war.'

McClinton, (John) Stuart (d. 1916), comrade and close friend of Ged's in the 7th South Lancs; an Ulsterman, he represented his province at rugby against Leinster; died on 5 July 1916 in the fighting around la-Boisselle; his body was never recovered and his name is inscribed on the Thiepval Memorial.

McKenna, Reginald (1863–1943), married, in 1908, Pamela *née* Jeykll, daughter of the gardener Gertrude Jeykll; entered Parliament as a Liberal, 1895; rose quickly under Asquith, and was home secretary, 1911–15; chancellor of the exchequer, 1915–16.

Maggie, Aunt, née Wilson, Christina Garvin's sister, from Newcastle; she lived in Whitley Bay.

Marchesi, Blanche (1863–1940), famed bel canto music teacher, and daughter of the renowned vocalist and teacher Mathilde Marchesi (d. 1913); the Marchesis lived on the opposite side of Greville Place and were friends of the Garvins.

Melican, Sergeant (d. 1916), physical training instructor and fencing instructor at Westminster School; held in high esteem by Ged, whom he taught fencing; he also instructed Una Garvin in foils; his straitened circumstances only became clear after his death, and the Garvins gave financial help to his widow.

Morant, Sir Robert Laurie (1863–1920), KCB, 1907; leading civil servant and educationalist; chairman of the national insurance commission, 1912–19; he married, in 1896, Helen *née* Cracknell.

Murray, (General) Sir Archibald (1860–1945), Chief of Staff to Sir John French, 1914–15; relieved in January 1915; briefly chief of Imperial General Staff, September 1915; commander of the Egyptian Expeditionary Force, 1916–17.

Northcliffe, Lord Alfred Harmsworth (1865–1922), cr. Viscount, 1917; journalist and newspaper proprietor; owner of *Daily Mail* (which he founded in 1896), *The Times*, and from 1905 the *Observer*; in 1908 Garvin became editor and one-fifth owner, but in 1911 Northcliffe decided to sell after they quarrelled, although he generously gave Garvin time to find a buyer; Northcliffe was a leading advocate of conscription and a strident critic of the Asquith government.

O'Sullivan family, American family who became close friends of the Garvins through the comradeship of Ged Garvin and Curtis O'Sullivan, who met at Westminster School. Curtis's father, Denis, was a singer, and his wife, Elisabeth ('Bess'), was a tremendous support to Christina Garvin, caring for her and her children; nicknamed 'Mrs O'S.', 'Step', or 'Stepmother' by the Garvins; Curtis served in the United States army during both world wars.

Redmond, John (1856–1918), Irish Nationalist politician, and leader of the Irish Parliamentary Party during the passage of third Home Rule bill; regarded as a moderate he quickly lost ground to more radical Nationalists after the outbreak of war in 1914.

Reid, Sir Robert Threshie (1846–1923), cr. 1st Earl Loreburn, 1911; Liberal politician and lawyer; lord chancellor, 1905–12.

Roze, Madame *née* Ponsin (1846–1926), French soprano for whom Bizet wrote the part of *Carmen*.

Sackville, Lady Victoria (1862–1936), mistress of Knole in Kent, which her father inherited; she married her cousin, Lionel Sackville West, 1890; their daughter was Vita Sackville West.

Saull, Annie, indispensable housekeeper and amanuensis of the Garvin family, 1909–47; she joined the Garvins in 1911, by which time she already had a large, young family, and an invalid husband; he died in 1918, and at least two of the children were sent to a Barnado's home.

Scott, Charles Prestwich ('C. P.') (1846–1932), renowned editor of the *Manchester Guardian*, 1872–1929; entered Parliament as a Liberal, 1895; opposed Boer War and also, initially, British intervention in the European war, August 1914; opposed conscription, 1916; favoured a negotiated peace, 1917.

Seely, J. E. B. ('Jack') (1868–1947), soldier and politician; secretary of state for war, June 1912–March 1914; resigned over 'Curragh' incident; special service with BEF, 1914; brigadier-general commanding the Canadian Cavalry Brigade, 1915–18.

Selfridge, (Harry) Gordon (1858–1947), American-born businessman; settled in England and founded Selfridge & Co., at the western end of Oxford Street, 1909.

Simon, Sir John Allsebrook (1873–1954), knighted, 1910; cr. Viscount, 1940; entered Parliament as Liberal, 1906; attorney-general, 1913–15; home secretary, 1915–16; considered resignation in opposition to the war, August 1914; eventually resigned over conscription, January 1916.

Smith, Frederick Edwin ('F.E.') (1872–1930), Baron Birkenhead, 1919; Earl, 1922; lawyer, politician and statesman; on opposition front bench in Commons from 1911; die-hard opponent of Parliament bill, 1911, and Irish home rule; solicitor-general, 1915; attorney-general, 1915–19.

Solano, (Captain) E. J., army officer, and frequent visitor to 9 Greville Place; author of *The Pacifist Lie: The Case for Sailors and Soldiers Against Conscientious Objectors* (1918), which argued the justness of the Allies' cause and the wickedness of the Germans'.

Spender-Clay, (Captain) Herbert Henry (1875–1937), one of the wealthiest commoners in England; served in Life Guards in Boer War; resigned commission, 1902; married, in 1904, Hon. Pauline Astor, daughter of William Waldorf; Unionist MP; served on Staff in European war, 1914–18.

Straubenzee, (Brigadier-General) Casimir Henry Claude van (1864–1943), served in the European War, 1914–17; CB, 1916.

Stead, Henry Wickham (1871–1956), foreign correspondent with *The Times* and later, 1919–22, editor; lived in Vienna in 1914, and as the European crisis unfolded in July of that year took a bellicose line in *The Times*.

Talbot, Lady Caroline Mary *née* Bertie, (Lady Edmund) (1859–1938), daughter of 7th Earl of Abingdon; married, in 1879, Edmund Talbot (aka Fitzalan-Howard) (1855–1947), chief Unionist whip, 1913–21.

Thomas, James Henry ('J. H.') (1874–1949), worked as an engine driver before becoming general secretary of the National Union of Railwaymen in 1918; joined Labour Party and entered Parliament, 1910; opposed conscription in 1916.

Vellacott, (Major) Paul Cairn (1891–1954), major, South Lancashire Regiment; brigade-major, with General Staff; DSO, 1917; headmaster of Harrow School, 1934–9; later master of Peterhouse, Cambridge; director of political warfare, Middle East, 1942–4.

Wiffles, Ged's dog, 'a smooth fox-terrier of the old type', who came to the Garvins by way of Madame Marchesi (see above).

Wilson, Lady Sarah (1865–1929), the youngest daughter of the 7th Duke of Marlborough, and Winston Churchill's aunt; war correspondent in the Boer War; her husband, Gordon Wilson, wrote for the *Daily Mail*.

Winser, Colonel (Charles Rupert) Peter (1880–1961), one of two ex-regulars recalled to the South Lancashire Regiment, September 1914, to lead the newly formed 7th (Service) Battalion; took command 27 September 1915; DSO, 1916; later brigadier-general; bar to DSO, 1918; described by Major-General Tom Bridges (above) as 'a stout fighter'.

GLOSSARY

A Note on Military Usage: 'Battalion, Brigade, Division'

The 7th (Service) Battalion of the South Lancashire Regiment, also known as 'The Prince of Wales's Volunteers', was included in the 56th Brigade of the 19th (Western) Division, and formed part of the Second New Army ('K.2') authorised by the army council on 11 September 1914. 'Service' battalions supplied the new armies and were numbered after a regiment's existing regular, reserve and territorial battalions. During the Somme offensive the 19th Division was part of Rawlinson's Fourth Army.

Army & Navy Store – London department store, in Victoria Street, which opened in 1872; it sold groceries, clothes and guns, and the clientele was originally restricted to the upper ranks of the armed forces and their widows.

Aunt Sally entertainment – popular game of medieval origin in which players throw wooden sticks, or batons, at a wooden skittle known as a 'doll'.

Babylon – J. L. Garvin's wry term for London, used to suggest its corruption; an allusion to the great city of Mesopotamia in ancient times.

'Bairnsfather's *Bystander* cartoons' – (Captain) Bruce Bairnsfather (1888–1959), of the Royal Warwickshire Regiment, studied art before the war, and his cartoons of trench life were published in *The Bystander* from 1915 as 'Fragments from France'; though frowned upon by officialdom they were immensely popular and the first collected volume (1916) sold out within weeks; others followed.

Balzac – an allusion to the works of Honoré de Balzac (1799–1850), French novelist and playwright; used by JLG to suggest an 'extraordinary mixture of ultra-romance and grim realism' (JLG to RGG, 3 January 1916).

bantams – British soldiers who were under the standard height for enlistment.

Barmecide breakfast – in the *Arabian Nights* one of the Barmecide princely family of Baghdad put a succession of empty dishes before a beggar, pretending that they contained a sumptuous repast – a fiction that the beggar good-humouredly accepted.

Barnardo's Home – a refuge for destitute and orphaned children, part of an international organisation begun by the evangelical Christian, Dr Thomas Barnado (1845–1905).

BEF – the British Expeditionary Force: a force for overseas service originating in the army reforms of 1908; on 5 August 1914 it was decided to send the BEF to France to support the French against the invading Germans; only five divisions, around 100,000 men, could be deployed, reflecting the small scale of Britain's professional army.

Bob Sawyer – character from Charles Dickens's *Pickwick Papers*, who 'had about him that sort of slovenly smartness and swaggering gait which is peculiar to young gentlemen who smoke in the streets by day, shout and scream in the same by night'.

boracic ointment – an antiseptic remedy then in common use.

bouleversement – an upheaval, especially a violent one.

brass-hats – high-ranking officers.

British Warm – the standard issue British army officer's overcoat.

Burberry – London outfitters renowned for its raincoats.

'Burke's denunciation of Hastings' – in 1786 Edmund Burke (1729–97) famously laid before Parliament twenty-two charges of tyrannical and arbitrary conduct against Warren Hastings, first Governor-General of Bengal (and effectively India), thus beginning Hastings's impeachment.

'Captain Fracasse' – an allusion to the eponymous hero of Théophile Gautier's (1811–72) *Le Capitaine Fracasse* (1863), a romantic adventure story that Ged read while at the front.

Casse-noisette – *The Nutcracker*, by Tchaikovsky (1892)

'cheers and a tiger' – in America a 'tiger' is a final yell given in a round of cheering.

Chinese paragons – relates to Guo Tujing's *The Twenty-Four Chinese Paragons of Filial Piety*, written in the Yuan dynasty; it describes the self-sacrificing behaviour of children for their parents.

compulsion – military conscription, also called 'national service' and 'general compulsion', and the subject of great political controversy. The Military Service Act of 27 January 1916 conscripted single men aged between eighteen and forty-one; a second Act, 25 May, extended conscription to married men.

Clausewitz – General Carl von Clausewitz (1780–1831), Prussian soldier and military theorist; the texts containing his influential work *On War* were published posthumously between 1832 and 1834.

Constitutional Club – Conservative political club in London, founded in 1883.

Cording – 'nautical and sporting waterproofers and tailors', according to their 1860 advertisement; founded by John Cording in the Strand in 1839, the business moved to Piccadilly in 1877, and specialised in boots and waterproof garments.

Dardanelles – the narrow straits dividing Asia Minor from the land mass of Europe, and connecting the Aegean with the Sea of Marmara; the straits offered a gateway to Constantinople from the west and were guarded by formidable Turkish defences.

'Daylight Saving Bill' – on 21 May 1916 the Summer Time Act became law, and all British clocks ran one hour before GMT between 21 May and 30 September, giving longer, lighter evenings. Although parents found it difficult to get their children to bed, the scheme was thought to increase national efficiency and was permanently instituted.

Der Letzte Tag – 'the day of expiation' (German).

Dolly Vardenish – *Dolly Varden* was a 1902 musical comedy based on Dickens's *Barnaby Rudge*: on stage the eponymous heroine is flirtatious and colourfully dressed, and in Dickens 'the very pink and pattern of good looks'.

Dundreary, Lord – a good-natured but brainless English aristocrat – a fictional character in Tom Taylor's 1858 play *Our American Cousin*.

F&M – Fortnum & Mason, off Piccadilly, famous and long-established purveyors of fine foods and provisions.

Faust – Goethe's *Faust* (1832) has two parts: at the end of the first, Faust, having sold his soul to the devil, is left remorseful and unfulfilled, but in the second he finds redemption and is ultimately borne aloft by angels.

field card – 'field service postcards' conveyed essential information through a series of statements that the sender deleted as applicable: e.g. 'I am quite well / I have been admitted to hospital'; the sender wrote only their name and the date – each card carried an official warning that it would be destroyed if more were added.

five-nine – a German 5.9-inch artillery shell.

flageolet – a small flute; Ged was an accomplished flautist and pianist.

Fullers – chain of teashops, famous for their walnut cake.

Gautier (Théophile) (1811–72) – French author, whose works Ged was likely to have first encountered at school.

Gideon – outnumbered by the Midianites, Gideon, 'a man of Israel', armed his three hundred men with empty pitchers which they broke in unison, while blowing trumpets and crying 'The sword of the Lord, and of Gideon'. The Midianites fled and their princes were slain: Book of Judges, Chapter 7.

grass-widower – a man who is divorced or separated from his wife.

grinding method – the concept of attrition: the destruction of the manpower of the opposing army; contrasts with 'breakthrough'. J. L. Garvin wrote in the *Observer* on 9 July: 'To gain ground is not our object; our business is to grind the enemy down where he stands.'

gründlich – thorough, or indepth (German).

guncotton – a form of nitrocellulose that came into common use as an ingredient in gunpowder in the mid-nineteenth century.

hate – the *Hymn of Hate* was an anti-British song popular in Germany at the outbreak of the war; it was sung in German trenches, and the British called an enemy artillery bombardment a 'hymn of hate', or simply a 'hate'.

Henry of Navarre – Henry III, King of Navarre, who became Henry IV of France (1553–1610).

Herzgeliebte – 'Heartbeloved' (German); used by Schiller in a letter to his parents.

Homeboarder – all day pupils at Westminster were assigned to one of two houses in the school set apart for them: one was called 'Ashburnham' and the other, more prosaically, 'Homeboarders', of which Ged was a member; in 1956 Homeboarders was renamed 'Wrens' after the great architect, who was an Old Westminster.

Homeric – applied by JLG to the Gallipoli campaign ('super-Homeric'), which was fought in the vicinity of ancient Troy.

Home Rule – the policy of re-establishing in Dublin a parliament that would legislate for the internal affairs of Ireland; it was proposed by the Liberal Party in three Bills, 1886, 1893 and 1912.

Hugo, Victor (1802–85) – French poet, novelist and dramatist, and the author of *Les Miserables* (1862).

Inferno – one of the three parts of Dante's *Divina Commedia* (the others being *Purgatorio* and *Paradiso*); in the third circle of hell are the gluttons, who are forced to lie in the slush created by freezing rain, black snow and hail – representing the waste of their lives on earth.

'The Slough of Despond' – in Part One of John Bunyan's *Pilgrim's Progress* (1678), the 'slough of despond' is a deep bog that Christian must cross to get to the wicket gate.

Jaeger – London clothes store renowned for its quality; during the First World War it produced sleeping bags, underwear and even horse blankets.

Keating's – vermin powder; used by Florence Nightingale during the Crimean War, it could be sprinkled on bedding to kill lice and fleas.

Leclair – Jean Marie Leclair (1697–1764), French violinist and composer.

Long Tom – type of swivel cannon used by the Navy; in J. M. Barrie's *Peter Pan* the pirate ship has a gun called 'Long Tom'.

Lyons – a teashop, one of a highly successful chain styled 'Lyons Corner Houses', and begun by John Lyons in 1884.

'Marlborough' – an allusion to John Churchill, 1st Duke of Marlborough, whose diplomatic and military skills were crucial to Britain's success during the war of the Spanish succession, 1701–14.

'Marconi interval' – a financial scandal in 1913 involving several senior members of Asquith's government including Lloyd George.

matric. – matriculation, the entrance exam to the University of Oxford; also the ceremony at which membership of the university is formally conferred.

Minenwerfer – German short-range trench mortar; sardonically named 'Minnie' by the British and much-feared by them.

Neuve Chapelle – the object of a surprise British attack on the Lys front on 10 March; though the town was captured, the operation exposed tactical and logistical failings, and British casualties were heavy.

New Armies – the five armies raised following Kitchener's appeal for volunteers on 7 August 1914; the first, 'K.1', came into being on 29 August.

Oliver – in Dickens's *Oliver Twist* (1837–8) the young orphan's pitiable request for more gruel famously sparks uproar in the workhouse.

Old Monarchy – the Ancien Régime of the Valois and Bourbon dynasties in France, which ended with the Revolution of 1789.

opéra bouffe – 'comic opera'; often draws on characters in everyday life.

Other Club – an exclusive cross-party parliamentary dining club founded in May 1911 by Winston Churchill and F. E. Smith, which met fortnightly when Parliament was in session; initially it had twelve Unionist, twelve Liberal and twelve distinguished non-aligned members. 'Rule 12' stated: 'Nothing in the rules or intercourse of the Club shall interfere with the rancour or asperity of party politics.' J. L. Garvin was a founder member.

Pagani's – famous London restaurant in Great Portland Street, which had an 'artists' room' decorated with graffiti, sketches and caricatures.

Pall Mall Gazette – London evening newspaper founded in 1865, and bought by William Waldorf Astor in 1893; in 1911 Astor, in search of an editor for the paper, acquired the services of J. L. Garvin by purchasing the *Observer* from Lord Northcliffe. Garvin edited the *Pall Mall Gazette* until it was sold in 1915, by which time it had become a heavy burden to him.

Pangloss – in Voltaire's *Candide* (1759) Pangloss adopted an attitude of unshakable optimism, believing that 'all is for the best in this best of all possible worlds'.

Pelion – a high, wooded mountain in Thessaly, famous in Greek mythology as the home of the centaur Chiron.

pip-squeaks – British army slang for a rifle-grenade or a small gas shell.

Pond's Extract – a cream for healing small cuts and abrasions, the principal active ingredient of which was witch-hazel.

Prince Otto – novel by Robert Louis Stevenson, published in 1885.

Rabelaisian cheer – after the bawdy style of the early French writer François Rabelais (1494–1553).

'the Revolution' – the French Revolution of 1789, beginning with the fall of the Bastille.

RFA – Royal Field Artillery.

Ronsard – Pierre de Ronsard, sixteenth-century French poet; in 1908 the *Selected Poems* were published by Oxford University Press.

Round Table – quarterly journal of imperial and international affairs begun by Philip Kerr, later Lord Lothian, 1910.

Royal Colonial Institute – founded in 1868 in London 'to promote colonial interests', with a fellowship of around four thousand and an extensive library.

Saguntum – city in Spain about nineteen miles north of Valencia; its alliance with Rome and capture by Hannibal, 218 BC, precipitated the Second Punic War (218–201).

St Gerard's medal – the patron saint of expectant mothers; devotional medals were (and still are) freely available from Roman Catholic suppliers.

secret session – in extreme circumstances the House of Commons can sit in a closed or 'secret' session, when its proceedings may not be reported in *Parliamentary Debates*.

Sesame Club – a progressive educational society, founded in London in 1895; by 1899 there were nine hundred members.

Sinn Féiners – supporters of the Irish nationalist party founded by Arthur Griffith in 1906, and devoted to freeing Ireland from Westminster rule; from the Gaelic, meaning 'ourselves'.

soixante dix – a reference to '1870' and the Franco-Prussian war.

Somerville – one of the three women's colleges at Oxford at the time of the Great War; Somerville admitted men in 1992.

Stores, the – see 'Army & Navy Store'.

strafe – to fire upon with rifle or artillery; from the German battle cry '*Gott Strafe England*'.

Strongbow – Richard de Clare (1130–76), Earl of Pembroke; led an army to invade Ireland, 1167–70, and was later King of Leinster.

sursum corde – a liturgical phrase in the Roman Catholic Mass meaning 'lift up your hearts'; said when the bread and wine are brought to the altar.

targe – archaic term for a shield.

Tariff movement – a political movement led by Joseph Chamberlain, and adopted by the Unionist Party from 1903, which favoured the imposition of tariffs on imported goods in order to protect home industry and agriculture, with preferential rates for goods from within the Empire ('imperial preference').

Tiptree – a popular brand of conserve, first produced in 1885 by Wilkin & Sons from a farm in the Essex village of Tiptree.

trenchscope – a trench periscope: different versions were on sale in shops in Britain.

twist – tobacco, which was sold in 'twists', that could be chewed as well as smoked; Ged did not use 'twist', but his mother sent it out for his men.

Ulster Division – the 36th (Ulster) Division was formed in September 1914, largely from the Protestant paramilitary 'Ulster Volunteer Force' that was raised in response to the threat of Home Rule; it was one of the few divisions to make progress on 1 July 1916, in spite of appallingly heavy casualties.

Unionism – the principle of upholding the union of Great Britain and Ireland, enshrined in the 1800 Act of Union; before 1914 the term 'Unionist' described British Conservatives as well as Irish (predominantly Ulster) opponents of Home Rule, and the Conservative Party was officially known as the 'Conservative and Unionist Party'.

'wait-and-see' ministry – a derogatory allusion to Asquith's pre-war government, suggesting inactivity and passiveness; in fact the phrase, as originally used by Asquith in speeches in 1910, carried menace, in the sense of 'wait and see what I do'.

Who is Sylvia – song by Franz Schubert, based on the song in Shakespeare's *Two Gentlemen of Verona*.

Wypers – Ged's idiosyncratic spelling of 'Wipers', the British army slang for Ypres.

Xenophon (*c.*428 BC–*c.*354 BC) – Athenian historian; author of a history of his times, *Hellenica*, a memoir of Socrates, with whom he studied, and *Anabasis*, an account of a military expedition to Asia Minor, in which he took part. Ged was given an edition of Xenophon for his twentieth birthday, bound in myrtle-green leather and edged in gold; it was kept in London awaiting his return.

Yukon – westernmost Canadian territory, famous for the Klondike gold rush from 1897.

A Note on Places

I. Associated with the Garvins

Cliveden – imposing Victorian mansion overlooking the River Thames in Buckinghamshire, the home of Waldorf Astor; J. L. Garvin was a regular visitor.

Constantine Bay – on the north Cornwall coast, west of Padstow; the Garvins spent summer holidays there (see Trevose Head, below).

9 Greville Place – the Garvin family home, just off Maida Vale, where it joins Kilburn High Road.

Knole – large fifteenth-century house in Sevenoaks, Kent, given to the Sackville family during the reign of Elizabeth I, and the setting for Virginia Woolf's *Orlando*.

7 Lansdowne Road – Notting Hill home of the O'Sullivans, friends of the Garvins; Christina Garvin sometimes stayed there, resting and recuperating.

Old Buckhurst – in Withyham, East Sussex, home of J. L. Garvin's friends the Colefaxes.

Orvieto – in Umbria, Italy; noted for its Gothic duomo and dramatic location; Christina and J. L. Garvin took a memorable three-month holiday in Italy early in 1907.

Shootlands – country house in Surrey, just south of the village of Wotton on the Guildford–Dorking road, and high above the valley running from Leith Hill; much-loved by the Garvins, who spent most of August and September 1915 there.

Trevose Head – spur of land adjacent to Constantine Bay in North Cornwall (see above), and a favourite haunt of Christina Garvin.

Wargrave Hall – on the banks of the Thames near Reading, Berkshire, the home of J. L. Garvin's great friend Sir Edward Goulding; much frequented by influential figures and leading Unionists of the day.

II. Associated with the 7th South Lancs

Bulford – training camp near Tidworth, on the Wiltshire–Hampshire border; there were firing ranges, and practice trenches that are still visible.

High Wood – between Martinpuich and Longueval, about a mile north-east of the Bazentins; the Flers Ridge ran through the wood and, although little more than a hundred feet high, it dominated the landscape around, providing a formidable defensive position.

Jellalabad Barracks, Tidworth, Hampshire – named after Jellalabad, eighty miles east of Kabul, from which the Somerset Light Infantry fought their way out after being besieged by Afghan tribesmen in 1841–2.

Mametz Wood – immediately to the south-west of the Bazentins, on the Logueval–Contalmaison Road; famous for its literary associations (it features in the work of Siegfried Sassoon and Robert Graves), as well as for the heavy fighting that took place there.

Somme – river in northern France that gives its name to the offensive of 1 July–18 November 1916, which was fought over the open, undulating country between the Somme and the Ancre (to the north). The rivers originate in the watershed of a long ridge running from the northern slopes of the Somme valley, near Peronne, to the Ancre at Thiepval. The ridge, which in places is as much as three hundred feet high, gave the Germans the advantage of high ground.

Tidworth – town on the eastern side of Salisbury Plain, one mile West of Andover, and home to Jellalabad Barracks (see above).

A Subaltern's Front-Line Reading

For his twentieth birthday Ged was given a luxury edition of Xenophon by his father, and the following April he returned the compliment on his father's birthday with a copy of William Milligan Sloane's beautifully illustrated *Life of Napoleon Bonaparte* (1911). A love of literature was a strong bond between them, and Ged's letters to his father reveal much about his front-line reading. The list below is very unlikely to be comprehensive, but it is nevertheless remarkable for its scope. There is no mention of any German work, although Ged – like his father – was fond of German literature. By contrast he writes of many French works, and while in France completed his research for an essay on the renowned seventeenth-century French general Marshal Turenne. Ged sent the finished manuscript home from the Lys front in January 1916: it was meant for private consumption only, but after his death his father published the essay in the *Observer*. In the same issue was a short memorial from a brother officer who observed Ged reading la Bruyère's satirical *Caractères* just before the night attack of 22 July: 'I remember him reading *Le Cid* and a book on Napoleon in these last days – also Shakespeare. He was never communicative about these things, but one could tell from the books he read of the kind of inner life he lived'.[1]

RGG's Reading List While at the Front, August 1915–July 1916

August 1915

Théophile Gautier, *Le Capitaine Fracasse* (1863)

1 The *Observer*, 30 July 1916. Ged's essay began: 'Except Napoleon, no general has led the French armies better than Turenne . . .'.

Molière, *Le Médecin Malgré Lui* (1666)
— *Le Bourgeois Gentilhomme* (1670)
Una Lucy Silberrad, *Sampson Rideout, Quaker* (1911) – found discarded in one of his billets; Ged thought it 'an historical novel of unusual merit'

September 1915

George Meredith, *The Adventures of Harry Richmond* (1871)
Molière, *Le Précieuses Ridicules* (1659)
— *L'Avare* (1668)
Williams Shakespeare, *Love's Labour's Lost* (1595)

October 1915

George Meredith, *The Adventures of Harry Richmond* (1871)
William Wordsworth, *Sonnets* – possibly the 1907 edition, a birthday present
— *The Excursion* (1814)

November 1915

George Meredith, *Beauchamp's Career* (1876)
— *The Adventures of Harry Richmond* (1871)
Molière, *Le Malade Imaginaire* (1673)
Alfred de Musset, *Carmosine* (1850)
Plutarch, *Life of Alexander* – in *Parallel Lives*; there were many translations in print
Thucydides, *History of the Peloponnesian War* – possibly *Thucydides' Peloponnesian War* translated by Richard Crawley, London, Dent, 1903, reprinted 1910

December 1915

Catullus, *Poetry* – there were numerous Latin and English editions in print
George Robert Gleig, *The Subaltern: A Chronicle of the Peninsular War* (1825)
Prosper Mérimée, *Colomba* (1841)
Abbé Prévost, *Manon Lescaut* (1731)
William Shakespeare, *Hamlet* (1601–2)

Thucydides, *History of the Peloponnesian War* (as above)
W. B. Yeats, *Countess Cathleen* (1899)

January 1916

Catullus, *Poetry* (as above)
Gustave Flaubert, *Trois Contes* (1877)
Ian Hay, *The First Hundred Thousand: Being the Unofficial Chronicle of a Unit of 'K (1)'* (1915)
Stephen Leacock, *Arcadian Adventures with the Idle Rich* (1915)
Henry Seton Merriman, *Barlasch of the Guard* (1903)
Sir Walter Scott, *A Legend of Montrose* (1819)
William Shakespeare, *As You Like It* (*c.*1599)
Thucydides, *History of the Peloponnesian War* (as above)

February 1916

George Meredith, *Rhoda Fleming* (1865)
Molière, *Le Misanthrope* (1666)
Sir Walter Scott, *A Legend of Montrose* (1819)
Thucydides, *History of the Peloponnesian War* (as above)

March 1916

George Meredith, *The Egoist* (1879)
Prosper Mérimée, *Dernières Nouvelles de Prosper Mérimée* (1873)
Charles Reade, *Griffith Gaunt; or, Jealousy* (1866)
Thucydides, *History of the Peloponnesian War* (as above)

April 1916

Jean de la Bruyère, *Les Caractères ou Les Moeurs de ce Siècle* (1688)
Nikolai Gogol, *The Inspector General* (1842)
George Meredith, *The Egoist* (1879)
Alexander Pope, *The Rape of the Lock* (1714)
Robert Sidney Waters, *Simple Tactical Schemes, with Solutions* (1913)
William Shakespeare, *The Tempest* (1611)

May 1916

Honoré de Balzac, *La Peau de Chagrin* (1831)

Jean de la Bruyère, *Les Caractères ou Les Moeurs de ce Siècle* (1688)
A. E. W. Mason, *Clementina* (1901)
Prosper Mérimée, *Lokis* (1870)
Henry Seton Merriman, *On Kedar's Tents* (1905)
William O'Connor Morris, *Napoleon, Warrior and Ruler* (1893)
Sir Walter Scott, *Guy Mannering* (1815)
William Shakespeare, *Merchant of Venice* (*c.*1598)

June 1916

Jean de la Bruyère, *Les Caractères ou Les Moeurs de ce Siècle* (1688)
William O'Connor Morris, *Napoleon, Warrior and Ruler* (1893)

July 1916

Jean de la Bruyère, *Les Caractères ou Les Moeurs de ce Siècle* (1688)
Pierre Corneille, *Le Cid: Tragédie en Cinq Actes* (1636)
Ernest William Hamilton, *The First Seven Divisions: Being a Detailed Account of the Fighting From Mons to Ypres* (1916)

A Subaltern's Front-Line Provisions

While J. L. Garvin sent his son books Christina Garvin dispatched virtually everything else – from food and toiletries to clothing and military equipment, including on one notable occasion a Smith and Wesson revolver. Christina shopped in London stores that are still well known today: Boots, Burberry, Fortnum and Mason, Harrods, Jaeger and Selfridges. Less well known are the Army & Navy (military supplies), Cording (boots), Truslove (stationery), and Withers (cakes). She delighted in supplying Ged's material needs every bit as much as his father delighted in satisfying his intellectual, and between them they kept their son well stocked. In fact Ged had to ask his mother to send fewer parcels, and smaller ones: he was constantly on the move, and the contents of a large hamper that could not be finished were all too likely to be left behind in billets, to the delight of the next occupants. The flow of parcels was not one way. Ged sent washing home to be laundered, and also mementoes from the front: much to his mother's relief he was dissuaded by his battalion's 'bomb expert', Captain Williams, from sending home an unexploded bomb. The following lists comprise the items that Christina said that she had sent, or which Ged specifically asked for, and they are very unlikely to be comprehensive.

Foodstuffs

baked beans – Ged also made a general request for tins of Heinz products
biscuits – sweet, i.e. chocolate creams, ginger snaps, shortbread
biscuits – savoury, i.e. Bath Olivers
Bovril
brandy – by the 'flask'; also sent out in a Schweppes dry ginger ale bottle
cakes – birthday, Christmas, iced, orange, etc.
calves-foot jelly
champagne
cheese – including Imperial brand
chocolate(s) – including Lindt
cigarettes – Woodbines, for his men
cocoa au lait – Milkmaid brand

coffee – tinned
Cognac – i.e. Gauthier Frères, six bottles were sent to Ged by Edward Goulding
corn – tinned
crème de menthe
dates
fruit – apples, bananas, oranges and pineapples
galantine
ginger marmalade
golden syrup
ham – tinned
Indian corn
jam – the favourite was Tiptree, especially strawberry, cherry and blackberry; sent in jars and tins
lemon squash tablets – 'in little croquette boxes' (from Fortnum and Mason's)
lemon crystals
macaroni – tinned
milk – tinned, including Milkmaid brand
mince pies
muscatels
nuts – including almonds and cashews
olives
port
potted meat
puddings – golden, plum and 'tinned'
raisins
shrimp paste
soup – cubes, tablets and tomato
'splits' – sent with cream and jam
sweets – i.e. acid-drops, crystallised fruits, lime juice, peppermint creams, peppermint lumps, peppermint rock and Turkish Delight
tea tabloids
toffee – Slade brand
tongue – tinned
twist – 'pretty black stuff', sold by the yard

Clothing

body belts – thick ones, especially useful at night
boots – Cordings, Fortnum and Mason, Hook Knowles and Jaeger
breeches
British Warm – overcoat
Burberry raincoat
collars
comforters
furry waistcoat
hankies
Jaeger cardigan jacket
Jaeger over-socks
mackintosh cape – large
mittens – knitted, long and short
puttees – ordinary and woollen knitted
pyjamas
Sam Browne belt
shirts
slippers – i.e. Jaeger wool-lined leather
socks – long and short
ties
tunic
underwear – vests and pants, in silk (for summer), linen mesh and wool
waistcoats
waterproof gloves, shorts

Toiletries

bromo – i.e. 'bromoseltzer', a powdered effervescent pain-killer habitually used by JLG
Eau de Cologne – i.e. 'solid'; Ged thought it 'grand, freshening one like anything'
foot powder
razors – made by Buckley and Gillette
hair-wash
iodine tubes – Burroughs & Wellcome
Keating's powder – 'Keating's Powder does the trick, / Kills all bugs and fleas off quick'
nail-cleaner
pocket comb

Pond's Extract
scent
soap – i.e. coal-tar tablet
toilet vinegar
tooth-paste, -powder and -soap – from Boots
vermin pad
vermin powder – from Boots
Virol – a toffee-flavoured medicinal syrup, commonly fed to children

Other

batteries – i.e. Ever Ready for a 'pocket-lamp'
bronze enamel stars – Ged's lieutenant 'pips'
candles – stumpy, long-lasting 'trench candles'
canvas bucket
electric lamp – a special lamp from Stewards
flageolet
folding knife, fork and spoon
fountain pencil refills
gold watch
illustrated papers – i.e. the *London News*
Leuco
'lamels'
matches
The *Observer* – copies sent weekly to Ged and his battalion
Orilux lamp – the 'trench torch' or 'officer's flashlight'
periscope
protractor – of the wooden 'service' type, about six inches by two inches
respirator
revolver – Smith and Wesson .45
rug
sheet music – for a flageolet
solid methylated spirits – sold in tins by Boots
steel mirror
strop
Tommy's Cooker – portable stoves fuelled by solidified alcohol (meths)
trenchoscope – a basic periscope consisting of parallel mirrors set in a long wooden box
writing blocks – i.e. pads

Select Bibliography and Note on Sources

I. Primary Sources

The correspondence published here is among the Garvin Papers in the British Library. The 7th South Lancs' involvement in the night attack of 22–23 July 1916 is recorded in the typescript war diary of the 56th Brigade, a contemporary document compiled by Captain J. N. Gilbey; the editors wish to thank the Museum of the Queen's Lancashire Regiment for access to this. The editors have been unable to trace the originals of two documents used by David Ayerst in the brief account of RGG's death that appears in his 1985 biography *Garvin of the Observer*: one is Second-Lieutenant Douglas Sharp's narrative of RGG's last hours, and the other 'Gerard Garvin's Diary'.

II. Secondary Sources

There is an especially rich literature for the First World War and it is beyond the scope of this bibliography to attempt an appraisal, or even offer pointers to the many excellent works. What follows is a list of the books most used in the editing of this volume. The place of publication is London unless otherwise stated. The editors had frequent recourse to *The Times Digital Archive* and the *Oxford Dictionary of National Biography*, both of which may be accessed online.

Ayerst, David, *Garvin of the Observer*, London and Dover, NH: Croom Helm, 1985.

Bairnsfather, Capt. Bruce, *'The Bystander's' Fragments from France*, London: The Bystander, 1916.

Beaver, Patrick, *The Wipers Times: a complete facsimile of the famous World War One trench newspaper* . . . London: P. Davies, 1973; Papermac edition, 1988.

Blunden, Edmund, *Undertones of War*, London: Richard Cobden-Sanderson, 1928.

Brittain, Vera, *Testament of Youth; An Autobiographical Study of the Years 1900–1925*, London: V. Gollancz, 1933.

Brock, Michael. '"The Eternal Lack of Motive": Raymond Asquith's Buried Talents', pp. 479–88, in *Winchester College: Sixth-Centenary Essays*, ed. Roger Custance, Oxford: Oxford University Press, 1982.

Brock, Michael and Eleanor (eds), *H. H. Asquith: Letters to Venetia Stanley*, Oxford: Oxford University Press, 1982.

Churchill, Winston S., *Great Contemporaries*, London: Thornton Butterworth, 1937; London: Cooper, 1990.

Corrigan, Gordon, *Loos 1915: The Unwanted Battle*, Staplehurst: Spellmount, 2004.

Edmonds, J. E., Sir, *History of the Great War Based on Official Documents: Military Operations France and Belgium, 1916*, London: Macmillan, 1932.

Foster, R. F., *Modern Ireland, 1600–1972*, London: Allen Lane, 1988.

Garvin, Katharine, *J. L. Garvin: A Memoir*, London: William Heinemann, 1948.

Germains, Victor Wallace, *The Kitchener Armies: The Story of a National Achievement*, London: P. Davies, 1930.

Gilbert, Martin, *Winston S. Churchill, Volume III: 1914–1916, The Challenge of War*. London: William Heinemann, 1971.

Gliddon, Gerald, *When the Barrage Lifts: A Topographical History of the Battle of the Somme, 1916*, Norwich: Gliddon, 1987; Stroud: Alan Sutton Publishing, 1994.

Gollin, Alfred M., *The* Observer *and J. L. Garvin, 1908–1914: A Study in Great Editorship*, London: Oxford University Press, 1960.

Graves, Robert, *Good-bye to All That: An Autobiography*, London: Jonathan Cape, 1929.

Hancock, Edward, *Bazentin Ridge*, Barnsley: Leo Cooper, 2001.

Hutton, John, *Kitchener's Men: The King's Own Royal Lancasters on the Western Front, 1915–1918*, Barnsley, Pen and Sword Military, 2008.

Jolliffe, John (ed.), *Raymond Asquith: Life and Letters*, London: Collins, 1980.

Liddell Hart, B. H., Sir, *The Real War, 1914–1918*, London: Faber and Faber, 1930.

Liddle, Peter, *The 1916 Battle of the Somme: A Reappraisal*, London: Leo Cooper, 1992.

Macdonald, Lyn, *The Somme*, London: M. Joseph, 1983.

Marwick, Arthur, *The Deluge: British Society and the First World War*, Boston: Little, Brown, 1965.

Middlebrook, Martin, *The First Day on the Somme, 1 July 1916*, London: Military Book Society, 1971.

Middlebrook, Martin and Mary, *The Somme Battlefields: A Comprehensive Guide From Crécy to the Two World Wars*, London: Viking, 1991.

Mullaly, B. R., *The South Lancashire Regiment: The Prince of Wales's Volunteers*, Bristol: White Swan Press, 1955.

O'Sullivan, Mrs Denis (Elizabeth) (ed.), *Harry Butters R.F.A.: 'An American Citizen': Life and War Letters*, New York, John Lane Company; London, John Lane, The Bodley Head, 1918.

Pope, Stephen and Elizabeth-Anne Wheal, *The Macmillan Dictionary of the First World War*, London: Macmillan, 1995.

Sheffield, Gary, *The Somme*, London: Cassell, 2003.

Simkins, Peter, *Kitchener's Army: The Raising of the New Armies, 1914–16*, Manchester: Manchester University Press, 1988.

Soames, Mary (ed.), *Speaking for Themselves: The Personal Letters of Winston and Clementine Churchill*, London: Doubleday, 1998.

Strachan, Hew, *The First World War: Vol. 1, To Arms*, Oxford: Oxford University Press, 2001.

— *The First World War: A New Illustrated History*, London: Simon and Schuster, 2003.

Stubbs, John, 'Appearance and Reality', pp. 320–38, in *Newspaper History from the Seventeenth Century to the Present Day*, George Boyce, James Curran and Pauline Wingate (eds.), London: Constable, 1978.

— 'Garvin, James Louis (1868–1947)', in *Oxford Dictionary of National Biography*, Oxford: Oxford University Press, 2004.

Tuchman, Barbara W., *The Guns of August*, New York: Macmillan, 1962.

Westlake, Ray, *British Battalions on the Somme, 1916*, Barnsley: Leo Cooper, 1994.

Whalley-Kelly, Captain H., *'Ich Dien': The Prince of Wales's Volunteers (South Lancashire) 1914–1934*, Aldershot: Gale and Polden, 1935.

Wyrall, Everard, *The History of the 19th Division, 1914–1918*, London: E. Arnold, 1932.

INDEX

Other books on the First World War published by Frontline include:

THE DAILY TELEGRAPH DICTIONARY OF TOMMIES' SONGS AND SLANG
John Brophy & Eric Partridge
Introduction by Malcolm Brown
ISBN 978-1-84415-710-5

THE GERMAN ARMY HANDBOOK OF 1918
Introduction by James Beach
ISBN 978-1-84415-711-2

SAGITTARIUS RISING
Cecil Lewis
ISBN 978-1-84832-519-7

THE SECRET BATTLE
A Tragedy of the First World War
A. P. Herbert
Foreword by Sir Winston Churchill
Introduction by Malcolm Brown
ISBN 978-1-84832-521-0

TWELVE DAYS ON THE SOMME
A Memoir of the Trenches, 1916
Sidney Rogerson
Introduction by Malcolm Brown
ISBN 978-1-84832-534-0